A New Take on Cake

Cake Pops
(page 292)

A New Take on Cake

175 Beautiful, Doable Cake Mix Recipes
for Bundts, Layers, Slabs, Loaves,
Cookies, and More!

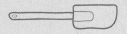

Anne Byrn

PHOTOGRAPHS BY DANIELLE ATKINS

Clarkson Potter/Publishers
New York

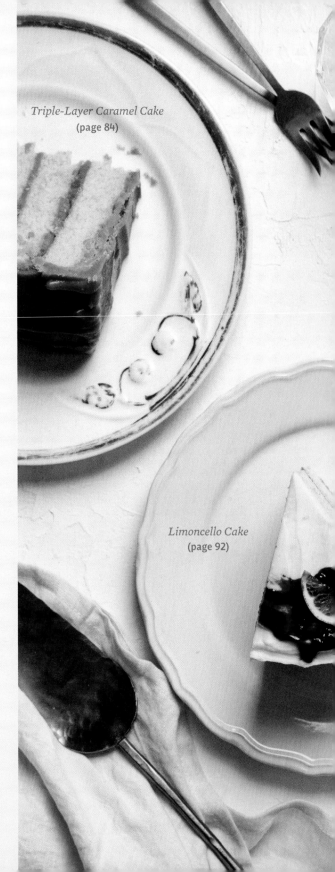

Triple-Layer Caramel Cake
(page 84)

Limoncello Cake
(page 92)

CLARKSON POTTER is a trademark
and POTTER with colophon is a registered
trademark of Penguin Random House LLC.

Some recipes originally appeared,
in different form, in *The Cake Mix Doctor*
(Workman Publishing, 1999).

Library of Congress Cataloging-in-Publication
Data is available upon request.

ISBN 978-0-593-23359-7
eBook ISBN 978-0-593-23360-3

Printed in the United States of America

Photographer: Danielle Atkins
Prop and Food Stylist: Teresa Blackburn
Food Styling Assistant: Martha Bowden
Author Photos: Bob Delevante
Editor: Raquel Pelzel
Designer: Catherine Casalino
Production Editor: Patricia Shaw
Production Manager: Jessica Heim
Composition: Merri Ann Morrell
Copy Editor: Kate Slate
Indexer: Elizabeth T. Parson

1st Printing

Cover cake: *Chocolate
Triple-Berry Cake* (page 194)

Gluten-Free Vanilla Cake
with Cherry Buttercream
(page 73)

For Bebe, again, and for my cake bakers—

Litton, Kathleen, and Gray

Chocolate Kahlúa Cake
(page 141)

Contents

1. Basic Butter Cake, p. 46

2. Peaches and Cream Cake, p. 47

3. New-Fashioned Yellow Cake with
Chocolate Buttercream, p. 48

4. Buttermilk Devil's Food Cake, p. 50

5. Vegan Seltzer Cake, p. 51

6. Chocolate Olive Oil Cake with
Chocolate Ganache, p. 52

7. Mint Chocolate Cookies
and Cream Cake, p. 55

8. Favorite German Chocolate Cake,
p. 57

9. Vegan Chocolate Cake with
Creamy Nutella Frosting, p. 61

10. Chocolate-Pistachio Ice Cream
Cake, p. 62

11. Boston Cream Pie, p. 64

12. Chocolate Chip Cake with Pan Frosting, p. 66

13. Perfect Sour Cream Chocolate Cake, p. 234

14. Pink Champagne Cake, p. 67

15. Reese's Peanut Butter Cake, p. 68

16. The Confetti Cake, p. 71

17. Gluten-Free Vanilla Cake with Cherry Buttercream, p. 73

18. Easy Red Velvet Cake, p. 76

19. Coconut Icebox Cake, p. 80

20. Deep South Strawberry Cake, p. 83

21. Triple-Layer Caramel Cake, p. 84

22. The Banana Cake, p. 86

23. Buttermilk Lime Cake, p. 87

24. Hummingbird Cake with Roasted Bananas, p. 88

25. Snickerdoodle Cake, p. 91

26. Blackberry Jam Cake, p. 145

27. Limoncello Cake, p. 92

28. Clementine Cake, p. 95

29. Orange Ricotta Birthday Cake, p. 98

30. Gluten-Free Pumpkin Spice Cake, p. 99

31. Vegan Mango Cake, p. 100

32. White Cake with White Frosting, p. 102

33. The DIY Wedding Cake, p. 105

34. Red Velvet Baby Cake with White Chocolate Glaze, p. 78

35. Strawberry Smash Cake, p. 111

36. Little Yellow Birthday Cake, p. 115

37. Chocolate Boozy Baby Cake, p. 116

38. Baked Alaska Baby Cake, p. 117

39. Banana Lime Baby Cake, p. 120

40. Lavender, Vanilla, Blueberry Baby Cake, p. 122

41. Little Brown Sugar–Grapefruit Cake, p. 124

42. Flowerpot Cakes, p. 126

43. Almond Cream Cheese Pound Cake, p. 130

44. Hershey's Bar Pound Cake, p. 132

45. Stacy's Chocolate Chip Cake, p. 134

46. White Chocolate–Peppermint Chiffon Cake, p. 137

47. Neapolitan Swirl Pound Cake, p. 138

48. Darn Good Chocolate Cake, p. 140

49. Chocolate Kahlúa Cake, p. 141

50. Tunnel of Fudge Cake, p. 142

51. Sour Cream Pound Cake, p. 144

52. Basic Buttermilk-Spice Cake, p. 145

53. Chocolate-Layered Pistachio Cake, p. 146

54. Apple Cider Cake with Cider Glaze, p. 148

55. Maple Nut Coffee Cake, p. 150

56. The Best Sock-It-to-Me Cake, p. 152

57. Sherry-Poppy Seed Cake, p. 155

58. My Bacardi Rum Cake, p. 156

59. Lemon and Sorghum Marble Spice Cake, p. 158

60. Susan's Lemon Cake, p. 161

61. Melted Ice Cream Cake, p. 162

62. Our Favorite Pumpkin Cake, p. 164

63. Pumpkin Icebox Cake, p. 165

64. 7Up Pound Cake, p. 167

65. Fab Five-Flavor Pound Cake, p. 168

66. Chocolate Chip Tahini Loaf, p. 169

67. Coconut, Banana, Chocolate Loaf, p. 170

68. Chocolate Nutella Loaf, p. 172

69. Ginger-Pear Loaf with Vanilla Drizzle, p. 173

70. Rosemary-Lemon Syrup Loaf, p. 174

71. Blood Orange Loaf
with Campari Glaze, p. 176

72. Fresh Raspberry Mojito Loaf,
p. 178

73. Earl Grey Tea Loaf, p. 180

74. Pumpkin and
Fresh Cranberry Loaf, p. 181

75. Pineapple Upside-Down Cake,
p. 184

78. Blueberry Cornmeal Skillet Cake, p. 189

76. Pumpkin Skillet Crumble, p. 186

77. Caramelized Bananas Foster
Skillet Cake, p. 188

79. Lemon, Caramel, Peach Skillet
Cake, p. 190

80. Apple Slice Skillet Cake, p. 192

81. Roasted Strawberry Upside-Down
Cake, p. 193

82. Chocolate Triple-Berry Cake, p. 194

83. Vegan Chocolate Tangerine Cake,
p. 195

84. Chocolate Praline Cake, p. 198

85. Gluten-Free Chocolate Swirled
Apricot Cake, p. 201

86. Strawberry-Lemon
Tres Leches Cake, p. 203

87. Chocolate Espresso
Tres Leches Cake, p. 205

88. "Cinnabon" Cake, p. 206

89. Italian Cream Cake, p. 208

90. Eggnog Cake with Bourbon Cream, p. 211

91. Orange-Pistachio Cake with Fresh Ginger Glaze, p. 212

92. Warm Chocolate Cookie Dough Cake, p. 214

95. Pumpkin Gingersnap Cheesecake, p. 218

93. Sour Cream Chocolate Chip Cheesecake, p. 215

94. Meyer Lemon Cheesecake, p. 219.

96. Basic Sour Cream Coffee Cake, p. 223

97. Chocolate Mayo Slab Cake, p. 224

98. Lazy Daisy Cake, p. 225

99. Texas Sheet Cake, p. 227

100. Chocolate Marbled Tiramisu, p. 228

101.Buttermilk Yellow Cake with Martha's Chocolate Fudge Icing, p. 230

102. The BTSC (Better Than Sex Cake), p. 233

103. The Pineapple Dump Cake, p. 235

104. Peanut Butter and Jelly Snack Cake, p. 237

105. Roasted Sweet Potato Snack Cake, p. 238

106. Costco Sheet Cake Reimagined, p. 240

107. Black- and Blueberry Buckle, p. 243

108. Vegan Cinnamon Applesauce Cake, p. 244

109. Sour Cream–Peach Kuchen, p. 246

112. Gingerbread Slab Cake with Lemon and Buttermilk Stripes, p. 251

110. Rhubarb and Spice Kuchen, p. 247

111. Easy Fruit Slab Pie, p. 249

113. Zucchini Chocolate Chip Slab Cake, p. 253

114. Birthday Cake for 50, p. 254

115. Big American Flag Cake, p. 256

116. Brown Butter Banana Pudding Slab Cake, p. 259

117. Chocolate-Covered Cherry Cake, p. 263

118. Chocolate Buttermilk Slab Cake with Caramel Frosting, p. 264

119. Basic Vanilla Cupcakes, p. 268

120. Orange Vanilla Chiffon Cupcakes with Raspberry Buttercream, p. 269

121. Vegan Dark Chocolate Cupcakes, p. 271

122. Matcha Mint Cupcakes, p. 272

123. Gluten-Free Chocolate Macaroon Cupcakes, p. 274

124. Chocolate Sour Cream Cupcakes, p. 275

125. Chocolate Peanut Butter Cupcakes, p. 278

126. Red Velvet Cupcakes with Mascarpone Frosting, p. 79

129. Key Lime Pie Cupcakes, p. 282

127. Sweet Tea Cupcakes with Lemon Buttercream, p. 279

128. Wedding Cake Cupcakes, p. 281

130. Lemon Curd Cupcakes with Leeann's Blackberry Frosting, p. 285

131. Chocolate Nutella Marbled Cupcakes, p. 286

132. Butternut Cupcakes with Cinnamon Buttercream, p. 287

133. Microwave Mug Sprinkle Cake, p. 289

134. Ice Cream Cone Cakes, p. 290

135. Cake Pops, p. 292

136. Chocolate Chunk Muffins, p. 295

137. Coffee Cake Muffins, p. 296

138. Lemon Buttermilk Poppy Seed Muffins, p. 298

139. Apple Butter Muffins, p. 299

140. Pear and Cardamom Muffins, p. 301

141. The Best Blueberry Muffins, p. 303

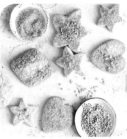
142. Basic Sugar Cookies, p. 307

143. Gluten-Free Slice-and-Bake Sugar Cookies, p. 308

144. Gluten-Free Chocolate Slice-and-Bake Sugar Cookies, p. 308

145. Cookie Pops, p. 309

146. Slice-and-Bake Toffee Maple Cookies, p. 310

147. Cashew Thumbprints, p. 311

148. Peanut Butter Cookies, p. 312

149. Almond Sandwich Cookies, p. 315

150. Brown Butter Chocolate Chip Cookies, p. 316

151. Double Chocolate Drop Cookies, p. 318

152. Ice Cream Sprinkle Cookie Sandwiches, p. 319

153. Easy Chocolate Walnut Cookies, p. 320

154. Gingerbread People, p. 321

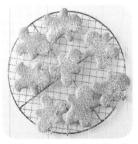
155. Gluten-Free Gingerbread People, p. 322

156. Brown Butter Blondies, p. 323

157. Spiced Tea Cakes with Chai Glaze, p. 324

158. Easy and Good Lemon Squares, p. 325

159. Whoopie Pies, p. 326

160. Petit Fours, p. 328

161. Cranberry-Orange Biscotti, p. 330

162. Chocolate-Almond Biscotti, p. 331

163. Plum Linzer Bars, p. 333

164. Orange Ricotta Cheesecake Bars, p. 334

165. Classic Gooey Butter Cake, p. page 336

166. Chocolate Brownie Gooey Butter Cake, p. 337

167. Chocolate Pecan Pie Squares, p. 338

168. Chocolate Fudge Peppermint Sticks, p. 339

169. Kahlúa Marbled Cheesecake Brownies, p. 340

170. Peanut Butter Chocolate Bars, p. 343

171. Little Brownie Pizza, p. 344

172. Buttermilk Spice Doughnuts, p. 346

Introduction: From Cake Mix to Cake Magnificent

I wrote *The Cake Mix Doctor* when my children were young and my family life was joyous but frantic. Baking for birthdays, potlucks, and bake sales often took place late at night when my kids were in bed, and it was so easy to reach in the pantry for a box of cake mix to get things started. My dirty little secret (and savior!) . . .

My mother, Bebe, had been doctoring up cake mixes and slathering them with homemade frosting for years. It was her idea that I developed into a newspaper story and then into a book. But little did I know that using mixes as a time-saving foundation for everything from rich chocolate layers to lemony Bundts would resonate with millions of cooks who embraced my hacks as well as my fearless heart to write about cake mixes in what seemed a from-scratch world. And little did I know that that book, which my daughters grew up with, would allow them to embrace baking at an early age and help them become the confident bakers they are today.

The Cake Mix Doctor became a bestseller nearly overnight, and to this day people arrive at my book signings with a ragged, stained, much-loved copy in hand. They've circled the postage stamp–size photos of their favorite recipes. And if not, I don't have to ask which recipes they've most baked—I just look at the batter-splattered pages!

Now more than twenty years later, I am writing a new book for a new time. I still believe that you can turn a mix into a masterpiece—and I still want to help you bake cakes with only a handful of ingredients and be able to effortlessly savor the joy of home baking. But this time, I explore new flavors, new shapes of pans, new methods for baking and frosting cakes, new ways to make cake inclusive and friendly for all, and share not only exciting new recipes but updates of many *Cake Mix Doctor* classics using today's smaller mixes. (Obviously, when companies downsized their mixes a decade ago, it perplexed a lot of us because favorite recipes didn't work anymore.) Well, they will now!

A New Take on Cake is built on what I originally created in *The Cake Mix Doctor*, but it clearly is for baking today—the cakes are still easy, but are bolder, fresher, more pantry-driven, and often adventurous while remaining simple enough to inspire everyone. This book is for bakers of all ages, regardless of how much you have to spend on ingredients, where you live, your baking preferences, whether you're vegan, gluten-free, or need to follow a sugar-free diet—and no matter your baking skill level.

Many home bakers have told me how much they relied on the basic cakes and frostings in *The Cake Mix Doctor* because the recipes were a roadmap to being creative in the kitchen. This book shares more of those flexible blueprint methods for cakes and frostings, too. You'll find a way to infuse basic chocolate ganache with fresh mint or create a distinctive buttercream frosting from just-picked summer blackberries or make a simple—and yummy—frosting from Nutella and peanut

Chocolate Marbled Tiramisu
(page 228)

butter, two pantry staples. And there are other ingredient revelations: coconut milk, Meyer lemons, plant butters, salted caramel, tahini, matcha, Greek yogurt—I had not baked with these ingredients two decades ago, but they now reside in my kitchen and my cakes are so much better for them. So even if you've read all my cookbooks and think you know everything, I encourage you to pay attention!

As I write this book at my kitchen table in Nashville, a global pandemic has forced most to stay home—from school, from work, from social gatherings. The good news is that we are baking more than ever to soothe ourselves and comfort one another, and just bring joy to our everyday routines. I welcome my old friends as well as newcomers to these pages. Let's go bake a cake and share it with someone we love. Not only will it taste good, but it will be beautiful and doable, too!

Enjoy!

Petit Fours
(page 328)

LET'S BAKE CAKE!

As much as I love baking a scratch cake—and I do have favorites—baking from scratch isn't for everyone. You've got to buy the right kind of flour and know how to measure it, which can be tricky. And you need ingredients at the right temperature. To seasoned bakers, this is second nature, but to the inexperienced, baking scratch cakes is stressful.

Not to mention the fact that the reason the cake is being baked—a birthday, special anniversary, significant homecoming—hangs on the precipice until that cake emerges from the oven. So much pressure! You can see why people bake with a mix to avert culinary mishaps, cope in a small kitchen, and survive a busy life. And it's why cake mixes have been sold for more than half a century to great success. To paraphrase what my friend Corabel's mother once said, "Why on Earth would I want to bake a scratch cake when Mr. Hines and Mrs. Crocker have been doing it so well for years?"

That sentiment was echoed in a letter I received from a reader who thanked me for penning what she called a "feminist cookbook." *The Cake Mix Doctor* allowed her to bake and enjoy the "tangible events of life" but not spend the entire day doing it. *That's why a cake mix.*

Why a Cake Mix?

When culinary historian and author Laura Shapiro researched the cultural phenomenon of cake mixes she found that home cooks realized how creative they could be with a box cake and they didn't have to sift flour or cream butter. "What's important about mixes, I've come to believe, isn't the cakes they produce but the cooks they produce."

Those cooks often turn to cake mixes not only to be creative but to economize. Cookbook author Von Diaz calls a box cake "a marker of true skill" in her Puerto Rican family. "Growing up, our finances were really tight. My mother would thank people who helped us out by baking a rum cake. Rum was cheap, and the cake mixes she would get on sale. Then she would turn them into something meaningful." *That's why a cake mix.*

But clearly it is what you do with a cake mix that makes a great cake. On their own and baked by package directions, these smaller mixes often cannot hold up to the weight of frosting. Plus, the flavor of most mixes is average at best. I don't blame you for being frustrated at what's on the grocer's shelves. I'm frustrated, too, and that's why I decided to write this book.

Choosing a Cake Mix

In The Cake Mix Doctor, *the biggest difference between brands of mixes was whether they contained pudding in the mix or not (plain cake mix). The pudding mixes were moister, but if you added a lot of additional ingredients to them, like eggs and sour cream, they got soggy and shrank while cooling in the pan. The plain mixes, on the other hand, were more successful to doctor up.*

Today, cake mixes come in all sorts of flavors; they may be gluten-free or not, natural, organic, or even single-serve. The pudding in the mix feature is no longer advertised on the package like it once was, and it's a little murky to figure out if mixes contain pudding—you really can't tell from the ingredient list. So for this go-around, my recipes don't call for them. Nowadays, I begin with just a simple mix—like white or butter or yellow or chocolate. For example, I turn white cake mix into an impressive Pink Champagne Cake (page 67); or butter cake mix into the much-adored Almond Cream Cheese Pound Cake (page 130); or a yellow mix into my sister Susan's Lemon Cake (page 161). The same goes for chocolate in the Darn Good Chocolate Cake (page 140) or Texas Sheet Cake (page 227). Shop the national brands, the store brands, and the "natural" brands of mixes. For many, the shortcoming of a cake mix is the use of artificial color and flavor. If these ingredients bother you, look for a mix without them.

All the recipes in this book begin with the 15.25-, 16-, and 16.25-ounce cake mixes. I add ingredients, like extra egg whites, cream cheese, ricotta, coconut milk, or half a package of pudding mix, to these smaller mixes to transform them into big layers, bountiful Bundts, even a sheet cake that rivals (dare I say is even better than!) the one at Costco. You don't need to worry about making any "upsizers," which are special mixtures of flour, sugar, and leavening popular with cake decorators to boost the size of a small mix. Every recipe in this book has upsizing built right into it.

Vegan Chocolate Cake with
Creamy Nutella Frosting
(page 61)

New Strategies and More Secrets for Beautifully Doable Cakes

Since I first shared secrets on how to bake cakes that don't look and taste like they started with a mix, I've come up with new ways you can improve on and fancy up a cake mix. Some of my most recent strategies are rediscovering the pantry and stocking it for easy cake baking. I've found new plant-based ingredients I really love and use them in recipes throughout this book. I have dialed up flavor since I wrote that first book, and I have dialed down sweet, reducing the sugar in many recipes. I also bake in new shapes of pans, which keeps baking interesting.

I'm expanding my taste for spices to include more than just the same old cinnamon and find myself turning to cardamom, turmeric, and crystallized ginger more often. And I stash coconut milk in my pantry. It's a plant-based ingredient that works just as well and often better than whole milk to create moist cakes and velvety frostings. Other new ingredients I am playing with include nondairy butters based on olive oil or avocado oil, which make lighter—and whiter—frostings. And Nutella. It's indispensable to the vegan baker and pretty darned delicious, too.

When it comes to more flavor, I think beyond adding water as a liquid ingredient and open the fridge instead. There I find orange juice, apple cider, seltzer, and coffee just to name a few. To economize, in lieu of expensive vanilla I look for other flavorings like lemon zest, almond extract, or espresso power. And I explore botanicals by introducing herbal flavors to cake. Some of my favorite pairings are rosemary with lemon, basil with lime, mint with chocolate, lavender with blueberries, even Earl Grey tea with vanilla.

It's also fun to introduce flavor partners in cakes and icings, like strawberry-lemon, pear-cardamom, and cinnamon-plum. I enjoy how caramel-chocolate, or lemon-

Rosemary-Lemon Syrup Loaf
(page 174)

caramel, as well as browned butter–vanilla and orange-ginger just seem to go naturally together.

And if I'm in a rut and out of recipe ideas, I look to smoothies and cocktails for flavor inspiration. A raspberry mojito, for example, inspired a loaf cake flavored with rum, lime, and fresh raspberries.

I've learned how to bring out more flavor of one ingredient by roasting and toasting. I roast bananas, strawberries, and peaches first so their sugars caramelize and flavors concentrate before adding them to a cake. I toast nuts and coconut—it's second nature.

And when it comes to sugar, there are ways to make the cake taste less sweet by adding ricotta, tahini, or cream cheese to a batter or frosting. Bitter, I've learned, can be a delicious surprise, so I use citrus or Campari to balance the sugar in a glaze. I think now before adding so much sugar and have updated some older recipes: For example I transformed the BTSC (Better Than Sex Cake) on page 233 into a bolder and more interesting cake with less sugar by making a scratch caramel sauce and topping. All the frostings in this book taste less sweet because they contain less confectioners' sugar—and a pinch of kosher or sea salt, a secret. And I frost less. Or not at all! We don't need so much icing anymore.

Thinking outside the box, you can turn heads simply by baking the same cake in a new pan. So instead of a Bundt, pour batter into a 10-inch loaf. Or bake a cake in a springform and then slice it horizontally into layers. Or just leave it whole. Or make baby cakes for smaller gatherings. Strive to be distinct and unusual. Anyone can make a lemon pound cake—why not make yours with Meyer lemon or clementines?

In essence, I want you to bake cakes so fabulous that no one knows they started with a mix. And I welcome scratch bakers who want to glean my tips and ideas while never opening a box!

Mixing the Cake Batter

Beating a cake mix batter is different than mixing a scratch cake. You don't cream sugar and butter to help the cake rise. Your cake rises because of leavening agents like baking powder already in the mix. In fact, you can do more harm by overbeating a cake mix than underbeating it because the overworking of the batter creates tunnels in the cake. So, follow the mixing times in the recipes. Have a light hand with the big powerful mixers. Use a hand mixer if you have one. But should you beat too long or too little, no worries. Cake-mix cakes nearly always rise!

And should you want to make a cake by hand without a mixer, it's quite simple. Stir for 15 to 20 soft strokes with a wooden spoon, followed by 35 to 50 stronger strokes to make a smooth batter. Should you want to use a food processor, pulse 15 times to combine the ingredients, then blend 1 minute for a smooth batter.

And what if there are still lumps in your batter in spite of mixing because the butter was too cold? Fill the kitchen sink to a 2-inch depth with very warm water. Place the mixing bowl of batter in the sink and leave it for 10 to 15 minutes. Remove the bowl from the sink, dry off the bottom of the bowl, and beat the batter until smooth.

Cake Pans: Layers, Bundts, Loaves, and More

Always invest in good pans. Choose metal instead of silicone or glass. Shiny and not dark, which darken the sides of your cake. And don't put baking pans in the dishwasher, which ruins their finish. Soak them in warm, soapy water in the sink and then hand-wash and dry. I avoid cooking sprays like Pam on dark pans because they contain propellants, which are alcohols, and cause the cake edges to bake hotter and darker. Instead, I fill a mister with my own vegetable oil.

LAYER PANS: Choose two 9-inch round shiny metal pans, possibly three. Love a taller cake on the stand? Bake in 8-inch pans. And if you need smaller cakes, use 6-inch.

THE BUNDT: Start simple with just the original fluted 12-cup Bundt. The lightweight aluminum Bundts are easy to prep, clean, and unmold. Graduate to heavier cast-iron Bundts if you want a crunchier exterior, to the smaller Bundt pans for mini-cakes, or to decorative Bundts like the Heritage pan to make a statement.

TUBE PAN: It screams pound cake and measures 10 inches across, holding slightly more batter than the 12-cup Bundt. The pan is named for its inner tube that brings heat to the center of the cake and allows dense cakes to bake evenly. Unlike the Bundt, which you invert so the bottom becomes the top of the finished cake, this cake is served the same way it goes into the oven.

THE 10-INCH LOAF PAN: Not only for making bread, this classic pan can bake beautiful cakes that don't need frosting. If you don't own a 10-inch loaf pan, you can pour the batter into the loaf pans you have, filling the pans about three-quarters full.

THE 13 × 9-INCH PAN: The most practical pan of all because you bake the cake, frost it, and serve it straight from the pan. And if you need layer cake, just cut the cake in half and stack.

AN 18 × 13-INCH HALF-SHEET PAN: Well known to the restaurant world, this workhorse of an aluminum pan will bake beautiful slab cakes.

SPRINGFORM PAN: Cakes (especially cheesecakes) are so easy to get out of the 9-inch pan with removable sides, and you can even slice it into layers. Tres leches cakes can soak up the milk syrup right in the pan.

CAST-IRON SKILLET: Famous for the Pineapple Upside-Down Cake (page 184), this old pan is new again. Recipes in this book call for a 12-inch skillet.

CUPCAKE/MUFFIN PANS: Two metal pans that each hold a dozen 2½-inch cupcakes or muffins are all you really need. If you want larger cupcakes, use Lotus-shape paper liners that fit into the standard pan but hold more batter.

Favorite Baking Tools from A to Z

Beyond pans, this equipment helps me bake beautiful cakes

- ☐ **ACETATE:** rigid plastic used by pastry chefs to wrap around cakes to build taller cakes with smooth sides. You'll find it where professional baking supplies are sold.

- ☐ **BOWLS:** stainless steel and glass

- ☐ **CAKE ROUNDS:** made of cardboard for moving, storing, and freezing cakes

- ☐ **CAKE SAVERS:** for toting

- ☐ **CAKE STANDS:** because cakes look more beautiful on them!

- ☐ **CHEF'S KNIFE:** for cutting chocolate into shavings

- ☐ **CHOPSTICKS:** for poking holes so glaze can seep into the cake

- ☐ **CUPCAKE LINERS:** for dressing up a simple cupcake

- ☐ **MICROPLANE:** for grating citrus zest and chocolate

- ☐ **PARCHMENT PAPER:** for lining pans so cakes don't stick

- ☐ **RULER:** for measuring pans, lengths of dough, and squares of cake

- ☐ **SCALE:** for measuring ingredients; also for weighing layer cakes before baking to make sure the same amount of batter is in each pan, creating equal layers to stack and frost

- ☐ **SCOOP:** like you use for ice cream; it evenly portions cupcake and muffin batter

- ☐ **SERRATED KNIFE:** for slicing cake layers in half

- ☐ **SPATULAS:** both rubber and silicone (heat tolerant) for mixing as well as metal icing spatulas, small and large, for frosting

- ☐ **SPRINKLES:** lots of them

- ☐ **THERMOMETER:** for icings and fillings and determining if a large cake is done

- ☐ **VEGETABLE PEELER:** for dragging across chocolate to make curls

- ☐ **WIRE RACKS, SMALL AND LARGE:** for cooling baked goods

- ☐ **WOODEN SPOONS:** for mixing everything

- ☐ **ZESTER:** to pull long thin strands off citrus

Well, wait just a minute. Read the recipe before you begin. Place the oven rack in the center of the oven and give your oven time to preheat—about 15 minutes. And keep the oven light on so you'll be able to see when the cake is done. *Now* we can begin.

Prep the Pan

Cakes can stick to a pan while baking, so you want to grease the sides of the pan with fat and flour to create a barrier to prevent this. Depending on how you prep the pan, you will get a slight difference in the outside texture. Brushing the pan with vegetable shortening and then dusting with flour creates a tender crust on cake layers that is easy to release from the pan and frost. This is super important when baking a cake like the red velvet because you want the crumbs to stay on the cake and not drag into the white frosting and turn it pink. And it is the preferred method for prepping a Bundt pan, especially one of those fancy Bundts with lots of crevices and detail. For gluten-free cakes, use rice flour or cornstarch in lieu of flour to dust the pans. Or dust a pan with cocoa for chocolate cakes.

Misting a pan with vegetable oil spray is fine for sheet and snack cakes that stay in the pan. It is sufficient for cakes baked in springform pans because of their removeable sides. And it works for muffins baked without paper liners. When to use butter to grease a pan? When you want a crumbly crust and a buttery flavor, wonderful for snack cakes, but not my choice on layers because it makes the frosting process messy. When to use cooking sprays like Pam? Never. They contain propellants, which are alcohols and create dark, tough cake edges.

Oven Temp . . . and When Is the Cake Done?

Most of the cakes in this book bake at 350°F. A rare exception is a larger cake baking more slowly at 325°F and a vegan or high-altitude cake baking more quickly at 375°F. Cookies and muffins also bake in a hotter oven.

After your oven preheats, take its temperature by placing an oven thermometer inside. If it registers lower than the preheated temp, your oven bakes cool, and if it's higher, your oven bakes hot. Calculate the difference between the thermometer reading and the temperature you set, and adjust the temperature on the oven up or down as needed to get the thermometer to reach the desired recipe temp.

Once your pans are in the oven, begin to time them. Look for visual signs of doneness—browning on a white or yellow cake, and possibly a chocolate cake that begins to pull away from the sides of the pan. Open the oven door briefly and carefully place a fingertip on the top of the center of the cake. Press down lightly. If it springs back, the cake is done. If not, give it a few more minutes.

The suggested baking times are just that—good suggestions. Set a kitchen timer with the minimum baking time. But when all else fails, know your oven!

Cool First, Then Frost

The best way to cool a cake is gradually. A cake needs to stay in the pan anywhere from 5 to 15 minutes, Bundts for 20 minutes, and a springform 15 minutes before unmolding. (An exception is a vegan layer cake that benefits from staying in the pan for 30 minutes before turning out.) After it has cooled in the pan per the recipe instructions, cool on a wire rack so air can circulate under the bottom and speed cooling. Once you turn them out of the pan and onto the rack, layers need to cool at least 30 minutes before frosting, but some Bundts can be glazed while warm. Cast-iron skillet cakes can be inverted onto a plate soon after they come out of the oven. It really depends on the pan and the recipe.

But sometimes you don't have the luxury of time. Sometimes you are in a mad rush to get the cake baked and frosted. And that is when you should stick the cake in the fridge or freezer.

Years ago, when I was on book tour with my first book, I visited St. Paul, Minnesota, and was baking cakes in the newspaper food writer's kitchen. It was bitterly cold outside and had been snowing all day. I was concerned because I had a cake in the oven and a plane to catch and needed to frost the cake in a hurry so I could get to the airport. I looked outside and there was this soft mound of snow on the deck—probably a foot deep. I nestled the yellow layers still in their pans right into that snow, and they cooled down in no time. Meanwhile I was beating chocolate frosting, which spread on that cooled cake like soft butter. And I made my plane.

New-Fashioned Yellow Cake with Chocolate Buttercream
(page 48)

While the cake bakes is a good time to either make the frosting or get all the ingredients at room temperature for frosting assembly. To bring butter and cream cheese to room temp in a hurry, microwave it on high power in 5- to 10-second intervals until soft. If you are making ganache, chop the chocolate and heat the cream to pour over. The ganache will come to the right spreading consistency by the time the cake is baked and has cooled. And if there are recipes that require a syrup or filling, you will be asked to make those first before you make the cake. Remember, too, that you can always use your refrigerator—and often the freezer—to speed up the process of making fillings, frostings, and other flourishes.

How to Frost Layers

Stacking and frosting layers isn't as difficult as it seems. If you have equal layers and they are baked and cooled, you are ready to frost. It is easier to frost flat cake layers, so to achieve this, slice the domed top off layers with a long serrated knife. (You can also press down on cake layers when they come out of the oven to flatten them. Or, flip the top layer upside down when frosting so the flat side is up.) Gently rub off any crumbs on the sides of the layers with your hands.

Place one layer—the larger one if your layers are not equal in size—on a serving plate or cake stand. And if you are a neat freak, place strips of wax or parchment paper— 3 × 12 inches—under the bottom layer to form a square around the cake and catch frosting run-offs. (You will gently pull the paper out from underneath after the cake is frosted.) But no worries if you don't have time for this, because even if you make a mess on the cake plate, you can always wipe it off with damp paper towels after frosting!

Spoon anywhere from ½ to 1 cup frosting onto the bottom layer, depending on the recipe (see photo 1, at right). If the bottom layer

is lopsided, this is a good time to build it up with frosting.

Place the second layer on top (see photo 2, opposite). Spread a modest amount of frosting on top (see photo 3). I like to make a "crumb" coat of frosting first—this captures any crumbs so when you spread on the second layer of frosting, it's bakery-perfect. To do this, spread a modest amount of frosting on the sides of the cake by holding a long metal spatula right against the cake with one hand and turning the cake plate with the other (see photo 4). You want the sides frosted thin enough to essentially see the cake peeking through. Once the sides are frosted, thinly frost the top of the cake and, if you have the time, place it in the fridge uncovered for 15 to 20 minutes (see photo 5). This sets the frosting and hardens it, making the cake easier to frost with a thicker final layer—especially when you are working in a hot kitchen or are baking in a humid climate.

Remove the cake from the fridge and finish frosting the top and sides to get the look you want. I use a small metal spatula and the back of a soupspoon to create drama, swirls, and dips on the top and use a long metal spatula to create either a sleek and smooth look or a patchy sort of layered look for the sides. You can also run a cake comb around the sides of the cake to create ridges and lines if you like.

CREATE A BARELY NAKED LOOK: Forget the first thin frosting coat. Spread frosting around the sides one way with a long metal spatula, then pull off half of it by running the spatula the other way, leaving some exposed cake edges. Frost the top of the cake.

FOR A NAKED LOOK: Don't frost the sides—just spread frosting between the layers and on top.

Simple Pleasures . . . Frost a Cupcake

Spread a couple of tablespoons of frosting onto a cooled cupcake with a short metal spatula or the back of a small spoon, just to the edge of the cupcake, still allowing a little bit of cake to peek out. Add something interesting on top, such as a chocolate curl, a few well chosen sprinkles, a small raspberry, or a toasted walnut. Peel back the paper liner and take a bite.

Wedding Cake Cupcakes
(page 281)

Easy Cake Decorations

I've never professed to be a cake decorator, and I have so much respect for people who do. It is an art and a craft that takes patience and practice. Bravo! My style of decorating a cake is a blend of homespun and modern. I follow the "less is more" mantra, and use ingredients on top of the cake to reflect what's inside. That's the way I baked and decorated most all the cakes photographed for this book. The challenge was to keep the adornment simple—no pastry bag allowed—so that anyone could attempt them.

Sometimes I suggest a garnish or decoration in the recipe. If I don't, it might be because the cake doesn't need it! And I think you'll find many of the cake garnishes right at your fingertips—nuts and candies, berries, citrus, chocolate shavings and curls, even sprinkles. Make sure you add the garnish immediately after frosting so the garnish sticks. If you've waited too long, and the berries on top of the cake roll off, just glue them back on with a dab of soft frosting.

Freezing Cake

The best cakes for freezing are unfrosted layers and Bundts, as well as unfrosted cookies and sheet cakes. First wrap a cooled cake in parchment or wax paper, then in foil, and then in a plastic resealable bag. Label the bag of cake and note the date you freeze it. Try to thaw—at room temp with the wrapping peeled back for a couple of hours—and use frozen cake within three months, the sooner the better.

Really Fast Cake Garnishes

☐ Sprinkles

☐ Berries or pomegranate seeds

☐ Finely chopped and toasted nuts—on the top or sides

☐ Chocolate shavings you make by slicing a chocolate bar with a heavy knife

☐ Edible flowers and herbs like rosemary flowers, nasturtiums, or violets, or mint leaves

☐ Toasted coconut

☐ Citrus zest—either grated or long strands of zest

☐ A dusting of confectioners' sugar, cocoa, or cinnamon. Get fancy and dust it over a stencil or a wire cooling rack to create a pattern

Strawberry Smash Cake
(page 111)

New Ways to Frost . . . or Not

If your frostings and garnishes need a refresh, here are some simple changes to make:

☐ Switch from white sugar to brown when making chocolate frosting.

☐ Add a pinch of sea or kosher salt to frostings to make them taste less sweet.

☐ Push a handful of fresh berries through a sieve and fold into vanilla buttercream frosting.

☐ Make homemade curd from citrus and fill cake layers.

☐ Or fill layers with whipped cream and fresh fruit.

☐ Make half a recipe of a different frosting and use it as a filling between cake layers.

☐ Add interest to the top of a cake with a praline, crumble, meringue, or streusel.

☐ Garnish with chocolate shavings, crumbled chocolate wafers, or cake crumbs so things don't look so plain. (Pulse cake—the dome you might have cut off—in a food processor to make these crumbs, and if you freeze the cake first it makes it easier to pulse.)

☐ Frost then drip. Stack and spread a thin layer of buttercream frosting on the top and sides of the cake and chill until firm. Then pour a caramel, white chocolate, or chocolate glaze over the top and return to the refrigerator until it sets.

☐ Or just frost less for barely or fully naked cakes.

More so now than ever, I realize we all need to bake differently. I tested many recipes for gluten-free, sugar-free, and vegan diets, and they are shared throughout this book. Here is a little more information on how to bake better when you have special situations:

Sugar-Reduced and Sugar-Free Cakes

For this book, I revisited frostings and glazes looking for ways to reduce sugar. I no longer add a box—about 4 cups—confectioners' sugar to a frosting recipe just because a recipe says so. Most of my buttercreams and cream cheese frostings call for 2 to 3 cups sugar, a significant reduction.

You will notice I suggest you forgo frosting on many cakes in this book because I feel the cake doesn't need it.

I also took a look at the sugar-free cake mixes to find out ways that those of you on a sugar-free diet can use them and bake well. I baked the Sugar-Free Darn Good Chocolate Cake (page 140) and the Sugar-Free Sock-It-to-Me Cake (page 153) using sugar-free versions of Pillsbury cake mixes, instant pudding mix, and chocolate chips. You could easily turn these recipes into cupcakes or a sheet cake. Enjoy these cakes warm, when they taste best and the chocolate is melted and the cinnamon more fragrant. And get creative with substitutes that are allowed on your diet. In the Sugar-Free Sock-It-to-Me Cake, for example, I replaced brown sugar in the streusel with finely chopped apple.

Vegan Cakes

When I wrote The Cake Mix Doctor, *the two options for vegan baking were Egg Beaters and Crisco, and that's about it. Now, coconut milk and nondairy plant butters made with avocado and olive oil have revolutionized how we can bake and frost a cake mix cake without dairy. But finding a suitable egg replacement involves trial and error. For someone accustomed to baking with eggs who wants vegan cakes to perform like a cake with eggs, it is less than perfect.*

My favorite substitute for eggs is unsweetened applesauce (¼ cup per egg). I've tried whipping aquafaba, the liquid found in a can of chickpeas or white beans, with a little cream of tartar. And I folded it into various cakes in lieu of eggs hopeful that the cake would rise to high heights like a chiffon. But it would rise and dip, and then I'd cover up the shortcomings with frosting. Vegan cakes can benefit from a slightly hotter oven.

Vegan Cinnamon Applesauce Cake
(page 244)

High-Altitude Cakes

I've experienced baking in mile-high cities on book tours and have heard from many of you. Thank you for your suggestions on making high-altitude baking more successful.

An area with an altitude over 3,500 feet is considered high altitude. There is less air pressure as elevation increases, which creates chaos for cakes. The leavening in the mix causes the cake to rise more rapidly, and so cakes bake up and overflow into the oven or rise up and fall flat. To counter this, set your oven 25°F hotter than the recipe suggests to help the cake create shape. And forgo pudding mixes and gelatin that contain sugar, which tenderizes and reduces the cake's structure.

Look for recipes in this book where I add some all-purpose flour to the cake mix—these are good candidates for high-altitude baking.

As for the size of pans that bake the best, choose 9-inch layers, Bundt and tube pans, or 9-inch squares instead of the 13 × 9-inch pan (which can yield a concave cake). Always grease and flour pans, because cakes tend to stick when baked in the clouds. And above all, embrace frosting!

Gluten-Free Cakes

Baking gluten-free has never been easier, and yet it is still a mystery. There are mixes, more ingredients at our fingertips, and better labeling. And yet everyone seems to search for a cake that doesn't taste "gluten-free," meaning gritty and with odd flavors from alternative flours. On top of that, because many gluten-free people follow a dairy-free diet, using dairy-free replacements presents challenges, too.

My advice is to experiment with gluten-free cake mixes and come up with ways to make them better using the recipes in this book. Rice flour is a main ingredient in most mixes and it is gritty, but I have found that acidic ingredients like orange juice tenderize it. Sugar, too, improves the cake's texture, and that's the reason I have success adding instant pudding mix to a gluten-free batter. Eggs help also. In fact, eggs are one of the most important ingredients in a gluten-free cake because they add structure in the absence of gluten. If you are baking gluten-free at a high altitude, add an extra egg white to the recipe for moisture and structure. Bake with cocoa and ground almonds because they both act like a "flour," and turn smaller mixes into a bigger cake.

Be aware that gluten-free cake batter is thicker than regular batter. You may need to beat it longer, and gluten-free cakes often take longer to bake. So be patient.

Cakes on a Budget

Thrift is a good reason people turn to cake mixes. The mixes are frequently on sale, and you can stock up. Compare brands and see how less expensive ones work with the recipes in this book.

Also stock up on staple ingredients like oil that are less expensive by unit—read the store shelf tag. Watch out for sales on chocolate chips and nuts and keep the nuts in the freezer to stay fresh longer. Right now one of the most basic ingredients—vanilla—is priced sky-high. With a clear conscience you can bake without it until the price comes down. Get creative with other flavorings, or look for markets that sell less expensive Mexican vanilla.

Bake ahead and freeze cakes for gifts or split a recipe into two pans and serve one now and freeze another for later. These are ways to reduce the amount of time you spend baking and also the amount of cake you consume. Both, in their own way, will save you money.

And lastly, don't buy one pricey ingredient like cardamom that sits in your pantry and is seldom used. When you look at a recipe, think of it as a blueprint. Think of what you have on hand. All of a sudden your baking will take on a new simplicity that works beautifully on a budget.

Cakes for Small Households

The easiest way to bake for one or two is to slice a whole cake into pieces and freeze it in portions. If you want to go one step further, make a half recipe of cake batter and bake it in a 6-inch round layer pan that is 3 inches deep.

How to do this? Invest in a kitchen scale. Combine the dry ingredients for your favorite recipe from this book in a bowl and with the help of the scale, divide the mixture in half. Place both halves in plastic resealable bags. When you are ready to bake a cake, pour the contents of one bag into a mixing bowl and add half the liquid called for in the recipe. If the recipe calls for 3 eggs, this is about 6 ounces. You can crack and lightly beat 2 eggs, then weigh 3 ounces of it on the kitchen scale. Or, you can use one whole egg and one egg yolk, which also weighs about 3 ounces. For frosting? Dust with confectioners' sugar or pour glaze over the top. Your smaller mixes will keep for several months, or until you feel like baking cake!

Banana Lime Baby Cake
(page 120)

*Gluten-Free Vanilla Cake
with Cherry Buttercream*
(page 73)

Layer Up

Layers of vanilla, chocolate, coconut, even clementine, are what we bake for birthdays and weddings, anniversaries and homecomings, all of life's sweet events. Their attraction is their classic architecture, the big statement they make on a cake stand (even if they're a baby cake), all the possibilities of intriguing fillings and frostings, and just before slicing, the photo-perfect garnishes.

Basic Butter Cake

SERVES 12

PREP: 10 MINUTES

BAKE: 20 TO 25 MINUTES
FOR 9-INCH LAYERS,
35 TO 40 MINUTES FOR A
13 × 9-INCH SHEET CAKE, 18 TO
22 MINUTES FOR CUPCAKES

CAKE

Vegetable oil spray or
vegetable shortening,
for greasing the pans

All-purpose flour,
for dusting the pans

1 (15.25-ounce) package
yellow or butter cake mix

4 tablespoons
(half a 3.4-ounce package)
vanilla instant pudding mix

3 large eggs

1 cup milk (whole,
evaporated, coconut,
or buttermilk)

8 tablespoons (1 stick)
unsalted butter,
melted and cooled

1 teaspoon vanilla extract

FROSTING CHOICES

Whipped Chocolate Ganache
(page 363), Clementine
frosting (from Clementine
Cake, page 95), Coffee
Buttercream (page 352)

This is the recipe for making layer cakes, cupcakes, sheet cake, you name it. It's a blank canvas and comes to life in various and delicious ways. If I have whole milk, I'll use it; if not, then there's probably some buttermilk in the fridge or coconut milk in the pantry that's an easy enough swap.

1. Make the cake: Place a rack in the center of the oven and preheat the oven to 350°F. Grease and flour two 9-inch round cake pans. Set the pans aside.

2. In a large mixing bowl, stir together the cake mix and pudding mix. Add the eggs, milk, melted butter, and vanilla. Beat with an electric mixer on low speed until blended, about 30 seconds. Stop the machine and scrape down the sides of the bowl with a rubber spatula. Beat on medium speed until the batter is well blended, about 1 minute. Divide the batter evenly between the prepared pans, smoothing it out with a rubber spatula.

3. Place the pans in the oven and bake until the cakes spring back when gently pressed in the middle and are golden brown, 20 to 25 minutes.

4. Let the cakes cool in the pans on wire racks for 10 to 15 minutes. Run a dinner knife around the edge of each pan, then invert each layer onto a rack. Invert the layers again so they are right-side up and allow the layers to cool completely, about 20 minutes longer.

5. Frost the cake: Place one cake layer right-side up on a cake plate. Spread some of the frosting over the top. Place the second layer on top of the first, right-side up. Spread some of the frosting over the top. Frost the sides of the cake with the remaining frosting. Slice and serve. Store, lightly covered, at room temperature for up to 4 days.

How to Make a Peaches and Cream Cake

Preheat the oven as directed. Grease a 9-inch springform pan and line the bottom with a round of parchment paper. Make the Basic Butter Cake batter, pour into the pan, and bake for 42 to 47 minutes. Cool in the pan, then slice horizontally into three layers. Place the bottom layer back in the reassembled springform pan. Fill and frost the layers with Homemade Cool Whip (page 368) and 2½ cups sliced fresh peaches. Chill until time to serve, then unsnap and remove the sides of the pan, slice, and serve.

New-Fashioned Yellow Cake
with Chocolate Buttercream

SERVES 12

PREP: 35 TO 40 MINUTES

BAKE: 20 TO 25 MINUTES

Vegetable oil spray or
vegetable shortening,
for greasing the pans

All-purpose flour,
for dusting the pans

1 (15.25-ounce) package
yellow or butter cake mix

3 large eggs

1 cup full-fat or light
canned coconut milk
(see Cook's Note)

⅓ cup vegetable oil

2 teaspoons vanilla extract

Chocolate Buttercream
Frosting (page 355)

COOK'S NOTE:
Buy a can of coconut
milk that yields at least
10 ounces: 8 ounces (1 cup)
for the cake and some
for the frosting. Or omit
the coconut milk and use
whole milk instead.

*Yellow cake with chocolate frosting is the classic birthday cake.
And in this update of an old favorite, canned coconut milk
is the surprising and new addition. While it doesn't impart
coconut flavor, boy, does it improve the texture of the cake!*

1. Place a rack in the center of the oven and preheat the oven
    to 350°F. Grease and flour two 9-inch round cake pans.
    Set the pans aside.

2. In a large mixing bowl, combine the cake mix, eggs, coconut
    milk, oil, and vanilla. Beat with an electric mixer on low speed
    until blended, about 30 seconds. Stop the machine and scrape
    down the sides of the bowl with a rubber spatula. Increase the
    mixer speed to medium and beat for 1 minute. The batter will
    be thick. Divide the batter evenly between the prepared pans,
    smoothing it out with a rubber spatula.

3. Place the pans in the oven and bake until the cakes are light
    golden brown and beginning to pull away from the sides of the
    pans, 20 to 25 minutes.

4. Let the cakes cool in the pans on wire racks for 10 to
    15 minutes. Run a dinner knife around the edge of each pan,
    then invert each layer onto a rack. Invert the layers again so
    they are right-side up and allow the cakes to cool completely,
    about 20 minutes longer.

5. To assemble the cake, place one cake layer right-side up on
    a cake plate and spread some frosting over the top. Place the
    second layer on top of the first, right-side up. Spread some
    frosting over the top. Frost the sides of the cake with the
    remaining frosting, or for a barely naked look, spread with
    frosting and then pull half of it back off with a long metal
    icing spatula. Slice and serve. Store, lightly covered, at room
    temperature for up to 4 days.

Buttermilk Devil's Food Cake

In spite of the name, there's nothing evil about this cake.
Devil's food cake was named because of the reddish hue
caused by the cocoa, baking soda, and buttermilk.

SERVES 12

PREP: 20 TO 25 MINUTES

BAKE: 22 TO 27 MINUTES

CAKE

Vegetable oil spray
or shortening,
for greasing the pans

All-purpose flour or
unsweetened cocoa powder,
for dusting the pans

1 (15.25-ounce) package
chocolate cake mix

2 tablespoons
unsweetened cocoa powder

3 large eggs

1¼ cups buttermilk,
preferably whole milk
(see Cook's Note)

½ cup vegetable oil

1 teaspoon vanilla extract

ASSEMBLY

Cream Cheese Frosting
(page 356) or Chocolate
Buttercream Frosting
(page 355)

White chocolate shavings,
for garnish

1. Make the cake: Place a rack in the center of the oven and preheat the oven to 350°F. Grease and flour two 9-inch round cake pans. Set the pans aside.

2. In a large mixing bowl, stir together the cake mix and cocoa. Add the eggs, buttermilk, oil, and vanilla. Beat with an electric mixer on low speed until blended, about 30 seconds. Stop the machine and scrape down the sides of the bowl with a rubber spatula. Increase the mixer speed to medium and beat for 40 seconds longer. The batter should be smooth, but it doesn't need a lot of beating time. Divide the batter evenly between the prepared pans, smoothing it out with a rubber spatula.

3. Place the pans in the oven and bake until the cakes spring back when gently pressed in the middle, 22 to 27 minutes.

4. Let the cakes cool in the pans on wire racks for 10 to 15 minutes. Run a dinner knife around the edge of each pan, then invert onto the rack. Invert the layers again so they are right-side up and allow the cakes to cool completely, about 20 minutes longer.

5. Assemble the cake: Place one cake layer right-side up on a cake plate and spread nearly 1 cup of frosting over the top. Place the second layer on top of the first, right-side up. Spread the rest of the frosting over the top and around the sides of the cake. Sprinkle the white chocolate shavings on the top.

COOK'S NOTE:

If you don't have buttermilk, make your own by adding 4 teaspoons distilled white vinegar or lemon juice to 1¼ cups whole milk. Let the mixture stand at room temperature for 10 minutes to thicken. Or you can substitute whole-milk kefir or plain full-fat yogurt.

Vegan Seltzer Cake

SERVES 12

PREP: 25 TO 30 MINUTES

BAKE: 25 TO 30 MINUTES

Vegetable oil spray
or shortening,
for greasing the pans

1 (15.25- or 16.25-ounce)
package yellow or white
cake mix

½ cup all-purpose flour

1 cup (8 ounces) unflavored
or vanilla seltzer or
sparkling water

⅔ cup vegetable oil

¼ cup unsweetened
applesauce

1 teaspoon vanilla extract
or grated lemon zest

Vegan Chocolate
Buttercream (page 353)

Sparkling water gives cake mix a boost, making it possible to create a cake without eggs. Be forewarned that while any flavored seltzer can be used since the flavor usually doesn't come through, the color of the seltzer can bake into some pretty "interesting" hues. For example, a reddish-purple pomegranate sparkling water will turn a cake gray! So watch those seltzers with colorings added to them!

1. Place a rack in the center of the oven and preheat the oven to 350°F. Grease two 8-inch round cake pans. Line the bottoms of the pans with rounds of parchment paper. Set the pans aside.

2. In a large mixing bowl, stir together the cake mix and flour. Add the seltzer, oil, applesauce, and vanilla. Beat with an electric mixer on low speed until blended, about 30 seconds. Stop the machine and scrape down the sides of the bowl with a rubber spatula. Increase the mixer speed to medium and beat for 1 minute. Divide the batter evenly between the two pans, smoothing it out with a rubber spatula.

3. Place the pans in the oven and bake until the cakes are lightly browned and spring back when gently pressed in the middle, 25 to 30 minutes.

4. Let the cakes cool in the pans on wire racks for at least 20 minutes. Run a dinner knife around the edge of each pan and invert each layer onto a rack and very carefully pull off the rounds of parchment paper. Invert the layers again so they are right-side up and allow the cakes to cool completely, about 20 minutes longer.

5. To assemble the cake, place one cake layer, right-side up, on a cake plate and carefully—vegan cakes are fragile—spread ¾ cup of the frosting over the top. Place the second layer, right-side up, on top of the first. Spread some of the frosting smoothly over the top. Slice and serve. Store, lightly covered, at room temperature for up to 4 days.

SERVES 12

PREP: 25 TO 30 MINUTES

BAKE: 20 TO 25 MINUTES

CAKE

Vegetable oil spray
or shortening,
for greasing the pans

All-purpose flour or
unsweetened cocoa powder,
for dusting the pans

1 (15.25-ounce) package
chocolate cake mix

2 tablespoons
unsweetened cocoa powder

2 teaspoons espresso powder
(see Cook's Notes)

3 large eggs

1¼ cups warm water

½ cup light olive oil

1 teaspoon vanilla extract

ASSEMBLY

Chocolate Ganache
(page 362)

Unsweetened cocoa powder,
for dusting

Chocolate Olive Oil Cake
with Chocolate Ganache

*Once you bake a chocolate and olive oil cake and spread
it with chocolate ganache, you'll do it again. Olive oil not only contains
heart-heathy monounsaturated fat, but it is a natural emulsifier,
providing a moist and rich crumb and good rise in the pan.
The best kind of olive oil for baking is light in flavor
and color—save the extra-virgin for salad!*

1. Make the cake: Place a rack in the center of the oven and preheat the oven to 350°F. Grease and flour two 9-inch round cake pans. Set the pans aside.

2. In a large mixing bowl, stir together the cake mix, cocoa, and espresso powder. Add the eggs, warm water, olive oil, and vanilla. Beat with an electric mixer on low speed until blended, about 30 seconds. Stop the machine and scrape down the sides of the bowl with a rubber spatula. Increase the mixer speed to medium and beat for 1 minute. The batter should be smooth. Divide the batter evenly between the prepared pans, smoothing it out with a rubber spatula.

3. Place the pans in the oven and bake until the cakes spring back when gently pressed in the middle and begin to pull away from the sides of the pans, 20 to 25 minutes.

4. Let the cakes cool in the pans on wire racks for 10 to 15 minutes. Run a dinner knife around the edge of each pan, then invert each layer onto a rack. Invert the layers again so the cakes are right-side up and allow the cakes to cool completely, about 20 minutes longer.

5. Assemble the cake: Place one layer right-side up on a cake plate and spread nearly 1 cup of frosting over the top. Place the second layer on top of the first, right-side up. Spread the rest of the frosting generously over the top and barely around the sides. Let sit for 30 minutes to let frosting set. Dust with cocoa. Slice and serve. Store, covered, in the refrigerator for up to 4 days.

COOK'S NOTES:
You can find espresso
powder in supermarkets in
the baking or coffee aisle.
In a pinch, substitute instant
coffee powder; or replace
the water in the recipe with
1¼ cups brewed coffee.

To make assembly neater,
wrap a piece of acetate
(see page 28) around the
cake before you frost the
top. Spoon the ganache on
top and chill until firm.

Mint Chocolate Cookies and Cream Cake

SERVES 12

PREP: 25 TO 30 MINUTES

BAKE: 23 TO 27 MINUTES

FREEZE: 1 HOUR

CAKE

Vegetable oil spray
or shortening,
for greasing the pans

All-purpose flour,
for dusting the pans

18 to 20 mint-chocolate
sandwich cookies
(see Cook's Note)

1 (15.25- or 16.25-ounce)
package white cake mix

3 large eggs

1 cup water

½ cup vegetable oil

1 teaspoon vanilla extract

TO FINISH

2 cups heavy cream

Whole mint-chocolate
sandwich cookies, for
garnish

When I shared Leigh Anne McInerney's cookies and cream cake in one of my earlier books, everyone loved it. Could it be the name, the ease, or the irresistible taste that makes it a favorite? Or that it's packed with more than 2 cups of crushed chocolate sandwich cookies? A few months back another reader, Dee Dee Dickey, emailed with a delicious tweak to that cake—using mint-flavored cookies instead of plain. Now we have the makings of another classic!

1.   Make the cake: Place a rack in the center of the oven and preheat the oven to 350°F. Grease and flour two 9-inch round cake pans. Set the pans aside.

2.   Place the cookies, including the filling, in a food processor. (Depending on the size of your food processor, you may need to do this in batches. If you first break up the cookies into large pieces by hand, it makes the process easier.) Pulse until you have coarse crumbs. You need 2¼ cups total cookie crumbs: 1 cup for the cake, 1 cup for the frosting, and ¼ cup for the garnish. Set aside.

3.   In a large mixing bowl, combine the cake mix, eggs, water, oil, and vanilla. Beat with an electric mixer on low speed until blended, about 30 seconds. Stop the machine and scrape down the sides of the bowl with a rubber spatula. Increase the mixer speed to medium and beat for 1 minute. Fold in 1 cup of the cookie crumbs until well distributed. Divide the batter evenly between the prepared pans, smoothing it out with a rubber spatula.

4.   Place the pans in the oven and bake until the cakes spring back when gently pressed in the middle and are lightly golden brown, 23 to 27 minutes.

CONTINUED

COOK'S NOTE:

Use whatever brand of mint-chocolate sandwich cookie–or plain–you like best. The number of cookies needed to make 2¼ cups crumbs will vary by brand.

5. Let the cakes cool in the pans on wire racks for 10 to 15 minutes. Run a dinner knife around the edge of each pan to loosen, then invert each layer onto a rack. Invert the layers again so they are right-side up and allow the cakes to cool completely, about 20 minutes longer.

6. To make slicing easier and more precise, wrap each layer in plastic wrap and place in the freezer for 1 hour.

7. To finish: Chill a mixing bowl and electric mixer beaters or the wire whisk attachment in the freezer for 10 minutes. Remove from the freezer and pour the cream into the bowl. Beat with the electric mixer on high speed until stiff peaks form, about 3 minutes. Fold in 1 cup of the reserved cookie crumbs, then cover the bowl with plastic wrap and chill the frosting until ready to use.

8. When ready to assemble the cake, remove the layers from the freezer and the frosting from the refrigerator. With a serrated knife, slice each layer in half horizontally to yield 4 thin layers. Place the bottom half of a cake layer cut-side up on a cake plate. Spread with some of the frosting. Top with the matching half of the layer, cut-side down. Spread with frosting. Add the bottom half of the second layer cut-side up, and spread with frosting. Top with the matching half of the layer, cut-side down. Spread the top and sides of the cake with the remaining frosting.

9. Sprinkle the remaining ¼ cup reserved crumbs on top of the cake. Decorate with whole cookies or halves. Place the cake in a cake saver or under a glass dome and refrigerate until ready to serve. Store in the fridge for up to 5 days.

CAKE

Vegetable oil spray
or shortening,
for greasing the pans

All-purpose flour or
unsweetened cocoa powder,
for dusting the pans

1 bar (4 ounces)
German's sweet chocolate

1 (15.25-ounce) package
yellow or butter cake mix

5 tablespoons (half a
3.9-ounce package) chocolate
instant pudding mix

3 large eggs

¾ cup evaporated milk
or water (see Cook's Note)

½ cup sour cream
or Greek yogurt

¼ cup vegetable oil

**Coconut Pecan Frosting
(page 58)**

COOK'S NOTE:
Buy a 12-ounce can of
evaporated milk. Use half
(¾ cup) in the cake and the
other half in the frosting.

Favorite German Chocolate Cake

German chocolate cake's popularity came out of frontier kitchens in Texas and Oklahoma where resourceful cooks grabbed a can of evaporated milk and a newfangled bar of German's sweet chocolate. Although some folks like to think this cake has German roots, its name comes from an English man—Sam German—who first manufactured the sweet chocolate used to make this cake. I not only love its story, but its taste, too!

1. Make the cake: Place a rack in the center of the oven and preheat the oven to 350°F. Grease and flour two 9-inch round cake pans. Set the pans aside.

2. Break the chocolate into 8 pieces and place in a microwave-safe bowl. Microwave on high power for 30 seconds, then stir. Microwave for another 20 to 30 seconds, until the chocolate is nearly melted. Stir until completely melted.

3. In a large mixing bowl, stir together the cake mix and pudding mix. Add the melted chocolate, the eggs, evaporated milk, sour cream, and oil. Beat with an electric mixer on low speed until blended, about 30 seconds. Stop the machine and scrape down the sides of the bowl with a rubber spatula. Increase the mixer speed to medium and beat for 1 minute. The batter will be thick. Divide the batter evenly between the prepared pans, smoothing it out with a rubber spatula.

4. Place the pans in the oven and bake until the cakes spring back when gently pressed in the middle, 25 to 30 minutes.

RECIPE AND INGREDIENTS CONTINUED

COCONUT PECAN FROSTING

¾ cup evaporated milk

¾ cup sugar

6 tablespoons unsalted butter

2 large egg yolks, lightly beaten

1 teaspoon vanilla extract

Pinch of salt

1 cup toasted unsweetened or sweetened shredded coconut (see Cook's Note)

¾ cup chopped toasted pecans (see Cook's Note)

COOK'S NOTE:
Toast both the coconut and pecans in a 350°F oven before making the frosting. Dried unsweetened coconut takes less time to toast than the sweetened coconut does. Allow 3 to 5 minutes for the unsweetened, and 5 to 7 minutes for the sweetened. Chopped pecans toast in 5 to 7 minutes.

5. Meanwhile, make the coconut pecan frosting: In a large saucepan, combine the evaporated milk, sugar, butter, egg yolks, vanilla, and salt. Cook over medium-low heat, stirring constantly, until thickened and golden, 10 to 12 minutes (reduce the heat to low if needed to gently cook the mixture). Remove from the heat. Stir in the coconut and pecans. Let the frosting cool to room temperature, about 30 minutes.

6. Let the cakes cool in the pans on wire racks for 10 to 15 minutes. Run a dinner knife around the edge of each pan, then invert onto the rack. Invert the layers again so they are right-side up and allow the cakes to cool completely while the frosting cools to room temperature.

7. To assemble the cake, place one cake layer, right-side up, on a cake plate and spread 1 cup of the frosting over the top. Place the second layer, right-side up, on top of the first. Pile the remaining frosting on top of the cake and spread it to the edges. Do not frost the sides of the cake. Slice and serve. Store this cake a few hours at room temp, but then place it in the fridge, lightly covered, where it will keep up to 5 days. For best slicing, remove from the fridge for 1 hour to come to room temperature.

SERVES 12

PREP: 20 TO 25 MINUTES

BAKE: 23 TO 27 MINUTES

CAKE

Vegetable oil spray
or shortening,
for greasing the pans

All-purpose flour or
unsweetened cocoa powder,
for dusting the pans

1 (15.25-ounce) package
chocolate cake mix
(see Cook's Note)

½ cup all-purpose flour

1 tablespoon unsweetened
cocoa powder

½ cup vegetable oil

¾ cup warm water

¾ cup (about two 3.9-ounce
containers) unsweetened
applesauce

ASSEMBLY

Creamy Nutella Frosting
(page 358)

Unsweetened cocoa powder,
for dusting

Vegan Chocolate Cake
with Creamy Nutella Frosting

*My adventure in vegan cake baking began with this recipe.
I tried various egg substitutes—a tablespoon of vinegar plus
a teaspoon of soda, as well as sparkling water, and finally arrived
at my favorite—unsweetened applesauce. I added a bit of flour
to bulk up the mix and give it more structure, and I baked
8-inch layers so the cake rises up higher in the pans. Nice!*

1. Make the cake: Place a rack in the center of the oven and preheat the oven to 350°F. Grease and flour two 8-inch round cake pans. Set the pans aside.

2. In a large mixing bowl, stir together the cake mix, flour, and cocoa. Add the oil, water, and applesauce. Beat with an electric mixer on low speed until blended, about 30 seconds. Stop the machine and scrape down the sides of the bowl with a rubber spatula. Increase the mixer speed to medium and beat for 1 minute longer. The batter will be thick. Divide the batter evenly between the prepared pans, smoothing it out with a rubber spatula.

3. Place the pans in the oven and bake until the cakes spring back when gently pressed in the middle, 23 to 27 minutes.

4. Let the cakes cool in the pans on wire racks for at least 20 minutes. It's important to let these vegan cakes cool a bit longer before you turn them out. Run a dinner knife around the edge of each pan, then invert each layer onto a rack. Invert the layers again so they are right-side up and allow the cakes to cool completely, about 20 minutes longer.

5. Assemble the cake: Place one cake layer, right-side up, on a cake plate and spread ¾ cup frosting over the top. Place the second layer, right-side up, on top of the first. Pile the remaining frosting on top of the cake. Swirl the frosting using the back of a spoon. Dust the top of the cake with cocoa. Slice and serve. Store, lightly covered, in the refrigerator for up to 4 days.

CAKE

Vegetable oil spray
or shortening,
for greasing the pans

All-purpose flour or
unsweetened cocoa powder,
for dusting the pans

1 (15.25-ounce) package
chocolate cake mix

2 tablespoons
unsweetened cocoa powder

3 large eggs

1¼ cups warm water

½ cup vegetable oil
or light olive oil

1 teaspoon vanilla extract

ASSEMBLY

2 pints (32 ounces)
pistachio or vanilla gelato
or ice cream

1 cup chopped salted
roasted pistachios

Whipped Chocolate Ganache
(page 363)

Chocolate-Pistachio Ice Cream Cake

Ice cream cakes are wonderfully efficient. No separate plates and bowls. No searching for the ice cream scoop once the cake has been cut. I hope you love the combination of chocolate cake and pistachio ice cream as much as I do, but if not, there's always mint chocolate or caramel!

1. Make the cake: Place a rack in the center of the oven and preheat the oven to 350°F. Grease and flour a 9-inch springform pan. Set the pan aside.

2. In a large mixing bowl, stir together the cake mix and cocoa. Add the eggs, water, oil, and vanilla. Beat with an electric mixer on low speed until blended, about 30 seconds. Stop the machine and scrape down the sides of the bowl with a rubber spatula. Increase the mixer speed to medium and beat for 1 minute. The batter should be smooth. Pour the batter into the pan, smoothing it out with a rubber spatula.

3. Place the pan in the oven and bake until the cake springs back when gently pressed in the middle, 48 to 52 minutes.

4. Let the cake cool in the pan on a wire rack for 15 minutes. Run a dinner knife around the edge of the pan, then unsnap and remove the sides of the pan. Allow the cake to cool completely, about 30 minutes longer.

5. Assemble the cake: Remove the ice cream from the freezer to soften slightly.

6. Slice the cooled cake horizontally into thirds, leaving the bottom third attached to the base of the pan. Spread one pint of ice cream over the bottom cake layer. Sprinkle with one-third of the pistachios. Place the second (middle) cake layer on top and spread it with the second pint of ice cream. Sprinkle with another one-third of the pistachios. Place the top third of the cake on top. Re-attach the pan sides around the cake and snap to secure. Cover with plastic wrap and place in the freezer while you prepare the ganache.

7. Remove the cake from the freezer. Remove the plastic wrap and the sides and bottom from the pan. Place the cake on a cake plate. Spread the top and sides of the cake with the ganache. Garnish with the remaining pistachios, if desired. Let the cake sit at room temperature until it is soft enough to slice, about 20 minutes. Slice and serve. Store, tightly covered, in the freezer for up to 1 week.

Boston Cream Pie

SERVES 12

PREP: 30 MINUTES

CHILL: 30 MINUTES
(FOR THE PUDDING)

BAKE: 20 TO 25 MINUTES

PUDDING FILLING

1 (5.1-ounce) package
vanilla instant pudding mix

2 cups whole milk
(see Cook's Note)

1 teaspoon vanilla extract

CAKE

Vegetable oil spray or shortening, for greasing the pans

All-purpose flour,
for dusting the pans

1 (15.25-ounce) package
yellow or butter cake mix

3 large eggs

1 cup whole milk
(see Cook's Note)

8 tablespoons (1 stick)
unsalted butter,
at room temperature

1 teaspoon vanilla extract

Shiny Chocolate Glaze
(page 371)

Boston cream pie is one of the first cakes I learned to bake because my dad loved it so. And the purist in me wants to make this cake from scratch each time. But now that I know how to tweak a yellow mix to make it more dense and rich by adding pudding mix, I can assemble this "homemade-ish" cake in about an hour.

1. Make the pudding filling: Measure out 3½ tablespoons of the pudding mix and set aside for the cake. Measure the remaining 9 tablespoons of the pudding mix into a medium bowl. Add the milk and vanilla and whisk until thickened, about 2 minutes. Let the pudding rest in the bowl for 5 minutes. Cover the bowl with plastic wrap and place in the refrigerator while you bake the cake.

2. Make the cake: Place a rack in the center of the oven and preheat the oven to 350°F. Grease and flour two 9-inch round cake pans. Set the pans aside.

3. In a large mixing bowl, stir together the cake mix and reserved 3½ tablespoons pudding mix. Add the eggs, milk, butter, and vanilla. Beat with an electric mixer on low speed until blended, about 30 seconds. Stop the machine and scrape down the sides of the bowl with a rubber spatula. Increase the mixer speed to medium and beat for 1 minute. The batter will be very thick. Divide the batter evenly between the prepared pans, smoothing it out with a rubber spatula.

4. Place the pans in the oven and bake until the cakes are lightly golden brown and the tops spring back when gently pressed in the middle, 20 to 25 minutes.

5. Let the cakes cool in the pans on wire racks for 10 to 15 minutes. Run a dinner knife around the edge of each pan, then invert each layer onto a rack. Invert the layers again so they are right-side up and allow the cakes to cool completely, about 30 minutes longer. (Or, place the cakes, uncovered, in the fridge for 5 to 10 minutes to speed-cool.)

Add a Touch of History

The original Boston cream pie from the Parker House hotel had a tablespoon of rum in the filling, and it was garnished around the sides with toasted sliced almonds.

6. To assemble the cake, remove the pudding filling from the refrigerator. Place one cake layer, right-side up, on a cake plate. Spoon the filling onto the center of the cake and spread until it barely reaches the edge. Place the second layer, right-side up, on top of the first. Spoon the glaze over the top of the cake and let it drip down the sides of the cake. Let the glaze firm up for 10 minutes before slicing and serving. Store, lightly covered, in the refrigerator for up to 4 days.

COOK'S NOTE:
You must use whole milk for this recipe because it gives the pudding and cake the fat they need to be creamy and moist, respectively.

Vegetable oil spray
or shortening,
for greasing the pans

All-purpose flour,
for dusting the pans

1 bar (4 ounces)
German's sweet chocolate

1 (15.25-ounce) package
yellow or butter cake mix

4 tablespoons (half a
3.4-ounce package) vanilla
instant pudding mix

3 large eggs

1 cup whole milk

¾ cup vegetable oil

1 cup (6 ounces) mini
semisweet chocolate chips

Chocolate Pan Frosting
(page 361)

Chocolate Chip Cake
with Pan Frosting

*These chocolate-flecked layers are so tempting when warm,
you need willpower to resist nibbling them as they cool. Packed
with semisweet and German sweet chocolate, this cake is based
on the much-loved Stacy's Chocolate Chip Cake (page 134)
and is a good match for my mom's chocolate pan frosting.*

1. Place a rack in the center of the oven and preheat the oven to
   350°F. Grease and flour two 9-inch round cake pans. Set aside.

2. Break the chocolate bar into 1-inch pieces. Turn on a food
   processor and drop the pieces in (or grate by hand). Process
   until the chocolate is grated. Set the grated chocolate aside.

3. In a large mixing bowl, stir together the cake mix and pudding
   mix. Add the eggs, milk, and oil. Beat with an electric mixer on
   low speed until blended, about 30 seconds. Stop the machine
   and scrape down the sides of the bowl with a rubber spatula.
   Increase the mixer speed to medium and beat for 1 minute
   more, until well blended. Fold in the grated chocolate and the
   mini chocolate chips. Divide the batter evenly between the
   prepared pans, smoothing it out with a rubber spatula.

4. Place the pans in the oven and bake until the cakes spring back
   and are lightly golden brown, 28 to 32 minutes.

5. Let the cakes cool in the pans on wire racks for 10 to 15 minutes.
   Run a dinner knife around the edge of each pan, then invert
   each layer onto a rack. Invert the layers again so they are right-
   side up and cool completely, about 20 minutes.

6. To assemble the cake, place one cake layer, right-side up, on
   a cake plate and ladle 1 cup of the warm frosting over the
   top. Place the second layer, right-side up, on top of the first.
   Ladle the remaining warm frosting over the top and, with a
   long metal spatula, smooth the top and spread the frosting
   around the sides. Let the cake rest for 30 minutes to allow the
   frosting to set. Slice and serve. Store, lightly covered, at room
   temperature for up to 4 days.

Pink Champagne Cake

SERVES 12

PREP: 35 TO 40 MINUTES

BAKE: 23 TO 28 MINUTES

Vegetable oil spray
or shortening,
for greasing the pans

All-purpose flour,
for dusting the pans

1 (15.25- or 16.25-ounce)
package white cake mix

½ cup all-purpose flour

¼ cup sugar

5 large egg whites

1 cup pink champagne

⅓ cup whole milk

12 tablespoons (1½ sticks)
unsalted butter,
at room temperature

2 teaspoons vanilla extract

1 drop pink food coloring
(optional)

Pink Champagne Frosting
(page 352)

Pink Cake for Nondrinkers

Instead of pink champagne, use 1⅓ cups milk in the cake and 3 to 4 tablespoons milk in the frosting. Use pink food coloring to tint both the cake and frosting.

I was challenged by a friend to create an easy cake mix recipe for this iconic West Coast cake that is flavored, obviously, with pink champagne and tinted pink. It was a delicious process!

1. Place a rack in the center of the oven and preheat the oven to 350°F. Grease and flour three 8-inch round cake pans. Set the pans aside.

2. In a large mixing bowl, stir together the cake mix, flour, and sugar. Add the egg whites, pink champagne, milk, butter, vanilla, and food coloring (if using). Beat with an electric mixer on low speed until blended, about 30 seconds. Stop the machine and scrape down the sides of the bowl with a rubber spatula. Increase the mixer speed to medium and beat for 1 minute, until well blended. Divide the batter evenly among the prepared pans, smoothing it out with a rubber spatula.

3. Place the pans in the oven and bake until the cakes are lightly browned and beginning to pull back from the sides of the pan, 23 to 28 minutes.

4. Let the cakes cool in the pans on wire racks for 10 to 15 minutes. Run a dinner knife around the edge of each pan, then invert each layer onto a rack. Invert the layers so they are right-side up and allow the cakes to cool completely, about 20 minutes longer.

5. To assemble the cake, place one cake layer, right-side up, on a cake plate and spread ¾ cup frosting over the top. Place the second layer, right-side up, on top of the first. Spread with ¾ cup frosting. Place the third layer, right-side up, on top. Spread frosting smoothly and generously over the top. Apply a thin "crumb coat" (see page 35) of frosting to the sides of the cake to seal in the crumbs. Then use the remaining frosting to apply a second, more generous layer to the sides of the cake. Slice and serve. Store, lightly covered, at room temperature for up to 4 days.

Reese's Peanut Butter Cake

CAKE

Vegetable oil spray
or shortening,
for greasing the pans

All-purpose flour,
for dusting the pans

1 (15.25-ounce) package
yellow or butter cake mix

⅓ cup all-purpose flour

2 large eggs

1¼ cups water

⅓ cup creamy peanut butter

⅓ cup vegetable oil

ASSEMBLY

38 Reese's bite-size
peanut butter cups

Peanut Butter Frosting
(page 354)

*Lucille Osborn, my friend and TV food stylist, always knows
how to make my recipes look fabulous. For a QVC airing with
a simple peanut butter layer cake, Lucille created an homage to
Reese's peanut butter cups. She scattered chopped peanut butter
cups between the layers and whole bite-size cups on top. When
my cakes were rolled off set, everyone backstage dove in!*

1. Make the cake: Place a rack in the center of the oven and
    preheat the oven to 350°F.

2. Grease and flour two 9-inch round cake pans. Set the pans aside.

3. In a large mixing bowl, stir together the cake mix and flour.
    Add the eggs, water, peanut butter, and oil. Beat with an electric
    mixer on low speed until blended, about 30 seconds. Stop the
    machine and scrape down the sides of the bowl with a rubber
    spatula. Increase the mixer speed to medium and beat for 1 minute
    longer. The batter should be well blended. Divide the batter evenly
    between the prepared pans, smoothing it out with a rubber spatula.

4. Place the pans in the oven and bake until the cakes are lightly
    golden brown and the tops spring back when gently pressed in
    the middle, 20 to 25 minutes.

5. Let the cakes cool in the pans on wire racks for 10 to 15 minutes.
    Run a dinner knife around the edge of each pan, then invert
    each layer onto a rack. Invert the layers again so they are
    right-side up and allow the cakes to cool completely, about
    20 minutes longer.

6. Assemble the cake: Freeze the peanut butter cups for 15 to
    20 minutes so they are easier to chop. Roughly chop 28 of these
    and set aside. Cut the remaining 10 peanut butter cups in half and
    set aside.

7. Place one cake layer, right-side up, on a cake plate and spread
    1 cup of the frosting over the top. Press half of the chopped
    peanut butter cups into this frosting. Place the second layer,

right-side up, on top of the first. Spread another cup of the frosting over the top. Press the remaining chopped peanut butter cups into this frosting. Frost the sides of the cake with the remaining frosting, or for a barely naked look, spread with frosting and then pull half of it off with a long metal icing spatula. Scatter the peanut butter cup halves on top of the cake. Slice and serve. Store, lightly covered, at room temperature for up to 1 day, then refrigerate for up to 4 days.

Slice and Serve: At Last, Your Homemade Cake

For the neatest slices of a layer cake, dip a long thin knife in hot water, dry it, then slice. Wipe off the knife between slices. For cakes with cream cheese frostings, chill the frosted cake 20 minutes before slicing. And use serrated knives for angel and chiffon cakes so you don't tear them.

The Confetti Cake

SERVES 12

PREP: 30 TO 35 MINUTES

BAKE: 25 TO 30 MINUTES

CAKE

Vegetable oil spray
or shortening,
for greasing the pans

All-purpose flour,
for dusting the pans

1 (15.25- or 16.25-ounce)
package white cake mix

½ cup all-purpose flour

¼ cup sugar

3 large eggs

1¼ cups whole milk or
full-fat canned coconut milk

12 tablespoons (1½ sticks)
unsalted butter,
at room temperature

½ cup sprinkles

ASSEMBLY

Cream Cheese Frosting
(page 356)

¼ cup sprinkles

This cake says party! The layers were cooling on the kitchen counter and I hadn't even stacked and frosted them yet when my son asked whose birthday we were celebrating. It's that kind of cake! And so much better than any of those confetti cake mixes. Mine is a sturdy and rich batter filled with sprinkles, spread with cream cheese frosting, and decorated with even more sprinkles on top or around the sides. It's the birthday cake you always wanted.

1. Make the cake: Place a rack in the center of the oven and preheat the oven to 350°F. Grease and flour two 9-inch round cake pans. Set the pans aside.

2. Place the cake mix in a large mixing bowl. Measure out 1 tablespoon of the flour and set it aside in a small bowl. Add the remaining flour, along with the sugar, to the cake mix and stir to combine. Add the eggs, milk, and butter and beat with an electric mixer on low speed until blended, about 30 seconds. Stop the machine and scrape down the sides of the bowl with a rubber spatula. Increase the mixer speed to medium and beat for 1 minute. The batter should be well blended.

3. Pour the sprinkles into the bowl with the reserved flour and toss with your fingers or a spoon to coat. Fold the sprinkles and flour into the batter. Divide the batter evenly between the prepared pans, smoothing it out with a rubber spatula.

4. Place the pans in the oven and bake until the cakes are lightly golden brown and the tops spring back when gently pressed in the middle, 25 to 30 minutes.

5. Let the cakes cool in the pans on wire racks for 10 to 15 minutes. Run a dinner knife around the edge of each pan, then invert each layer onto a rack. Invert the layers again so they are right-side up and allow the cakes to cool completely, about 20 minutes longer.

CONTINUED

How to Roll a Cake in Sprinkles

Place a cake layer on a cardboard round the same size. Frost the surface and place a second layer on top. Frost the sides of the cake with a thin layer of frosting to make a "crumb coat" (see page 35) to seal in the crumbs. Refrigerate the cake for at least 15 minutes. Once the crumb coat is chilled, frost the sides with a more generous coat of frosting, reserving 1 cup of frosting for the top of the cake (but don't frost the top yet). Place the cake, uncovered, in the freezer for 20 minutes. Remove the cake from the freezer and place a second cardboard round on top of the cake. Pour 1 cup sprinkles into a rectangular pan or tray. With one hand on the cake bottom and one on the top, run the sides of the cake through the sprinkles like a wheel running through gravel. Patch any bare places with sprinkles using your hands. When the sides are well coated with sprinkles, place the cake upright on a stand or platter. Remove the cardboard round on top and frost the top of the cake.

6. Assemble the cake: Place one cake layer, right-side up, on a cake plate and spread 1 cup of the frosting over the top. Place the second layer, right-side up, on top of the first. Spread another cup of the frosting over the top. Frost the sides of the cake with the remaining frosting. Decorate the top with the sprinkles. (For a more elaborate presentation, see How to Roll a Cake in Sprinkles, left). Slice and serve. Store, lightly covered, at room temperature for up to 4 days.

Gluten-Free Vanilla Cake
with Cherry Buttercream

To create this spectacular cake, you need two gluten-free mixes to make enough batter to fill three cake layers, which, after baking, are split in half to yield six impressive layers. The cherry preserves spread between three of the layers provide a blast of flavor and color, too.

CAKE

Vegetable oil spray
or shortening,
for greasing the pans

2 (15-ounce) packages
gluten-free yellow cake mix

1 (3.4-ounce) package
vanilla instant pudding mix

⅓ cup granulated sugar

2 large eggs

4 large egg whites

1 cup sour cream

¾ cup vegetable oil

½ cup water

2 tablespoons vanilla extract

½ teaspoon almond extract

CHERRY FILLING

1 jar (13 ounces) cherry
preserves (a generous 1 cup)

1. Make the cake: Place a rack in the center of the oven and preheat the oven to 350°F. Grease three 8-inch round cake pans and line the bottoms with parchment rounds. Set aside.

2. In a large mixing bowl, combine the cake mixes, pudding mix, granulated sugar, whole eggs, egg whites, sour cream, oil, water, vanilla, and almond extract. Beat with an electric mixer on low speed until blended, about 30 seconds. Stop the machine and scrape down the sides of the bowl with a rubber spatula. Increase the mixer speed to medium and beat for 1 minute. The batter will be thick. Divide the batter evenly among the prepared pans, smoothing it out with a rubber spatula.

3. Place the pans in the oven and bake until the cakes are lightly golden brown and the tops spring back when gently pressed in the middle, 32 to 37 minutes.

4. Let the cakes cool in the pans on wire racks for 10 to 15 minutes. Run a dinner knife around the edge of each pan, then invert each layer onto a rack and remove the parchment round. Invert the layers again so they are right-side up and allow the cakes to cool completely, about 20 minutes longer.

5. Make the cherry filling: Pulse the cherry preserves in a food processor for 15 to 20 seconds to chop up the cherry pieces. Measure out 2 tablespoons and set aside for the frosting.

RECIPE AND INGREDIENTS CONTINUED

CHERRY BUTTERCREAM FROSTING

12 tablespoons (1½ sticks) unsalted butter, at room temperature

3 to 3½ cups confectioners' sugar

1 to 2 tablespoons milk

1½ teaspoons vanilla extract

Edible rose petals or fresh cherries, for garnish

6. Make the cherry buttercream frosting: In a large mixing bowl, beat the butter with an electric mixer on low speed until fluffy, about 30 seconds. Stop the machine and add 3 cups of the confectioners' sugar, 1 tablespoon milk, 1 tablespoon of the reserved cherry preserves, and the vanilla. Beat on low speed until the sugar is well incorporated, about 1 minute. Increase the speed to medium and beat until the frosting is light and fluffy, about 1 minute longer, adding more confectioners' sugar, milk, or preserves as needed to produce a spreadable frosting.

7. To assemble the cake, with a serrated knife, slice the layers in half horizontally to yield 6 thin layers. Place the bottom half of one cake layer, cut-side up, on a cake plate. Spread with one-third of the cherry filling, spreading nearly to the edges. Top with the matching top half of the layer, cut-side down. Spread with ½ cup of the frosting. Add the bottom half of the second layer, cut-side up, and spread with another one-third of the filling. Top with the matching top half of the layer, cut-side down, and spread with another ½ cup of the frosting. Add the bottom half of the third layer, cut-side up, and spread with the final one-third of the filling. Top with the matching top half of the layer, cut-side down. Frost the top and sides of the cake with the remaining frosting. Decorate with rose petals or fresh cherries, then slice and serve. Store, lightly covered, at room temperature for up to 4 days.

Easy Red Velvet Cake

SERVES 12

PREP: 30 TO 35 MINUTES

BAKE: 22 TO 27 MINUTES

CAKE

Vegetable oil spray
or shortening,
for greasing the pans

All-purpose flour,
for dusting the pans

1 (15.25-ounce) package
yellow or butter cake mix

4 tablespoons (half a
3.4-ounce package) vanilla
instant pudding mix

2 tablespoons
unsweetened cocoa powder

3 large eggs

1 cup buttermilk,
preferably whole milk

½ cup vegetable oil

1 bottle (1 ounce)
red food coloring

ASSEMBLY

Cream Cheese Frosting
(page 356)

Fresh raspberries,
edible roses, and
confectioners' sugar,
for garnish

Before you pull a red velvet cake mix off the shelf, try this recipe. I add cocoa for flavor, buttermilk for moisture, and the customary red food coloring. And it bakes into a grand cake as well as a baby cake or cupcakes (variations follow). These red velvets will surely get attention!

1. Make the cake: Place a rack in the center of the oven and preheat the oven to 350°F. Grease and flour two 9-inch round cake pans. Set the pans aside.

2. In a large mixing bowl, stir together the cake mix, pudding mix, and cocoa. Add the eggs, buttermilk, oil, and food coloring. Beat with an electric mixer on low speed until blended, about 30 seconds. Stop the machine and scrape down the sides of the bowl with a rubber spatula. Increase the mixer speed to medium and beat for 1 minute. The batter should be well blended. Divide the batter evenly between the prepared pans, smoothing it out with a rubber spatula.

3. Place the pans in the oven and bake until the cakes spring back when gently pressed in the middle, 22 to 27 minutes.

4. Let the cakes cool in the pans on wire racks for 10 to 15 minutes. Run a dinner knife around the edge of each pan, then invert onto a rack. Invert the layers again so that they are right-side up and let cool completely while you make the frosting.

5. Assemble the cake: Place one cake layer, right-side up, on a cake plate and spread some of the frosting over the top. Place the second layer, right-side up, on top of the first. Spread the top with some of the frosting. Frost the sides of the cake with just a thin coat to seal in the red crumbs (see page 35). Refrigerate the cake for 15 minutes. Finish frosting the sides of the cake with the remaining frosting. For a barely naked look, spread the sides of the cake with one layer of frosting and then pull half of it off with a long metal icing spatula, letting the red cake crumbs bleed into the frosting, tinting it slightly pink. Decorate the top with the raspberries, roses, and confectioners' sugar. Slice and serve. Store, lightly covered at room temperature for up to 1 day and in the refrigerator for up to 4 days.

Red Velvet Baby Cake with White Chocolate Glaze

Make the batter for the Easy Red Velvet Cake, but reduce the oil to ¼ cup and add 4 tablespoons unsalted butter, melted. Bake in two 6-inch round cake pans that are 3 inches deep. Grease and flour the pans and line the bottoms with rounds of parchment. Bake at 350°F for 38 to 42 minutes. Frost with a double recipe of White Chocolate Glaze (page 370) to completely cover the cake with frosting, or just spread White Chocolate Glaze between the layers and on top. Garnish with red cake crumbs you make by pulsing cake in the food processor. Slice the ½-inch dome off the top of each layer to get enough cake to make crumbs.

Red Velvet Cupcakes with Mascarpone Frosting

Make the batter for the Easy Red Velvet Cake. Line 18 to 20 cups of two muffin tins with paper liners. Scoop ⅓ cup (about 2 ounces) batter into each lined cup, filling it three-quarters of the way full. Bake at 350°F for 18 to 22 minutes. Frost with the Mascarpone Frosting (page 357) and garnish with white chocolate shavings.

Red Velvet Peppermint Cupcakes

Make the Red Velvet Cupcakes (above) and add ½ teaspoon peppermint extract to both the batter and the frosting. Garnish with crushed candy canes.

Coconut Icebox Cake

SERVES 12

PREP: 35 TO 40 MINUTES

BAKE: 20 TO 25 MINUTES

CAKE

Vegetable oil spray
or shortening,
for greasing the pans

All-purpose flour,
for dusting the pans

1 (15.25- or 16.25-ounce)
package white cake mix

3 large eggs

1 cup canned full-fat
or light coconut milk

⅓ cup vegetable oil

¼ teaspoon coconut extract
or ½ teaspoon vanilla extract

COCONUT FROSTING

1 cup sour cream

3 cups frozen whipped
topping (Cool Whip), thawed
(see Cook's Notes)

½ cup confectioners' sugar

2 (6-ounce) packages frozen
unsweetened shredded
coconut, thawed, or 2½ cups
sweetened or unsweetened
shredded coconut (see
Cook's Notes)

Sweetened shredded coconut,
for decoration (optional)

Everyone loved Grandma's Coconut Icebox Cake in the original The Cake Mix Doctor *because they could make it ahead and let it "marinate" for three days in the fridge—during which time it got even more moist and coconutty. I admit that while it was delicious, it was also problematic because if you tried slicing and serving before day three, the frosting would slide off the cake! With this recipe I revisited Grandma's cake and can now share a cake that still benefits from a few days in the fridge but has a frosting that stays put the minute you spread it on the cake. This way you have more flexibility: Serve the cake on day one and it's delicious—by day three, it's beyond!*

1. Make the cake: Place a rack in the center of the oven and preheat the oven to 350°F. Grease and flour two 9-inch round cake pans. Set the pans aside.

2. In a large mixing bowl, combine the cake mix, eggs, coconut milk, oil, and coconut extract. Beat with an electric mixer on low speed until blended, about 30 seconds. Stop the machine and scrape down the sides of the bowl with a rubber spatula. Increase the mixer speed to medium and beat until smooth, about 1 minute. Divide the batter evenly between the prepared pans, smoothing it out with a rubber spatula.

3. Place the pans in the oven and bake until the cakes are lightly golden brown and the tops spring back when gently pressed in the middle, 20 to 25 minutes.

4. Let the cakes cool in the pans on wire racks for 10 to 15 minutes. Run a dinner knife around the edge of each pan, then invert each layer onto a rack. Invert the layers again so they are right-side up and allow the cakes to cool completely, about 20 minutes longer.

5. To make slicing easier and more precise, wrap each layer in plastic wrap and freeze for 1 hour.

6. Meanwhile, make the coconut frosting: In a large mixing bowl, combine the sour cream, whipped topping, and confectioners'

Generally, I am not a big fan of Cool Whip, but in this recipe it makes the cake easier to assemble. You could substitute Homemade Cool Whip (page 368).

Use frozen unsweetened coconut or sweetened shredded coconut (from the baking aisle), whichever you prefer. I like the unsweetened frozen because it has more coconut flavor, but the shredded coconut in the baking aisle is pretty and best for garnishing the top.

sugar. Beat with the electric mixer on medium speed until well combined, 30 to 45 seconds. Refrigerate until you are ready to assemble the cake.

7. When ready to assemble the cake, remove the layers from the freezer and the frosting from the refrigerator. With a serrated knife, slice each layer in half horizontally to yield 4 thin layers. Place the bottom half of a cake layer, cut-side up, on a cake plate. Spread with 1 cup of the frosting. Sprinkle one-quarter of the coconut (about a heaping ½ cup) on top of the frosting. Top with the matching top half of the layer, cut-side down. Spread with another 1 cup frosting and one-quarter of the coconut. Add the bottom half of the second layer, cut-side up, and spread with 1 cup of frosting and one-quarter of the coconut. Top with the matching half of the layer, cut-side down. Spread the top of the cake with the remaining frosting and coconut.

8. Place the cake in a cake saver or under a glass dome in the refrigerator until time to serve, preferably 4 hours, and up to 4 days. If desired, garnish the top with more coconut.

COOK'S NOTE:
Half a package of
strawberry gelatin adds
plenty of strawberry flavor
and color in this cake if
you'd like to reduce sugar.
Save the remainder
for another cake!

Deep South Strawberry Cake

SERVES 12

PREP: 35 TO 40 MINUTES

BAKE: 25 TO 30 MINUTES

CAKE

Vegetable oil spray
or shortening,
for greasing the pans

All-purpose flour,
for dusting the pans

1 (15.25-ounce) package
yellow or butter cake mix

⅓ cup all-purpose flour

1 (3-ounce) package
strawberry gelatin
(see Cook's Note)

3 large eggs

1 cup mashed fresh
strawberries (from 1½ cups
hulled sliced berries)

½ cup vegetable oil

½ cup whole milk

ASSEMBLY

Strawberry Cream Cheese
Frosting (page 360)

1 whole strawberry,
for garnish

If you visit bakeries, diners, and home kitchens in the South, you will find this cake—bright pink and packed with strawberry flavor. It comes at that flavor both honestly (with fresh strawberries) and maybe not so much (with strawberry-flavored gelatin)—but who's to tell?

1. Make the cake: Place a rack in the center of the oven and preheat the oven to 350°F. Grease and flour two 9-inch round cake pans. Set the pans aside.

2. In a large mixing bowl, stir together the cake mix, flour, and gelatin. Add the eggs, strawberries, oil, and milk. Beat with an electric mixer on low speed until blended, about 30 seconds. Stop the machine and scrape down the sides of the bowl with a rubber spatula. Increase the mixer speed to medium and beat for 1 minute, until well blended. Divide the batter evenly between the prepared pans, smoothing it out with a rubber spatula.

3. Place the pans in the oven and bake until the cakes are lightly browned and spring back when gently pressed in the middle, 25 to 30 minutes.

4. Let the cakes cool in the pans on wire racks for 10 to 15 minutes. Run a dinner knife around the edge of each pan, then invert each layer onto a rack. Invert the layers again so they are right-side up and allow the cakes to cool completely, about 20 minutes longer.

5. Assemble the cake: Place one cake layer, right-side up, on a cake plate and spread ¾ cup frosting over the top. Place the second cake layer, right-side up, on top of the first. Spread some of the frosting smoothly over the top. Frost the sides of the cake with the remaining frosting, first applying a thin "crumb coat" (see page 35) to seal in the cake crumbs and then adding a second, more generous layer of frosting. (If desired, pull the frosting off the sides of the cake for a barely naked look.) Place the whole strawberry on top. Slice and serve. Store, lightly covered, in the refrigerator for up to 4 days.

Triple-Layer Caramel Cake

SERVES 12

PREP: 40 TO 45 MINUTES

BAKE: 15 TO 20 MINUTES

Vegetable oil spray
or shortening,
for greasing the pans

All-purpose flour,
for dusting the pans

1 (15.25-ounce) package
yellow or butter cake mix

4 tablespoons (half a
3.4-ounce package) vanilla
instant pudding mix

3 large eggs

1 cup whole milk

8 tablespoons (1 stick)
unsalted butter,
melted and cooled

2 teaspoons vanilla extract

Quick Caramel Frosting
(page 364)

While from-scratch caramel cake is a sight to behold and requires much skill, there is a simpler path. My mother taught me how to make this frosting, and it pulls together in less than 10 minutes. And considering you can bake the cake in half an hour, you are well on your way to making the simplest and most delicious three-layer caramel cake imaginable.

1. Place a rack in the center of the oven and preheat the oven to 350°F. Grease and flour three 9-inch round cake pans. Set the pans aside.

2. In a large mixing bowl, stir together the cake mix and pudding mix. Add the eggs, milk, melted butter, and vanilla. Beat with an electric mixer on low speed until blended, about 30 seconds. Stop the machine and scrape down the sides of the bowl with a rubber spatula. Increase the mixer speed to medium and beat until the batter is smooth, about 1 minute. Divide the batter evenly among the prepared pans, smoothing it out with a rubber spatula.

3. Place the pans in the oven and bake until the cakes are golden brown and spring back when gently pressed in the middle, 15 to 20 minutes.

4. Let the cakes cool in the pans on wire racks for 10 to 15 minutes. Run a dinner knife around the edge of each pan, then invert each layer onto a rack. Invert the layers again so they are right-side up and allow the cakes to cool completely, about 20 minutes longer.

5. To assemble the cake, place one cake layer, right-side up, on a cake plate and spread ¾ cup of warm frosting over the top. Place the second layer, right-side up, on top of the first. Spread ¾ cup of warm frosting over the top. Place the remaining layer on top and pour about 1 cup frosting over the top, spreading with smooth strokes. Frost the sides of the cake with the remaining frosting. If the frosting hardens, place it over low heat and stir until warm and spreadable. Slice the cake and serve. Store, lightly covered, at room temperature for up to 5 days.

The Banana Cake

SERVES 12

PREP: 25 TO 30 MINUTES

BAKE: 23 TO 27 MINUTES

CAKE

Vegetable oil spray
or shortening,
for greasing the pans

All-purpose flour,
for dusting the pans

1 (15.25-ounce) package
yellow or butter cake mix

4 tablespoons (half a
3.4-ounce package) vanilla
instant pudding mix

1 teaspoon
ground cinnamon

3 large eggs

1 cup mashed ripe bananas
(2 large or 3 small)

½ cup vegetable oil

½ cup water

FROSTING CHOICES

Quick Caramel Frosting
(page 364) or Cream Cheese
Frosting (page 356)

Very rarely did my mother buy a premade dessert, but one of the rare exceptions was frozen Sara Lee banana cake with cream cheese frosting. I had pretty much forgotten this bit of my history until Alex Witchel of the New York Times *asked if I would come to New York and bake a banana cake in her kitchen. While we baked, she confessed her nostalgic love of the Sara Lee banana cake, too, and as I was leaving I told Alex she could stash the rest of the cake in her freezer. We both knew it would freeze well! Here is the cake, and you have the choice of caramel frosting as it was presented in* The Cake Mix Doctor *or the cream cheese to duplicate Sara Lee.*

1. Make the cake: Place a rack in the center of the oven and preheat the oven to 350°F. Grease and flour two 9-inch round cake pans. Set the pans aside.

2. In a large bowl, stir together the cake mix, pudding mix, and cinnamon. Add the eggs, mashed banana, oil, and water. Beat with an electric mixer on low speed until blended, about 30 seconds. Stop the machine and scrape down the sides of the bowl with a rubber spatula. Increase the mixer speed to medium and beat for 1 minute, until well blended. Divide the batter evenly between the pans, smoothing with a rubber spatula.

3. Place the pans in the oven and bake until the cakes are lightly browned and spring back when gently pressed in the middle, 23 to 27 minutes. Remove the pans from the oven and cool on wire racks for 10 to 15 minutes. Run a dinner knife around the edge of each pan and invert the cakes onto a rack, then invert them again onto another rack so they are right-side up and allow the cakes to cool completely, about 20 minutes longer.

4. To assemble the cake, place one cake layer, right-side up, on a cake plate and spread ¾ cup frosting over the top. Place the second layer, right-side up, on top of the first. Spread some frosting smoothly over the top. Frost the sides of the cake with the remaining frosting. Slice and serve. With caramel frosting, store, lightly covered, at room temperature for up to 4 days. With cream cheese frosting, store in the refrigerator for up to 4 days.

Buttermilk Lime Cake

SERVES 12

PREP: 50 TO 55 MINUTES

BAKE: 40 TO 45 MINUTES

CAKE

1 cup whole milk

1 tablespoon fresh lime juice

Vegetable oil spray
or shortening,
for greasing the pan

All-purpose flour,
for dusting the pan

1 (15.25-ounce) package
yellow or butter cake mix

4 tablespoons (half a
3.4-ounce package) vanilla
instant pudding mix

3 large eggs

8 tablespoons (1 stick)
unsalted butter,
at room temperature

ASSEMBLY

Homemade Fruit Curd
(page 365), made with
lime juice

Lime Buttercream
(page 352)

Grated lime zest,
for garnish

This cake infused with lime is so easy to love. From the simplest lime buttercream to the lime-scented velvety curd spread between lime-flavored layers—which takes a little time to make, but is so worth it—it doesn't miss one chance to say "lime." There's even a faux buttermilk you make with whole milk and lime juice to curdle it.

1. Make the cake: Pour the milk into a small bowl and stir in the lime juice. Let sit, uncovered, at room temperature for 10 minutes.

2. Place a rack in the center of the oven and preheat the oven to 350°F. Grease and flour a 9-inch springform pan. Set the pan aside.

3. In a large mixing bowl, stir together the cake mix and pudding mix. Add the lime buttermilk, eggs, and butter. Beat with an electric mixer on low speed until blended, about 30 seconds. Stop the machine and scrape down the sides of the bowl with a rubber spatula. Increase the mixer speed to medium and beat for 1 minute, or until smooth. Turn the batter into the prepared pan, smoothing it out with a rubber spatula.

4. Place the pan in the oven and bake until the cake is golden brown and the top springs back when gently pressed in the middle, 40 to 45 minutes.

5. Let the cake cool in the pan on a wire rack for 15 minutes. Run a dinner knife around the pan edge and unsnap and remove the sides of the pan. Allow the cake to cool completely, about 20 minutes longer.

6. Assemble the cake: Slice the cake horizontally into thirds. Remove the bottom layer from the pan base by sliding a long knife underneath it. Place this bottom layer, cut-side up, on a cake plate and spread about half of the curd (½ cup) almost to the edges. Place the second layer on top of the first. Spread with the remaining lime curd. Place the final layer over the curd, right-side up. Frost the top and sides of the cake with the buttercream. Scatter lime zest over the top. Chill the cake for 30 minutes to make slicing easier. Slice and serve. Store, lightly covered, in the refrigerator for up to 4 days.

Hummingbird Cake
with Roasted Bananas

SERVES 12

PREP: 35 TO 40 MINUTES

BAKE: 25 TO 30 MINUTES

CAKE

Vegetable oil spray
or shortening,
for greasing the pans

All-purpose flour,
for dusting the pans

2 large or 3 medium
bananas, halved lengthwise

1 tablespoon light
brown sugar

¼ teaspoon ground nutmeg

1¼ teaspoons
ground cinnamon

1 (15.25-ounce) package
yellow or butter cake mix

¼ cup all-purpose flour

3 large eggs

1 (8-ounce) can juice-
packed crushed pineapple,
undrained

¼ cup vegetable oil

ASSEMBLY

Cream Cheese Frosting
(page 356) or Cinnamon
Buttercream (page 351)

Ground cinnamon,
for dusting

When this cake originated in the 1970s, it was baked in a Bundt. Throughout the years, the banana-pineapple-cinnamon Hummingbird has been made into layers, cupcakes, and so many other configurations. I now roast the bananas first to add even more flavor to this great cake.

1. Make the cake: Place a rack in the center of the oven and preheat the oven to 375°F. Grease and flour two 9-inch round cake pans. Set the pans aside.

2. To roast the bananas, line a small baking sheet or toaster oven pan with foil. Place the banana slices, cut-side up, on the pan and sprinkle with the brown sugar, nutmeg, and ¼ teaspoon of the cinnamon. Place in the oven and roast until bubbling on top, about 15 minutes. Remove the bananas from the oven, but leave the oven on and reduce the temperature to 350°F.

3. Carefully drain off any liquid from the pan of bananas, transfer the bananas to a bowl, and mash. Measure out ¾ cup mashed banana and set aside to cool.

4. In a large mixing bowl, stir together the cake mix, flour, and remaining 1 teaspoon cinnamon. Add the mashed roasted bananas, eggs, pineapple and juices, and oil. Beat with an electric mixer on low speed until blended, about 15 seconds. Stop the machine and scrape down the sides of the bowl with a rubber spatula. Increase the mixer speed to medium and beat for 1 minute, until well blended. Divide the batter evenly between the prepared pans, smoothing it out with a rubber spatula.

5. Place the pans in the oven and bake until the cakes are golden brown and beginning to pull away from the sides of the pan, 25 to 30 minutes.

6. Let the cakes cool in the pans on wire racks for 10 to 15 minutes. Run a dinner knife around the edge of each pan, then invert each layer onto a rack. Invert the layers again so they are right-side up and allow the cakes to cool completely, about 20 minutes longer.

7. Assemble the cake: Place one cake layer, right-side up, on a cake plate and spread ¾ cup frosting over the top. Place the second layer, right-side up, on top of the first. Spread the rest of the frosting smoothly over the top. Or, spread some on the top and frost the sides of the cake with the remaining frosting, first applying a thin "crumb coat" (see page 35) to seal in the cake crumbs and then adding a second, more generous layer of frosting. Dust the top with cinnamon. Slice and serve. Store, lightly covered, at room temperature for up to 1 day, then in the refrigerator for up to 3 days.

Snickerdoodle Cake

SERVES 12

PREP: 35 TO 40 MINUTES

BAKE: 20 TO 25 MINUTES

CAKE

Vegetable oil spray
or shortening,
for greasing the pans

All-purpose flour,
for dusting the pans

1 (15.25-ounce) package
yellow or butter cake mix

2 teaspoons
ground cinnamon

3 large eggs

1 cup whole milk

8 tablespoons (1 stick)
unsalted butter,
at room temperature

1 teaspoon vanilla extract

FROSTING CHOICES

Cinnamon Buttercream
(page 351) or Cereal Milk
Frosting (page 352), using
Cinnamon Toast Crunch for
the cereal milk

Ground cinnamon,
for dusting (optional)

Snickerdoodles are beloved cinnamon-sugar cookies with the funny name, and this cake reminds me of those cookies. You begin with a yellow cake mix, add a generous dose of cinnamon, and bake into layers—or whatever shape you like. Then frost with a buttercream infused with cinnamon. Yum!

1. Make the cake: Place a rack in the center of the oven and preheat the oven to 350°F. Grease and flour two 9-inch round cake pans. Set the pans aside.

2. In a large mixing bowl, stir together the cake mix and cinnamon. Add the eggs, milk, butter, and vanilla. Beat with an electric mixer on low speed until blended, about 30 seconds. Stop the machine and scrape down the sides of the bowl with a rubber spatula. Increase the mixer speed to medium and beat for 1 minute. The batter will be thick. Divide the batter evenly between the prepared pans, smoothing it out with a rubber spatula.

3. Place the pans in the oven and bake until the cakes are lightly browned and spring back when gently pressed in the middle, 20 to 25 minutes.

4. Let the cakes cool in the pans on wire racks for 10 to 15 minutes. Run a dinner knife around the edge of each pan, then invert each layer onto a rack. Invert the layers again so they are right-side up and allow the cakes to cool completely, about 20 minutes longer.

5. To assemble the cake, place one cake layer, right-side up, on a cake plate and spread ¾ cup of the frosting over the top. Place the second layer, right-side up, on top of the first. Spread some of the frosting smoothly over the top. Frost the sides of the cake with the remaining frosting, first applying a thin "crumb coat" (see page 35) to seal in the cake crumbs and then adding a second, more generous layer of frosting. Dust with cinnamon, if desired. Slice and serve. Store, lightly covered, at room temperature for up to 4 days.

Limoncello Cake

SERVES 12

PREP: 35 TO 40 MINUTES

BAKE: 25 TO 30 MINUTES FOR
8-INCH AND 20 TO 25 MINUTES
FOR 9-INCH LAYERS

CAKE

Vegetable oil spray
or shortening,
for greasing the pans

All-purpose flour,
for dusting the pans

1 (15.25- or 16.25-ounce)
package white cake mix

¼ cup all-purpose flour

¼ cup sugar

3 large eggs

1 cup limoncello,
plus 2 tablespoons for
brushing the layers

⅓ cup whole milk

12 tablespoons (1½ sticks)
unsalted butter,
at room temperature

FILLING

1 jar (13 ounces) blueberry
preserves (a generous 1 cup;
see Cook's Note)

1 tablespoon limoncello

Chilled limoncello is summertime in a glass. Sipping the Italian lemon liqueur evokes sweet memories . . . that summer in Tuscany renting the villa with friends when our kids were younger, laughter, homemade pasta, tiramisu till you could eat no more, and then that quenching cold glass of limoncello. I've wanted to bake a cake with limoncello for years, and after I spread the lemony layers with blueberry preserves and a lemon buttercream, I wondered what took me so long!

1. Make the cake: Place a rack in the center of the oven and preheat the oven to 350°F.

2. Grease and flour two 8-inch or 9-inch round cake pans.

3. In a large mixing bowl, stir together the cake mix, flour, and sugar. Add the eggs, limoncello, milk, and butter. Beat with an electric mixer on low speed until blended, about 30 seconds. Stop the machine and scrape down the sides of the bowl with a rubber spatula. Increase the mixer speed to medium and beat for 1 minute. The batter will be thick. Divide the batter evenly between the prepared pans, smoothing it out with a rubber spatula.

4. Place the pans in the oven and bake until the cakes are lightly golden and spring back when gently pressed in the middle, 25 to 30 minutes for 8-inch pans, 20 to 25 minutes for 9-inch pans.

5. Let the cakes cool in the pans on wire racks for 10 to 15 minutes. Run a dinner knife around the edge of each pan, then invert each layer onto a rack. Invert the layers again so they are right-side up and allow the cakes to cool completely, about 20 minutes longer. Brush each layer with 1 tablespoon limoncello.

6. Make the filling: In a small bowl, stir together the blueberry preserves and limoncello. Measure out 2 tablespoons and set aside for the garnish.

RECIPE AND INGREDIENTS CONTINUED

COOK'S NOTE:
You can use other preserves such as seedless blackberry between the layers, but if the fruit is in large pieces, pulse it in the food processor first.

Lemon Buttercream
(page 352)

¼ cup fresh blueberries

Lemon slices

7. To assemble the cake, with a large serrated knife, slice the layers in half horizontally to yield 4 layers. Place the bottom half of one cake layer, cut-side up, on a cake plate. Spread half of the filling nearly to the edges. Top with the matching half of the layer, cut-side down. Spread with ¾ cup of the frosting. Add the bottom half of the second layer, cut-side up, and spread with the rest of the filling. Top with the matching half of the layer, cut-side down. Frost the top and sides of the cake with the remaining frosting. Pull the frosting off the sides for a barely naked look. Garnish the top with the reserved 2 tablespoons filling and scatter with blueberries. Decorate with lemon slices. Slice and serve. Store, lightly covered, in the refrigerator for up to 4 days.

Clementine Cake
(opposite)

Clementine Cake

SERVES 12

PREP: 1 HOUR 15 MINUTES

BAKE: 20 TO 25 MINUTES

CAKE

Vegetable oil spray
or shortening,
for greasing the pans

All-purpose flour,
for dusting the pans

1 (15.25-ounce) package
yellow or butter cake mix

4 tablespoons (half a
3.4-ounce package) vanilla
instant pudding mix

3 large eggs

¾ cup whole milk, warmed

¼ cup clementine juice
(2 to 3 clementines)

8 tablespoons (1 stick)
unsalted butter,
at room temperature

Last summer a few of us gathered to celebrate my friend Beth's birthday, and of course I volunteered to bake the cake. What's nice about sharing food with friends is that they are eager to taste the recipes that you've been working on, and if they like it enough, they can't wait to try it out in their kitchen afterward. I often get feedback—and even new ideas for the next book! If you can't find clementines, tangerines work nicely, too.

1. Make the cake: Place a rack in the center of the oven and preheat the oven to 350°F. Grease and flour two 9-inch round cake pans. Set the pans aside.

2. In a large mixing bowl, stir together the cake mix and pudding mix. Add the eggs, milk, clementine juice, and butter. Beat with an electric mixer on low speed until blended, about 30 seconds. Stop the machine and scrape down the sides of the bowl with a rubber spatula. Increase the mixer speed to medium and beat until the batter is smooth, about 1 minute. Divide the batter evenly between the prepared pans, smoothing it out with a rubber spatula.

3. Place the pans in the oven and bake until the cakes are golden brown and spring back when gently pressed in the middle, 20 to 25 minutes.

4. Let the cakes cool in the pans on wire racks for 10 to 15 minutes. Run a dinner knife around the edge of each pan, then invert each layer onto a rack. Invert the layers again so they are right-side up and allow the cakes to cool completely, about 20 minutes longer.

RECIPE AND INGREDIENTS CONTINUED

CLEMENTINE FROSTING

8 tablespoons (1 stick) unsalted butter, at room temperature

2 cups confectioners' sugar

2 tablespoons whole milk

1 teaspoon grated clementine or orange zest

1 tablespoon clementine or orange juice

Pinch of salt

ASSEMBLY

Homemade Fruit Curd (page 365), made with clementine juice

Clementine zest, for garnish (optional)

5. Make the clementine frosting: In a medium mixing bowl, beat the butter with an electric mixer on low speed until fluffy, about 30 seconds. Stop the machine and add the confectioners' sugar, milk, clementine zest, clementine juice, and salt and beat with the mixer on low speed until the confectioners' sugar is well incorporated, about 1 minute. Increase the mixer speed to medium and beat until the frosting is light and fluffy, about 1 minute.

6. Assemble the cake: Slice each layer in half horizontally. Place the bottom half of one layer, cut-side up, on a cake plate and spread about half of the curd (½ cup) almost to the edges. Place the matching half of this layer, cut-side down, on top. Spread the top with about ¾ cup of the frosting. Place the bottom half of the second layer, cut-side up, on top. Spread the remaining half of the curd (½ cup) almost to the edges. Place the matching half of this layer, cut-side down, on top. Frost the top and sides of the cake with the remaining frosting. Garnish with clementine zest if desired. Chill the cake for 30 minutes to make slicing easier. Store, lightly covered, in the refrigerator for up to 4 days.

Add Zest to Cakes

The outermost colored layer of a lemon, lime, or orange is called the zest. Underneath it is the bitter white pith. Together, the zest and pith make up the rind. What makes zest so essential in baking is this is where the fruit's aromatic oils are located. So with a simple swipe of a zester, you can add more flavor to a batter than if you had folded in all the fruit's juice. The amount of zest you get depends on the size of the citrus—an average lemon has about 2 teaspoons of grated zest with limes yielding less and oranges more. I like to use a Microplane grater to zest right into the bowl. To create long pieces of zest for garnish, use a zesting tool that you drag across the fruit. And remember—always zest before juicing!

Orange Ricotta Birthday Cake

SERVES 12

PREP: 30 TO 35 MINUTES

BAKE: 25 TO 30 MINUTES FOR
8-INCH AND 20 TO 25 MINUTES
FOR 9-INCH LAYERS

Vegetable oil spray
or shortening,
for greasing the pans

All-purpose flour,
for dusting the pans

1 (15.25-ounce) package
yellow or butter cake mix

4 tablespoons (half a
3.4-ounce package) vanilla
instant pudding mix

3 large eggs

1 tablespoon grated orange
zest (optional; from 2 oranges)

1 cup orange juice
(see Cook's Note)

½ cup light olive oil

½ cup whole-milk
ricotta cheese

Orange Cream Cheese
Frosting (page 360)

COOK'S NOTE:
Fresh orange juice or OJ
from the carton work in
this recipe. If you use fresh
juice, then you have the
oranges to zest, which adds
so much more intense flavor
to the cake and frosting.

*This cake is a wonderful mix of old memories and new flavors.
The recipe was inspired by my grandmother, who baked a dense orange
layer cake each Christmas. For my shortcut version, I add grated
orange zest, orange juice, and ricotta, which gives a cake mix cake
richness and texture and more resembles one baked from scratch.*

1. Place a rack in the center of the oven and preheat the oven to
    350°F. Grease and flour two 8-inch or 9-inch round cake pans.

2. In a large mixing bowl, stir together the cake mix and pudding
    mix. Add the eggs, orange zest (if using), orange juice, olive
    oil, and ricotta. Beat with an electric mixer on low speed until
    blended, about 30 seconds. Stop the machine and scrape down
    the sides of the bowl with a rubber spatula. Increase the mixer
    speed to medium and beat until the batter is smooth, about
    1 minute. Divide the batter evenly between the two prepared
    pans, smoothing it out with a rubber spatula.

3. Place the pans in the oven and bake until the cakes are lightly
    browned and spring back when gently pressed in the middle,
    25 to 30 minutes for 8-inch pans, 20 to 25 minutes for 9-inch pans.

4. Let the cakes cool in the pans on wire racks for 10 to 15 minutes.
    Run a dinner knife around the edge of each pan, then invert
    each layer onto a rack. Invert the layers again so they are
    right-side up and allow the cakes to cool completely, about
    20 minutes longer.

5. To assemble the cake, place one cake layer, right-side up, on a
    cake plate and spread ½ to ¾ cup of the frosting over the top.
    Place the second layer, right-side up, on top of the first. Spread
    some of the frosting smoothly over the top. Frost the sides of the
    cake with the remaining frosting, first applying a thin "crumb
    coat" (see page 35) to seal in the cake crumbs, and then adding a
    second, more generous layer of frosting. If desired, for a barely
    naked look, pull off some of the frosting from the sides. Slice and
    serve. Store, lightly covered, at room temperature for up to 4 days.

Gluten-Free Pumpkin Spice Cake

SERVES 12

PREP: 20 TO 25 MINUTES

BAKE: 25 TO 30 MINUTES

CAKE

Vegetable oil spray
or shortening,
for greasing the pans

1 (15-ounce) package
gluten-free yellow cake mix

4 tablespoons (half a
3.4-ounce package) vanilla
instant pudding mix

1½ teaspoons
ground cinnamon

½ teaspoon ground ginger

¼ teaspoon ground cloves

3 large eggs

1 cup canned unsweetened
pumpkin puree

1 teaspoon grated orange
zest (optional)

½ cup orange juice

½ cup vegetable oil

2 teaspoons vanilla extract

ASSEMBLY

Orange Cream Cheese
Frosting (page 360)

Fresh orange zest and
chopped pecans, for garnish

Years ago I had the wonderful opportunity to immerse myself in gluten-free cake baking. It was a project I took on because so many of my readers had requested gluten-free recipes—yet they still wanted to be able to bake (and, more importantly, eat!) cake. What I learned is this: Citrus not only adds flavor but also improves the texture of the gluten-free mixes. Plus, citrus is a nice flavor match for pumpkin and melds well with the warm spices.

1. Make the cake: Place a rack in the center of the oven and preheat the oven to 350°F. Grease two 8-inch round cake pans. Line the bottoms of the pans with rounds of parchment paper. Set aside.

2. In a large mixing bowl, stir together the cake mix, pudding mix, cinnamon, ginger, and cloves. Add the eggs, pumpkin, orange zest (if using), orange juice, oil, and vanilla. Beat with an electric mixer on low speed until blended, about 30 seconds. Stop the machine and scrape down the sides of the bowl with a rubber spatula. Increase the mixer speed to medium and beat for 1 minute. The batter will be thick. Divide the batter evenly between the prepared pans, smoothing it out with a rubber spatula.

3. Place the pans in the oven and bake until the cakes are firm when gently pressed in the middle, 25 to 30 minutes.

4. Let the cakes cool in the pans on wire racks for 10 to 15 minutes. Run a dinner knife around the edge of each pan, then invert each layer onto a rack and pull off the rounds of parchment paper. Invert the layers again so they are right-side up and allow the cakes to cool completely, about 20 minutes longer.

5. Assemble the cake: Place one cake layer, right-side up, on a cake plate and spread ½ cup of the frosting over the top. Place the second layer, right-side up, on top of the first. Spread some of the frosting smoothly over the top. Frost the sides of the cake with the remaining frosting. Garnish the top with orange zest and pecans. Slice and serve. Store, lightly covered, in the refrigerator for up to 4 days.

Vegan Mango Cake

SERVES 12

PREP: 25 TO 30 MINUTES

BAKE: 30 TO 35 MINUTES

CAKE

Vegetable oil spray
or shortening,
for greasing the pans

All-purpose flour,
for dusting the pans

2 to 3 ripe mangoes (about
2 pounds), cut into 1-inch
chunks (see Cook's Notes)

1 (15.25-ounce) package
yellow cake mix

2 tablespoons
all-purpose flour

½ teaspoon
ground cardamom

¼ teaspoon
ground cinnamon

½ cup vegetable oil

1 teaspoon vanilla extract

ASSEMBLY

Vegan Vanilla Buttercream
Frosting (page 353; see
Cook's Notes)

Fresh mango slices, for
garnish

*Mango not only blends into a delicious smoothie, but it can
add structure to a vegan cake. In fact, it has just the right texture
to add moisture and body as well to this cake made without eggs.
(We also tried this recipe with bananas and loved it.)
Frost with vegan buttercream—I like to add more pureed mango
or perhaps a squeeze of lemon juice or splash of vanilla.*

1. Make the cake: Place a rack in the center of the oven and preheat the oven to 350°F. Grease and flour two 8-inch round cake pans.

2. Pulse the mango chunks in a food processor until nearly smooth, about 30 seconds. Measure out 1¼ cups of the mango puree and transfer to a large mixing bowl. (Reserve some mango puree for the frosting; see Cook's Notes.)

3. Add the cake mix, flour, cardamom, cinnamon, oil, and vanilla to the mango puree. Beat with an electric mixer on low speed until blended, about 30 seconds. Stop the machine and scrape down the sides of the bowl with a rubber spatula. Increase the mixer speed to medium and beat until the batter is smooth, about 1 minute. Divide the batter evenly between the two pans, smoothing it out with a rubber spatula.

4. Place the pans in the oven and bake until the cakes are lightly browned and spring back when gently pressed in the middle, 30 to 35 minutes.

5. Let the cakes cool in the pans on wire racks for at least 20 minutes. Run a dinner knife around the edge of each pan, then invert each layer onto a rack. Invert the layers again so they are right-side up and allow the cakes to cool completely, about 20 minutes longer.

6. Assemble the cake: Place one cake layer, right-side up, on a cake plate and spread ½ to ¾ cup of the frosting over the top. Place the second layer, right-side up, on top of the first. Spread some frosting smoothly over the top. Frost the sides of the cake with the remaining frosting, first applying a thin

Thaw frozen mango chunks from Trader Joe's and puree them. Or substitute 1¼ cups canned mango pulp, which you can find in South Asian markets. In a pinch, use mango baby food puree.

When making the vegan buttercream frosting, substitute 1 tablespoon mango puree for an equal quantity of liquid in the recipe.

"crumb coat" (see page 35) to seal in the cake crumbs, then adding a second, more generous layer of frosting. If desired, for a barely naked look, pull off some of the frosting from the sides. Garnish the top with mango slices. Slice and serve. Store, lightly covered, in the refrigerator for up to 4 days.

VEGAN BANANA CAKE: Replace the pureed mango with 3 mashed ripe bananas. Increase the cinnamon to 1 teaspoon and omit the cardamom.

Baking Times for 8-inch vs. 9-inch Pans

If you want to bake a cake in 8-inch pans when the recipe calls for 9-inch, add about 5 minutes cooking time. And if you bake in 9-inch but the recipe calls for 8-inch, subtract about 5 minutes. The smaller pans are taller in height, so it takes a little longer to bake in them.

White Cake
with White Frosting

SERVES 12

PREP: 30 MINUTES

BAKE: 22 TO 27 MINUTES

Vegetable oil spray
or shortening,
for greasing the pans

All-purpose flour,
for dusting the pans

⅔ cup white chocolate chips
or chopped white chocolate
(4 ounces)

1 (15.25- or 16.25-ounce)
package white cake mix

5 tablespoons
all-purpose flour

5 large egg whites

¾ cup warm water

½ cup sour cream

¼ cup vegetable oil

White Chocolate Cream
Cheese Frosting (page 356)

COOK'S NOTE:
You can use a bar of white
chocolate in this recipe and
chop it into pieces before
microwaving. You will
use a total of 10 ounces:
4 ounces in the cake
and 6 in the frosting.

My daughter went through a phase when the only birthday cake she wanted was "white cake with white frosting." Fear not, it passed, and she moved on to more adventurous flavors. But it reminds me there is always someone who prefers white cake and frosting—so bake a cake for them!

1. Place a rack in the center of the oven and preheat the oven to 350°F. Grease and flour two 9-inch round cake pans. Set the pans aside.

2. Place the white chocolate in a large microwave-safe bowl and microwave for 45 seconds on high power. Stir until the chocolate is melted. Add the cake mix, flour, egg whites, water, sour cream, and oil to the bowl. Beat with an electric mixer on low speed until blended, about 30 seconds. Stop the machine and scrape down the sides of the bowl with a rubber spatula. Increase the mixer speed to medium and beat for 1 minute longer. The batter will be thick. Divide the batter evenly between the prepared pans, smoothing it out with a rubber spatula.

3. Place the pans in the oven and bake until the cakes spring back when gently pressed in the middle, 22 to 27 minutes.

4. Let the cakes cool in the pans on wire racks for 10 to 15 minutes. Run a dinner knife around the edge of each pan, then invert each layer onto a rack. Invert the layers again so they are right-side up and allow the cakes to cool completely, about 20 minutes longer.

5. To assemble the cake, place one cake layer, right-side up, on a cake plate and spread nearly a cup of frosting over the top. Place the second layer, right-side up, on top of the first. Spread the rest of the frosting over the top and around the sides of the cake. Store, lightly covered, at room temperature for up to 4 days.

The DIY Wedding Cake

SERVES 52 TO 86

PREP: 40 TO 45 MINUTES

BAKE: ABOUT 55 MINUTES
FOR THE 6-INCH PAN, 1 HOUR
5 MINUTES FOR THE 8-INCH
PAN, AND 1 HOUR 15 MINUTES
FOR THE 12-INCH PAN

COOL: AT LEAST 1 HOUR,
THEN STORE OVERNIGHT

ASSEMBLE: 3 HOURS

CAKE

Vegetable shortening,
for greasing the pans

All-purpose flour,
for dusting the pans

4 (15.25- or 16.25-ounce)
packages butter or white
cake mix

2 (3.4-ounce) packages
white chocolate or vanilla
instant pudding mix

4 sticks (1 pound) unsalted
butter, at room temperature

12 large eggs

4 cups whole milk or full-fat
coconut milk, warmed

1 cup vegetable oil

¼ cup vanilla extract

1 to 2 teaspoons almond
extract (optional)

One of the most frequent questions I receive from home bakers is how to bake a wedding cake. And not being a professional baker, I was at first shy about offering advice. But I challenged myself to make a three-layer wedding cake and was pleasantly surprised—and proud!—of my success.

A few of the most clever suggestions I picked up were from Rose Levy Beranbaum in The Cake Bible: *She suggests using plastic drinking straws as dowels to support the cake layers. She also came up with the brilliant idea of turning the cake pan upside down on top of the bottom layer to mark the spot where the next layer goes.*

For my first wedding cake test, I made sure to give myself enough time—I shopped on one day, baked the layers the next, and finished the cake on the third day. In the end, I was amazed at what I learned and what a beautiful cake it was! It just requires a bit of patience and planning. For this book, I revisited that recipe using the smaller cake mixes and went with a slightly different formula because I wanted the layers to be sturdy enough to stack and frost. I added fillings I had not thought of before and a blueprint way of designing and customizing the cake.

1. Make the cake: Place a rack in the center of the oven and preheat the oven to 325°F. Generously grease the sides of the 12-inch, 8-inch, and 6-inch round cake pans. Dust the sides with flour and shake out the excess. Lightly grease the bottoms of the pans, then line the bottoms with rounds of parchment paper (cut to fit the bottom of each pan). Set the pans aside.

2. In a large mixing bowl, stir together the cake mixes and pudding mixes. Set the bowl aside.

3. Place the butter in a very large mixing bowl and beat on low speed with an electric mixer until creamy, 1 to 2 minutes.

RECIPE AND INGREDIENTS CONTINUED

1 jar (8.2 ounces) apricot fruit spread or 1 cup apricot preserves

Homemade Fruit Curd (page 365), made with lemon or orange juice

Brown Sugar Cream Cheese Frosting (page 358)

FROSTING

4 (8-ounce) packages cream cheese, at room temperature

16 tablespoons (2 sticks) unsalted butter, at room temperature

1 tablespoon vanilla extract

12 to 16 cups (3 to 4 pounds) confectioners' sugar, sifted

Add the eggs, milk, oil, vanilla, and almond extract (if using) and beat on low speed until incorporated, 1 to 2 minutes. Increase the mixer speed to medium and beat until smooth, about 1 minute. Add the mixture of the cake and pudding mixes, about 3 cups at a time, beating on low speed until just incorporated, about 15 seconds for each addition. When all of the dry ingredients have been added, increase the mixer speed to medium and beat until the batter is smooth, about 1½ to 2 minutes.

4. Add 3 cups of the batter to the 6-inch pan. (If you have a kitchen scale, place the empty pan on the scale, zero it out, and fill the pan with 1½ pounds of batter.) Add 5 cups (or 2½ pounds) of the batter to the 8-inch pan. Add 10 cups (or 5 pounds) of the batter to the 12-inch pan. Smooth the top of the batter in all three pans with a rubber spatula. Place the pans in the oven.

5. If your oven is not large enough to hold all three pans on one rack, place two pans on the center rack and the third pan in the center of a rack in the upper third of the oven. Or, bake the two smaller layers first, followed by the 12-inch layer. Bake the cake layers until they just begin to pull away from the sides of the pans and the tops are lightly browned. A toothpick inserted in the center of the layers should come out clean. (Although I usually don't advise using a toothpick to test for doneness, these cake layers are dense and thicker than usual.) The 6-inch round will bake in about 55 minutes, the 8-inch in about 1 hour 5 minutes, and the 12-inch in about 1 hour 15 minutes.

6. Transfer the pans to wire racks to cool. Immediately press down gently on each layer for 10 to 15 seconds with your hands or the bottom of a saucepan the same size as the layer (make sure the pans are clean) to level the layers and make them easier to stack. Let the cakes cool in the pans for 10 minutes. Run a knife around the edge of each pan, gently shake the pans to loosen the cakes, then invert each layer onto a wire rack and peel off the parchment rounds. Invert the layers again so they are right-side up and allow to cool to room temperature, at least 1 hour.

One 12-inch round cake pan,
3 inches deep

One 8-inch round cake pan,
3 inches deep

One 6-inch round cake pan,
3 inches deep

3 cardboard cake rounds:
one 12 inches in diameter,
one 8 inches, and one
6 inches (see Cook's Notes)

Long, thin metal icing
spatula

Double-sided tape
or masking tape

15- to 16-inch round cake
plate or cake base

Plastic drinking straws

Fresh flowers of your choice
(tulips, roses, peonies,
carnations, orchids, or
edible flowers; see
Cook's Notes)

Florist's wire or 1 twist tie

7. Once cooled, wrap the layers well in plastic wrap and store at room temperature for up to 1 day before filling and frosting. Or, wrap the layers in plastic wrap and then in heavy-duty foil and freeze them for up to 1 month. (Thaw slightly before filling and frosting.) In warm weather, make sure the cake layers are cold before frosting them; chill them in the freezer, if needed.

8. Fill the layers: If you wish to fill the layers, slice each layer in thirds horizontally with a serrated knife. Spread the filling of choice on two of the split layers. Reassemble the split layers, place on sheet pans, cover with plastic wrap, and chill.

9. Make the frosting: Place the cream cheese and butter in a very large mixing bowl and beat with an electric mixer on medium-low speed until creamy, 1 to 1½ minutes. Add the vanilla and confectioners' sugar, 2 cups at a time, beating on low speed until the sugar is incorporated and the consistency you desire. Stop the machine and scrape down the bowl with a rubber spatula. Increase the mixer speed to medium and beat until fluffy, 1 to 2 minutes. Set aside.

10. To frost the cake, dab 2 tablespoons of frosting each onto the 12-inch cardboard cake round, the 8-inch, and the 6-inch and spread it across the round in a thin layer. Place each cake layer on top of its matching size of cake round. The dab of icing will keep the layers from sliding. Frost the top and sides of the cake layers with a long, thin metal icing spatula. Begin by spreading a thin coat all the way around the sides to seal in the crumbs, then go back and apply a thicker coat. Frost the 12-inch and 8-inch layers flat across the top. Frost the top of the 6-inch layer more generously, as it will be placed on top of the cake Set the cake layers, uncovered, in the refrigerator to chill. You should have about 2 cups of frosting remaining.

11. To assemble the cake, place a few pieces of double-sided tape or loops of masking tape in the center of a cake plate or base that is 15 to 16 inches in diameter, or 3 to 4 inches larger than the largest cake layer. Place the 12-inch cake layer, still on its cardboard base, on the cake plate or base; the tape will hold it securely.

CONTINUED

Cardboard cake rounds can be found at baking supply stores or online.

Choose a different filling to spread in each of three tiers. A nice combination is apricot on one tier, a citrus curd on another, and a brown sugar frosting on the third. Or use the same filling throughout. You will need about 6 cups.

When decorating your cake, flowers are a fresh and easy garnish. But make sure that the blooms you use are free from pesticides and organically grown. Match the flowers on the cake with the colors for the big day.

12. Overturn the empty 8-inch baking pan and set it in the center of the 12-inch cake layer, using the rim of the pan to make a mark in the frosting where you'll place the 8-inch layer. Insert a drinking straw vertically into the center of the 12-inch layer all the way to the base and mark where the top of the cake meets the straw. Remove the straw and cut it and 7 more straws into pieces of this length (these will be used to support the 8-inch layer). Insert 1 straw back into the center of the cake layer and place the other 6 in an upright spoke pattern around it, halfway between the center and the circle you made with the 8-inch pan. Carefully place the 8-inch layer with its cardboard base on top of the 12-inch layer, matching with the circle marked in the frosting.

13. Overturn the empty 6-inch baking pan and set it in the center of the 8-inch cake layer, using the rim of the pan to make a mark in the frosting where you'll place the 6-inch layer. Insert a straw into the center of the 8-inch layer and mark where the top of the cake meets the straw. Remove the straw and cut it and 5 more straws to this length. Insert 1 straw in the center of the 8-inch cake layer and the remaining 5 straws in spokes around it. Carefully place the 6-inch layer with its cardboard base on top of the 8-inch layer, matching with the circle you marked in the frosting.

14. With the remaining frosting and a small metal spatula, fill any gaps and spread frosting around the base of each cake layer to create a seamless look. For the top, trim flowers so they have 1 to 2 inches of stem. Tie them together with florist's wire or a twist tie. Insert the flower bundle into the top of the cake. Feel free to decorate the sides and the base of the plate with more flowers. Store the finished cake in the refrigerator until time to serve.

TIPS FOR BAKING THE BEST WEDDING CAKE

1. This recipe makes 86 small servings or 52 more generous ones. If the bride and groom want to keep the top layer for their first anniversary, reduce those numbers by 10. And always consult with your wedding planner, with Wilton books, and online for the number of servings you get from different sizes of pans.

2. Use all white cake mix if you want a very white cake. Use a mix of both white and butter if you want a slightly richer cake, and use only butter mixes for a more pound cake–like cake.

3. Vanilla instant pudding mix turns this cake slightly golden, so opt for the white chocolate pudding mix to keep a white cake white.

4. Need more cake? Bake the cakes in half-sheet pans. Each 18 × 13-inch pan will yield about 50 servings. Or add a 16-inch layer (3 inches deep) on the bottom of the cake and the servings increase dramatically. (You will need 8 more cups of frosting to cover this layer.)

5. Bake this cake in two batches to make mixing easier and to be able to fit the layers in your oven. Fill the 6-inch and 8-inch pans first, reserving 1 cup of batter, then add that to the remaining batter and fill the 12-inch cake pan.

6. Bake at 325°F for a longer, slower bake and better texture.

Step by Step, How to Cut the Cake

1. Make a cut all the way around the bottom layer using the middle layer as a guide. Cut this 2-inch-wide ring of cake into 20 to 24 generous slices or 40 smaller ones.

2. Carefully remove the top layer from the middle layer and set it aside. Slice it last into 8 to 10 slices or save it for the bride and groom.

3. Cut the middle layer as you would a round layer cake, cutting through to the cardboard round. Remove the 8-inch cardboard round. You should get at least 12 generous slices or 18 smaller ones.

4. Cut the remaining part of the bottom layer as you would a round layer cake. It should yield at least 12 generous slices or 18 smaller ones.

Baby Cakes

I've fallen in love with baking baby cakes—these adorable 6-inch tiers. They're perfect for small gatherings and whenever you just want a bite of cake. Or at least, you want it to *look* that way. In truth, these pans hold the same amount of batter as a regular layer cake. From strawberry to yellow birthday to grapefruit to lavender to Baked Alaska, the flavors are anything but small!

*Chocolate Boozy
Baby Cake*
(page 116)

*Little Brown Sugar–
Grapefruit Cake*
(page 124)

*Red Velvet Baby Cake with
White Chocolate Glaze*
(page 78)

Vegetable oil spray,
for misting the pans

1 (15.25-ounce) package
yellow or butter cake mix

4 ounces cream cheese,
at room temperature

3 large eggs

½ cup warm water

½ cup vegetable oil

1 teaspoon vanilla extract

3 tablespoons strawberry
gelatin (see Cook's Note)

Strawberry Cream Cheese
Frosting (page 360)

8 to 12 fresh strawberries,
capped and sliced vertically,
for garnish

Strawberry Smash Cake

*My granddaughter is crazy about fresh strawberries.
So I created this recipe for her first birthday, and it is named
because this is when children have permission to stick their
hands in the icing and—smash!—the cake if they like. Everyone,
meanwhile, is taking photos! To have a little fun, I tinted one of
the layers with strawberry gelatin and made alternating layers
of pink and vanilla. On top? One birthday candle, surrounded
by a strawberry flower. It's really too pretty to smash!*

1. Place a rack in the center of the oven and preheat the oven
    to 350°F. Mist the bottom and sides of two 6-inch round cake
    pans that are 3 inches deep. Line the bottoms with rounds of
    parchment paper and mist the parchment. Set the pans aside.

2. In a large mixing bowl, combine the cake mix, cream cheese,
    eggs, water, oil, and vanilla. Beat with an electric mixer on
    low speed until blended, about 30 seconds. Stop the machine
    and scrape down the sides of the bowl with a rubber spatula.
    Increase the mixer speed to medium and beat until the batter
    is smooth, about 1 minute. Pour half of the batter into one of
    the prepared pans, smoothing the top with a rubber spatula.
    Stir the strawberry gelatin into the remaining batter until
    combined. Pour the strawberry batter into the second
    prepared pan, smoothing the top with a rubber spatula.

3. Place the pans in the oven and bake until the cakes spring
    back when gently pressed in the middle, 40 to 45 minutes.
    (The layer with strawberry gelatin takes a minute or two
    longer than the plain layer.)

4. Let the cakes cool in the pans on a wire rack for 10 minutes.
    Run a knife around the edges of each pan, then invert each
    layer onto a rack and pull off the rounds of parchment paper.
    Invert the layers again so they are right-side up and allow to
    cool completely, about 30 minutes.

CONTINUED

COOK'S NOTE:

You can omit the gelatin in one layer, or you can add the whole package of gelatin to the entire batter to make a completely strawberry cake. By changing the color—and flavor—of the gelatin, you can create a cake of pretty much any color for birthdays, game days, baby showers, or holidays.

5. To assemble the cake, slice the rounded dome (about ½ inch) off the top of each cake with a long serrated knife and discard. Slice each cake in half horizontally.

6. Place the bottom half of the vanilla cake cut-side up on a cake plate. Frost with ½ cup of the frosting, spreading it to the edges. Top with the bottom half of the strawberry cake cut-side up and spread with ½ cup frosting. Add the top half of the vanilla cake cut-side down and spread with ½ cup frosting. Finally, set the top half of the strawberry cake on top cut-side down. Spread the remaining frosting on the top and sides of the cake.

7. Place one small, rounded slice of strawberry in the center of the cake to form the center of the flower. Arrange the rest of the strawberry slices, closely together and at an angle, in concentric circles, beginning at the center and moving out as far as you want to go, to create a flower. Place the cake, uncovered, in the refrigerator to chill at least 30 minutes before slicing. Store, lightly covered, in the refrigerator for up to 5 days.

Little Yellow Birthday Cake

SERVES 8 TO 12

PREP: 25 TO 30 MINUTES

BAKE: 38 TO 42 MINUTES

Vegetable oil spray,
for misting the pans

1 (15.25-ounce) package
yellow or butter cake mix

4 tablespoons (half a
3.4-ounce package) vanilla
instant pudding mix

3 large eggs

10 tablespoons (1¼ sticks)
unsalted butter or plant
butter, at room temperature
(see Cook's Note)

1¼ cups whole milk or
full-fat canned coconut
milk, warmed

1 teaspoon vanilla extract

Chocolate Cream Cheese
Frosting (page 359),
Strawberry Cream Cheese
Frosting (page 360), or
Matcha Buttercream
(page 352)

½ cup chocolate decorating
sprinkles or shavings,
for garnish

*This might be the only birthday cake you need for children,
a best friend, or anyone overwhelmed by the thought of baking
a big cake. It's small in stature but substantial in flavor.
Spread with the customary chocolate cream cheese frosting or
a pastel buttercream tinted with strawberries or matcha.*

1. Place a rack in the center of the oven and preheat the oven to 350°F. Mist the bottom and sides of two 6-inch round cake pans that are 3 inches deep. Line the bottoms with rounds of parchment and mist the parchment. Set the pans aside.

2. In a large mixing bowl, stir together the cake mix and pudding mix. Add the eggs, butter, milk, and vanilla. Beat with an electric mixer on low speed until blended, about 30 seconds. Stop the machine and scrape down the sides of the bowl with a rubber spatula. Increase the mixer speed to medium and beat until the batter is smooth, about 1 minute. Divide the batter evenly between the prepared pans, smoothing the tops with a rubber spatula.

3. Place the pans in the oven and bake until the cakes are golden brown and the top springs back when gently pressed in the middle, 38 to 42 minutes.

4. Let the cakes cool in the pans on a wire rack for 5 minutes. Run a knife around the edges of each pan, then invert each layer onto the rack and pull off the parchment paper rounds. Invert the layers again so they are right-side up and allow to cool at least 20 minutes longer.

5. To assemble the cake, slice the rounded dome (about ½ inch) off the top of each cake with a long serrated knife and discard. Slice each cake in half horizontally.

CONTINUED

6. Place the bottom half of one cake cut-side up on a cake plate. Frost the top with about ½ cup of the frosting, spreading it to the edges. Top with the matching half of the cake cut-side down and spread with ½ cup frosting. Then top with the bottom half of the second cake cut-side up and spread with ½ cup frosting. Finally, top with the second layer cut-side down. Spread the remaining frosting over the top and sides of the cake.

7. Garnish the cake with the sprinkles. (For how to garnish the sides of a frosted cake with sprinkles, see How to Roll a Cake in Sprinkles, page 72.) Place the cake, uncovered, in the refrigerator to chill for at least 30 minutes before slicing. Store, lightly covered, in the fridge for up to 4 days.

How to Make a Chocolate Boozy Baby Cake

Bake the Darn Good Chocolate Cake (page 140) in two greased, floured, and parchment-lined 6-inch round pans that are 3 inches deep at 350°F for 35 to 40 minutes. Cool, then slice the ½-inch dome off the top of each cake (save to make crumbs). Set aside. Slice each cake horizontally in half. Stack the layers on a cake plate, spreading each layer with Whipped Chocolate Ganache (page 363) and Sweetened Whipped Cream (page 366) that you flavor with brandy, bourbon, or Kahlúa. Reserve enough whipped cream to spread on the top. Pulse the cake scraps in a food processor—or with your fingers—to make crumbs. Scatter the cake crumbs and some shaved semisweet chocolate on top of the cake. Store in the fridge for up to 3 days.

Baked Alaska Baby Cake

MAKES TWO 6-INCH CAKES,
EACH SERVING 4 TO 6

PREP: 40 TO 45 MINUTES, PLUS
1 HOUR FOR FREEZING

BAKE: 35 TO 40 MINUTES

CAKE

Vegetable oil spray,
for misting the pans

1 (15.25-ounce) package
yellow or butter cake mix

3 large eggs

1 cup full-fat canned
coconut milk or whole milk

⅓ cup vegetable oil

2 teaspoons vanilla extract

ICE CREAM

2 pints (4 cups) chocolate,
banana, or strawberry
ice cream

MERINGUE

4 large egg whites,
at room temperature

¼ teaspoon cream of tartar

1 cup sugar

Baked Alaska, made with cake, ice cream, and a browned meringue on top, is generally not for the fearful, but it is awfully impressive looking. I found some ways to actually make Baked Alaska for a dinner party at home that doesn't require a lot of steps. I start with a cake mix. And buy the ice cream. The meringue? It's a little different than the way my mother showed me—has a bit more sugar—but stays sturdy and glossy and browns gloriously.

1. Make the cake: Place a rack in the center of the oven and preheat the oven to 350°F. Mist the bottom and sides of two 6-inch round cake pans that are 3 inches deep. Line the bottoms with rounds of parchment and mist the parchment. Set the pans aside.

2. In a large mixing bowl, combine the cake mix, eggs, milk, oil, and vanilla. Beat with an electric mixer on low speed until blended, about 30 seconds. Stop the machine and scrape down the sides of the bowl with a rubber spatula. Increase the mixer speed to medium and beat until the batter is smooth, about 1 minute. Divide the batter evenly between the prepared pans, smoothing the tops with a rubber spatula.

3. Place the pans in the oven and bake until the cakes are golden brown and the top springs back when gently pressed in the middle, 35 to 40 minutes.

4. Let the cakes cool in the pans on a wire rack for 10 minutes. Run a knife around the edge of each pan, invert each layer onto the rack and pull off the rounds of parchment paper. Invert the layers again so they are right-side up and allow to cool for at least 20 minutes longer. Wash and dry the cake pans and set aside.

5. Remove the ice cream from the freezer. Slice the rounded dome (about ½ inch) off the top of each cake with a long serrated knife and discard. Place the cakes back in the pans. Spoon about

CONTINUED

If you want to completely
enrobe the frozen cake
and ice cream in meringue,
spread it around the sides
of the cake and pile it in
swirls on top. You can place
under the broiler to brown
the top, but you will need
a kitchen torch to brown
the sides. Or you can omit
the broiler and brown the
entire meringue using a
blow torch. This cake needs
to be enjoyed immediately.

If you only need to serve 4 to
6, bake both cakes, freeze
one, but only assemble one
Baked Alaska. You need
just 1 pint of ice cream
and should divide the
meringue recipe in half.

2 cups of ice cream on top of each cake, filling the pans all the way to the top. Cover with plastic wrap and freeze for 1 hour.

6. Make the meringue: In a large mixing bowl, combine the egg whites and cream of tartar and beat with an electric mixer on high speed until the egg whites are soft and foamy, about 2 minutes. Continue to beat on high speed, adding ¼ cup of the sugar at a time, until the whites are stiff and glossy, about 2 minutes.

7. When you are ready to serve, preheat the broiler to high. Remove the cake pans from the freezer, unmold the cakes from the pans, and transfer to a sheet pan. Spoon the meringue on top of the cakes (see Cook's Notes), then quickly broil until golden brown, about 1 minute. Slice and serve at once.

BANANA JAM

4 large ripe bananas

⅔ cup granulated sugar

2 tablespoons packed
dark brown sugar

Grated zest of 1 lime

Juice of 2 medium limes

Pinch of salt

2 tablespoons dark
or golden rum

CAKE

Vegetable oil spray,
for misting the pans

1 (15.25-ounce) package
yellow cake mix

4 tablespoons (half a
3.4-ounce package) vanilla
instant pudding mix

1 teaspoon
ground cinnamon

3 large eggs

1 cup mashed ripe banana
(2 large or 3 small bananas)

½ cup vegetable oil

½ cup full-fat or light
canned coconut milk

Banana Lime Baby Cake

With baby cakes, you bake a celebration each time you preheat the oven. And the island flavors of bananas, lime, and rum in this recipe do not disappoint. Banana lovers will adore what's spread between the layers—a jam made with, what else?: bananas, limes, and a spot of rum.

1. Make the banana jam: Cut the bananas into pieces and place in a medium saucepan with the granulated sugar and brown sugar. Cook over low heat, mashing the bananas with a potato masher or fork, until mostly smooth with some chunks remaining, 4 to 5 minutes.

2. Add the lime zest, lime juice, salt, and rum. Increase the heat a bit to bring the mixture to a boil, then reduce the heat and simmer on low, stirring frequently, until thickened and caramel-colored, about 10 minutes. Remove from the heat and let cool in the pan while you make the cake.

3. Make the cake: Place a rack in the center of the oven and preheat the oven to 350°F. Mist the bottom and sides of two 6-inch round cake pans that are 3 inches deep. Line the bottoms with rounds of parchment and mist the parchment. Set the pans aside.

4. In a large mixing bowl, stir together the cake mix, pudding mix, and cinnamon. Add the eggs, mashed banana, oil, and coconut milk. Beat with an electric mixer on low speed until blended, about 30 seconds. Stop the machine and scrape down the sides of the bowl with a rubber spatula. Increase the mixer speed to medium and beat until the batter is smooth, about 1 minute. Divide the batter evenly between the prepared pans, smoothing the top with a rubber spatula.

5. Place the pans in the oven and bake until the top of the cakes spring back when gently pressed in the middle, 38 to 42 minutes.

1 teaspoon grated lime zest

Small-Batch Cream Cheese Frosting (page 357)

1 lime, thinly sliced and cut into halves, for garnish (optional)

6.   Let the cakes cool in the pans on a wire rack for 5 minutes. Run a knife around the edges of each pan, then invert each layer onto the rack and pull off the rounds of parchment paper. Invert the layers again so they are right-side up and allow to cool for at least 20 minutes longer.

7.   Assemble the cake: Fold the lime zest into the cream cheese frosting. Slice the rounded dome (about ½ inch) off the top of each cake with a long serrated knife and discard. Slice each layer in half horizontally.

8.   Place the bottom half of one cake cut-side up on a cake plate and spread one-third (about ½ cup) of the banana jam almost to the edges. Place the matching half of this cake cut-side down on top. Spread the top of this layer with about ¾ cup of the frosting. Refrigerate the cake for 5 minutes for the frosting to set a bit.

9.   Spread the frosting with another one-third of the banana jam. Place the bottom half of the second cake cut-side up on top. Spread the remaining one-third of the banana jam almost to the edges. Place the matching half of this cake cut-side down on top. Frost the top and sides of the cake with the remaining frosting.

10. Refrigerate the cake for 30 minutes to make slicing easier. Garnish with the lime slices, if desired. Store this cake, lightly covered, in the refrigerator for up to 5 days.

LAVENDER "TEA"

1 tablespoon dried lavender
(see Cook's Note)

1 cup boiling water

CAKE

Vegetable oil spray,
for misting the pans

1 (15.25-ounce) package
yellow or butter cake mix

⅓ cup all-purpose flour

2 tablespoons sugar

3 large eggs

8 tablespoons (1 stick)
unsalted butter,
melted and cooled

¼ cup vegetable oil

1 teaspoon vanilla extract

ASSEMBLY

Vanilla Buttercream Frosting
(page 351)

1½ cups fresh or frozen
(thawed) wild blueberries

Sprig fresh lavender,
for garnish

Lavender, Vanilla, Blueberry Baby Cake

*Once I figured out how to perfume a tea loaf with Earl Grey
(see page 180), I was on to lavender. In much the same way
you brew a cup of tea with loose tea leaves, you pour boiling
water over dried lavender blossoms and let them steep for
24 hours. The water will turn faintly pink and smell of lavender.
This is a lovely cake to bake for small tea parties, intimate
book clubs, or to nibble on while you read Jane Austen.*

1. Make the lavender "tea": Place the dried lavender in a small
    glass bowl and pour the boiling water over it. Let it steep,
    uncovered, for at least 6 hours or preferably overnight.

2. Make the cake: Place a rack in the center of the oven and
    preheat the oven to 350°F. Mist the bottom and sides of two
    6-inch round cake pans that are 3 inches deep. Line the bottoms
    with rounds of parchment and mist the parchment. Set the
    pans aside.

3. In a large mixing bowl, stir together the cake mix, flour, and
    sugar. Add the eggs, butter, oil, and vanilla. Strain the lavender
    tea into the bowl (discard the lavender buds). Beat with an
    electric mixer on low speed until blended, about 30 seconds.
    Stop the machine and scrape down the sides of the bowl with
    a rubber spatula. Increase the mixer speed to medium and beat
    until the batter is smooth, about 1 minute. Divide the batter
    evenly between the prepared pans, smoothing the top with
    a rubber spatula.

4. Place the pans in the oven and bake until the cakes are golden
    brown and the top springs back when gently pressed in the
    middle, 35 to 40 minutes.

5. Let the cakes cool in the pans on a wire rack for 5 minutes.
    Run a knife around the edge of each pan, then invert each
    layer onto the rack and pull off the rounds of parchment paper.
    Invert the layers again so they are right-side up and allow to
    cool for at least 20 minutes longer.

6. To assemble the cake, slice the rounded dome (about ½ inch) off the top of each cake with a long serrated knife and discard. Slice each layer in half horizontally. Set aside. Set aside 1 tablespoon of the blueberries for garnish.

7. Place the bottom half of one layer, cut-side up, on a cake plate. Frost with about ½ cup of the frosting, spreading it nearly to the edges. Scatter with ½ cup of the blueberries. Top with the top half of the cake layer cut-side down, spread it with ½ cup frosting, then scatter with ½ cup blueberries. Top with the bottom half of the second layer cut-side up, spread with ½ cup frosting, and scatter with the remaining blueberries. Place the top half of the second layer cut-side down on top. Spread the remaining frosting on top of the cake and thinly around the sides to create a barely naked look. Scatter the reserved blueberries on top of the cake and decorate with a sprig of fresh lavender, if desired. Store, lightly covered, at room temperature for one day or in the refrigerator for up to three days.

Little Brown Sugar-Grapefruit Cake

SERVES 8 TO 12

PREP: 1 HOUR 15 MINUTES

BAKE: 35 TO 40 MINUTES

CAKE

Vegetable oil spray,
for misting the pans

1 (15.25-ounce) package
yellow or butter cake mix

4 tablespoons (half a
3.4-ounce package) vanilla
instant pudding mix

3 large eggs

4 tablespoons (½ stick)
unsalted butter,
at room temperature

¾ cup whole milk, warmed

¼ cup vegetable oil

¼ cup fresh pink grapefruit
juice (from 1 large or 2 small
grapefruit; see Cook's Notes)

ASSEMBLY

Homemade Fruit Curd
(page 365), made with
pink grapefruit juice

Brown Sugar Cream Cheese
Frosting (page 358)

Pink grapefruit suprêmes
(see Cook's Notes),
for garnish (optional)

This sweet little cake was modeled after the classic grapefruit chiffon cake born 100 years ago in Hollywood at the Brown Derby restaurant. The key ingredient in that cake was vegetable oil, which kept the cake moist. And the grapefruit? It was the diet pill of the '20s—movie starlets thought it would melt the pounds away, so bakers added it to cake, too! I've incorporated a cake mix, added a fresh grapefruit curd, and introduced grapefruit's flavor partner—brown sugar—in the frosting. A star is born!

1. Make the cake: Place a rack in the center of the oven and preheat the oven to 350°F. Mist the bottom and sides of two 6-inch round cake pans that are 3 inches deep. Line the bottoms with rounds of parchment and mist the parchment. Set the pans aside.

2. In a large mixing bowl, stir together the cake mix and pudding mix. Add the eggs, butter, milk, oil, and grapefruit juice. Beat with an electric mixer on low speed until blended, about 30 seconds. Stop the machine and scrape down the sides of the bowl with a rubber spatula. Increase the mixer speed to medium and beat until the batter is smooth, about 1 minute. Divide the batter evenly between the prepared pans, smoothing the top with a rubber spatula.

3. Place the pans in the oven and bake until the cakes are golden brown and spring back when gently pressed in the middle, 35 to 40 minutes.

4. Let the cakes cool in the pans on a wire rack for 10 to 15 minutes. Run a dinner knife around the edge of each pan, then invert each layer onto the rack and pull off the rounds of parchment paper. Invert the layers again so they are right-side up and allow the cakes to cool completely, about 30 minutes longer.

5. Assemble the cake: While the cakes are cooling, remove the grapefruit curd from the refrigerator and let it come to room temperature.

COOK'S NOTES:

If you have leftover grapefruit juice or zest after making the curd, fold it into the frosting.

To create what are called "suprêmes" to garnish the top of the cake, peel a pink grapefruit, then slice down between the membranes that enclose the fruit segments to expose the fruit inside. Place these grapefruit suprêmes on top of the cake.

6. Slice the rounded dome (about ½ inch) off the top of each cake with a long serrated knife and discard. Slice each layer in half horizontally. Place the bottom half of one cake cut-side up on a cake plate. Spread about half (½ cup) of the curd almost to the edges. Place the matching half of this cake on top, cut-side down, and spread with about ¾ cup of the frosting. Place the bottom half of the second cake cut-side up on top. Spread with the remaining curd almost to the edges. Place the matching top half of this cake on top cut-side down. Frost the top and sides of the cake with the remaining frosting. Garnish with grapefruit suprêmes, if desired. Refrigerate for 30 minutes to make slicing easier. Slice and serve. Store, lightly covered, in the refrigerator for up to 4 days.

Flowerpot Cakes

MAKES 6 FLOWERPOT CAKES,
EACH SERVING 2

PREP: 45 TO 50 MINUTES

BAKE: 35 TO 40 MINUTES

CAKE

Six 4-inch new clay
flowerpots

Vegetable oil spray,
for misting the pots

1 cup (6 ounces)
semisweet chocolate chips

1 (15.25-ounce) package
chocolate cake mix

5 level tablespoons
(half a 3.9-ounce package)
chocolate instant
pudding mix

3 large eggs

1 cup full-fat or light
canned coconut milk

½ cup vegetable oil

ASSEMBLY

Cake crumbs or crumbled
chocolate wafer cookies
(to look like dirt)

½ recipe Chocolate
Buttercream Frosting
(page 355)

Pesticide-free edible
flowers, such as zinnias,
with sturdy stems

Let's time-travel to the 1960s when flowerpot cakes were all the rage. The late Helen Corbitt of Texas was the Martha Stewart of the time and created grand table settings for presidents' wives using decorated flowerpot cakes. I channeled my inner Helen Corbitt for this retro recipe and loved baking cakes in these little clay pots. Be sure to use new flowerpots or flowerpots that have not been used for potting plants. Wash them with soap and rinse and dry them well. Mist the insides with oil and fit a small piece of aluminum foil in the bottom to cover the hole. That's it! I baked chocolate flowerpot cakes, but you could use the batter for Basic Vanilla Cupcakes (page 268).

1. Make the cake: Place a rack in the center of the oven and preheat the oven to 350°F. Wash, rinse, and pat dry 6 clay flowerpots measuring 4 inches across and 4 inches deep. Mist the pots and place them on a sheet pan. Cut 6 small pieces of aluminum foil and use to cover the hole in the bottom of the pots. Set aside.

2. Place the chocolate chips in a microwave-safe bowl and microwave on high power until nearly melted, 30 to 40 seconds. Stir until the chocolate is completely melted. Set aside for 10 minutes to cool.

3. In a large mixing bowl, stir together the cake mix and pudding mix. Add the melted chocolate, eggs, coconut milk, and oil. Beat with an electric mixer on low speed until blended, about 30 seconds. Stop the machine and scrape down the sides of the bowl with a rubber spatula. Increase the mixer speed to medium and beat until the batter is smooth, about 1 minute. Divide the batter evenly among the flowerpots, filling them slightly more than half full (but less than two-thirds).

4. Place the pan with the flowerpots in the oven and bake until the top of the cakes spring back when gently pressed in the middle, 35 to 40 minutes.

5. Carefully transfer each pot to a wire rack and let cool for 20 minutes. If you want to use crumbs as garnish, slice ½ inch off the top of 2 of the cakes and set aside.

6. Spread the top of each cake with chocolate frosting. With your fingers, crumble the reserved cake tops into coarse crumbs and scatter on top of the frosting. Stick the flowers into the cake. If the flower stems aren't sturdy enough to pierce the cake, use green drinking straws like flower stems and place the flowers into the straws. Store uncovered at room temperature for up to 3 days.

Bundts, Pounds, and Loaves

Refreshingly hands-off, these frank and honest cakes are anything but plain Jane. You pop them in the oven, unmold them (or serve straight from the pan), drizzle a glaze over the top—or not—then slice and eat. Plus, they stash in the freezer for unexpected company or last-minute bakes. Most of these cakes can be baked either as a Bundt, pound (tube pan), or loaf—it's up to you!

Almond Cream Cheese Pound Cake

MAKES 12 SERVINGS

PREP: 10 TO 15 MINUTES

BAKE: 40 TO 45 MINUTES

Vegetable oil spray
or shortening,
for greasing the pan

All-purpose flour,
for dusting the pan

1 (15.25-ounce) package
yellow or butter cake mix

1 (8-ounce) package cream
cheese, at room temperature

3 large eggs

½ cup warm water

½ cup vegetable oil

1 teaspoon vanilla extract

1 teaspoon almond extract

1 teaspoon confectioners'
sugar, for dusting (optional)

COOK'S NOTE:

If you use a tube pan for
this cake, add 2 tablespoons
flour and increase the baking
time by about 5 minutes.

This cake is close to my heart. The original recipe was sent to me by the late Ross Beck of Texarkana, Arkansas. Through the years, his recipe became the go-to of many good cooks until the mixes decreased in size, and then that threw this recipe's devotees into a tailspin. I tested this recipe many different ways in order to perfect it and get it to work with the smaller cake mixes, and in the end, it tastes just like the original! Yet, I did omit the extra sugar and poured it into a Bundt pan this go-around, which gives it the support it needs to rise high, be moist and rich, and make everyone happy, including me!

1. Place a rack in the center of the oven and preheat the oven to 350°F. Grease and flour a 12-cup Bundt pan. Set the pan aside.

2. In a large mixing bowl, combine the cake mix, cream cheese, eggs, water, oil, vanilla, and almond extract. Beat with an electric mixer on low speed until blended, about 30 seconds. Stop the machine and scrape down the sides of the bowl with a rubber spatula. Increase the mixer speed to medium and beat until the batter is smooth and fluffy, about 1 minute. Pour the batter into the prepared pan, smoothing the top with a rubber spatula.

3. Place the pan in the oven and bake until the cake springs back when gently pressed in the middle, 40 to 45 minutes.

4. Let the cake cool in the pan on a wire rack for 20 minutes. Run a long knife around the edges of the cake, shake the pan gently, and invert the cake onto a wire rack or cake plate. Let the cake cool for at least 20 minutes longer. Sift the confectioners' sugar over the top, if desired. Slice and serve. Store, tightly covered, at room temperature for up to 5 days.

MEYER LEMON CREAM CHEESE POUND CAKE: Make the batter for the Almond Cream Cheese Pound Cake, but omit the vanilla and almond extracts and add the grated zest and juice of 1 Meyer lemon to the batter. (A Meyer lemon is a little sweeter than a regular lemon and is actually a cross between a lemon and a mandarin orange.) Bake as directed.

Hershey's Bar Pound Cake

Vegetable oil spray
or shortening,
for greasing the pan

All-purpose flour,
for dusting the pan

½ cup sliced almonds,
coarsely chopped

6 (1.55-ounce) bars
Hershey's milk chocolate

1 (15.25-ounce) package
yellow or butter cake mix

5 tablespoons (half a
3.9-ounce package)
chocolate instant
pudding mix

3 large eggs

1 cup buttermilk,
preferably whole milk

⅓ cup water

8 tablespoons (1 stick)
unsalted butter,
at room temperature

½ teaspoon almond extract

1 cup (6 ounces)
mini semisweet chocolate
chips or shaved semisweet
chocolate (optional)

Hershey's Bar cakes date to the late 1950s. Some are scratch cakes and some start with a cake mix. My recipe, made with buttermilk for moist richness and melted milk chocolate for flavor, beats all other recipes hands down. Plus, I sprinkle sliced almonds in the bottom of the Magnolia-shaped Bundt pan before pouring in the batter so they toast and make a beautiful decoration on what will end up as the top of the cake. Even if you use a regular Bundt pan, they will look fabulous as well!

1. Place a rack in the center of the oven and preheat the oven to 350°F. Grease and flour a 12-cup Bundt pan. Scatter the almonds in the bottom of the pan. Set the pan aside.

2. Break the Hershey's bars into quarters and place in a glass pie plate or small glass bowl. Microwave on high power until the chocolate is nearly melted, 45 to 50 seconds. Stir with a silicone spatula until completely melted. Set aside.

3. In a large mixing bowl, stir together the cake mix and pudding mix. Add the eggs, buttermilk, water, butter, and almond extract. Beat with an electric mixer on low speed until blended, about 30 seconds. Stop the machine and scrape down the sides of the bowl with a rubber spatula. Increase the mixer speed to medium and beat until the batter is smooth and fluffy, about 1 minute. Pour in the melted chocolate and beat on low speed until blended, about 30 seconds. Fold in the chocolate chips (if using). Pour the batter into the prepared pan, smoothing the top with a rubber spatula.

4. Place the pan in the oven and bake until the cake springs back when gently pressed in the middle, 49 to 54 minutes.

5. Let the cake cool in the pan on a wire rack for 20 minutes. Run a long knife around the edges of the cake, shake the pan gently, then invert the cake onto a wire rack or cake plate. Let the cake cool for at least 20 minutes longer. Slice and serve. Store, tightly covered, at room temperature for up to 5 days.

Stacy's Chocolate Chip Cake

Vegetable oil spray
or shortening,
for greasing the pan

All-purpose flour,
for dusting the pan

1 bar (4 ounces)
German's sweet chocolate

1 (15.25-ounce) package
yellow or butter cake mix

4 tablespoons (half a
3.4-ounce package) vanilla
instant pudding mix

3 large eggs

1 cup whole milk

¾ cup vegetable oil

1 teaspoon vanilla extract

1 cup (6 ounces) regular
or mini semisweet
chocolate chips

1 teaspoon confectioners'
sugar or 1 teaspoon each
confectioners' sugar and
unsweetened cocoa powder,
for garnish (optional)

The sign of a great cake recipe is when you open the cookbook and you turn to a page splattered with batter—proof of every time someone has baked that cake. This is that cake, the recipe everyone wants to talk about at book signings. Stacy Ross of Nashville sent me this recipe back when I was writing The Cake Mix Doctor *in 1998. I baked it for my family, and my mother, who was particular about baking, kept sneaking back into the kitchen to grab another slice. That's how I knew it was a keeper. Stacy once told me she liked to bake this cake for gifts and I agree—it's the perfect cake to share with everyone you love, another sign of a great recipe.*

1. Place a rack in the center of the oven and preheat the oven to 350°F. Grease and flour a 12-cup Bundt pan. Set the pan aside.

2. Break the chocolate bar into 4 pieces and finely grate in a food processor (drop the pieces in one at a time with the processor running) or with a hand grater. Set the grated chocolate aside.

3. In a large mixing bowl, stir together the cake mix and pudding mix. Add the eggs, milk, oil, and vanilla. Beat with an electric mixer on low speed until blended, about 30 seconds. Stop the machine and scrape down the sides of the bowl with a rubber spatula. Increase the mixer speed to medium and beat until the batter is smooth and fluffy, about 1 minute. Fold in the grated chocolate and the chocolate chips. Pour the batter into the prepared pan, smoothing the top with a rubber spatula.

4. Place the pan in the oven and bake until the cake springs back when gently pressed in the middle, 45 to 50 minutes.

5. Let the cake cool in the pan on a wire rack for 20 minutes. Run a long knife around the edges of the cake, shake the pan gently, and invert the cake onto a wire rack or cake plate. Let the cake cool at least 20 minutes longer. Sift the confectioners' sugar over the top, if desired. Slice and serve. Store, tightly covered, at room temperature for up to 5 days.

COOK'S NOTE:
This cake is baked in a
Heritage Bundt pan.

COOK'S NOTE:
For the best rise, do not
grease the sides of the
pan, only the bottom.

SERVES 12

PREP: 20 MINUTES

BAKE: 30 TO 35 MINUTES

CAKE

Vegetable oil spray or shortening, for greasing the bottom of the pan (see Cook's Note)

3 large eggs, separated

½ teaspoon cream of tartar

1 (15.25-ounce) package chocolate cake mix

5 tablespoons (half a 3.9-ounce package) chocolate instant pudding mix

¾ cup water

½ cup vegetable oil

1 teaspoon vanilla extract

½ to 1 teaspoon peppermint extract

1 cup (6 ounces) white chocolate chips

ASSEMBLY

White Chocolate Glaze (page 370) or Shiny Chocolate Glaze (page 371)

Chopped peppermint candy, for garnish

White Chocolate-Peppermint Chiffon Cake

Chiffon cakes are the best of both worlds: They are moist and tender as well as light and fluffy. In this recipe, I've added peppermint extract and white chocolate chips to the batter, so not only is this cake visually stunning, it's delicious. Finish it with white chocolate glaze and chopped peppermint candies if you're feeling over the top!

1. Make the cake: Place a rack in the center of the oven and preheat the oven to 350°F. Grease just the bottom of a 10-inch tube pan (see Cook's Note). Set the pan aside.

2. In a medium mixing bowl, combine the egg whites and cream of tartar. Beat with an electric mixer on high speed until stiff peaks form, about 3 minutes. Set the bowl aside.

3. In a large mixing bowl, combine the cake mix, pudding mix, egg yolks, water, oil, vanilla, and peppermint extract. With the same beaters used for the egg whites—no need to wash them—beat on low speed until blended, about 30 seconds. Stop the machine and scrape down the sides of the bowl with a rubber spatula. Increase the mixer speed to medium and beat until the batter is smooth and fluffy, about 1 minute. Fold the beaten egg whites into the batter with a rubber spatula until the mixture is well combined but light. Fold in the white chocolate chips. Pour the batter into the prepared pan, smoothing the top with the rubber spatula.

4. Place the pan in the oven and bake until the cake springs back when gently pressed in the middle, 30 to 35 minutes.

5. Let the cake cool in the pan on a wire rack for 20 minutes. Run a long knife around the edges of the cake, shake the pan gently, and invert the cake once and then again so it rests right-side up on a wire rack or cake plate.

6. Assemble the cake: Pour warm glaze over the top. Press candy onto the glaze, if desired. Let cool 20 minutes. Store at room temperature for up to 5 days.

Neapolitan Swirl Pound Cake

SERVES 12

PREP: 25 TO 30 MINUTES

BAKE: 45 TO 50 MINUTES

Vegetable oil spray
or shortening,
for greasing the pan

All-purpose flour,
for dusting the pan

1 (15.25- or 16.25-ounce)
package white cake mix

¼ cup all-purpose flour

¼ cup granulated sugar

3 large eggs

1⅓ cups whole milk, warm

12 tablespoons (1½ sticks)
unsalted butter,
at room temperature

2 teaspoons vanilla extract

3 tablespoons
strawberry gelatin

½ cup (3 ounces)
semisweet chocolate chips

1 teaspoon confectioners'
sugar, for dusting, optional

Clever mothers like mine bought Neapolitan ice cream because it was a peacemaker. But I was the peace breaker, because once everyone had their chosen flavor of vanilla, chocolate, or strawberry, I ran the scoop from right to left, grabbing some of each! Not only did I think it tasted better this way, but my bowlful was a beauty. Those memories came rushing back when we baked this pound cake with its swirls of vanilla, chocolate, and strawberry and sliced it to reveal its Neapolitan charms.

1. Place a rack in the center of the oven and preheat the oven to 350°F. Grease and flour a 12-cup Bundt pan. Set the pan aside.

2. In a large mixing bowl, stir together the cake mix, flour, and granulated sugar. Add the eggs, milk, butter, and vanilla. Beat with an electric mixer on low speed until blended, about 30 seconds. Stop the machine and scrape down the sides of the bowl with a rubber spatula. Increase the mixer speed to medium and beat until the batter is smooth and fluffy, about 1 minute. Divide the batter into thirds, using your eye or a kitchen scale. Place one-third of the batter in a medium bowl and set aside. Place another one-third in a second medium bowl, whisk in the strawberry gelatin, and set aside. Place the final third of the batter in a third medium bowl. Microwave the chocolate chips in a small glass bowl on high power until partially melted, 20 to 30 seconds. Stir until completely melted, then fold into the third bowl of batter.

3. Using a separate ice cream scoop or soupspoon for each bowl, randomly dollop one flavor of the batter at a time into the prepared pan. You can be organized about this or not. Just make sure the level of batter in the pan stays about the same. (You do not need to swirl the batter because the batter swirls on its own as it bakes.)

4. Place the pan in the oven and bake until the cake springs back when gently pressed in the middle, 45 to 50 minutes.

5. Let the cake cool in the pan on a wire rack for 20 minutes. Run a long knife around the edges of the cake, shake the pan gently, and invert the cake onto a wire rack or cake plate. Let the cake cool at least 20 minutes longer. Sift the confectioners' sugar over the top, if desired, then slice and serve. Store, lightly covered, at room temperature for up to 5 days.

Darn Good Chocolate Cake

SERVES 12

PREP: 15 TO 20 MINUTES

BAKE: 42 TO 47 MINUTES

Vegetable oil spray
or shortening,
for greasing the pan

All-purpose flour,
for dusting the pan

1 (15.25-ounce) package
chocolate cake mix

5 tablespoons
(half a 3.9-ounce package)
chocolate instant
pudding mix

3 large eggs

¾ cup water

½ cup sour cream

½ cup vegetable oil

1⅔ cups (10 ounces) mini
semisweet chocolate chips

1 teaspoon unsweetened
cocoa powder or
confectioners' sugar,
for dusting (optional)

COOK'S NOTE:
Add a teaspoon of vanilla
extract or espresso powder
to the batter if you like.

When I named this cake two decades ago, I took a little liberty as to how Aunt Louise described. She called it "Damn Good Chocolate Cake," which does have a stronger message! It's the cake that everyone knows and loves.

1. Place a rack in the center of the oven and preheat the oven to 350°F. Grease and flour a 12-cup Bundt pan. Set the pan aside.

2. In a large mixing bowl, stir together the cake mix and pudding mix. Add the eggs, water, sour cream, and oil. Beat with an electric mixer on low speed until blended, 30 seconds. Stop the machine and scrape down the sides of the bowl with a rubber spatula. Increase the mixer speed to medium and beat until the batter is smooth, about 1 minute. Fold in the chocolate chips. Pour the batter into the prepared pan, smoothing the top.

3. Place the pan in the oven and bake until the cake springs back when gently pressed in the middle, 42 to 47 minutes.

4. Let the cake cool in the pan on a wire rack for 20 minutes. Run a long knife around the edges of the cake, shake the pan gently, and invert the cake onto a wire rack or cake plate. Let the cake cool. Sift the cocoa over the top, if desired. Slice and serve. Store, tightly covered, at room temperature for up to 5 days.

SUGAR-FREE DARN GOOD CHOCOLATE CAKE: Make the batter for Darn Good Chocolate Cake substituting a 16-ounce package of Pillsbury sugar-free chocolate cake mix and a 1.4-ounce package of sugar-free chocolate instant pudding mix for those mixes. Use plain nonfat Greek yogurt instead of the sour cream and a 9-ounce package (1½ cups) of Lily's brand stevia-sweetened semisweet chocolate chips. All other ingredients stay the same. Note that the batter is very thick. It does not pour into the pan; instead, you must dollop large spoonfuls of it into a 12-cup Bundt pan. Bake at 350°F until the cake springs back when lightly pressed, 38 to 43 minutes. The cake is best warm, while the chocolate is still melted.

Chocolate Kahlúa Cake

SERVES 12

PREP: 15 TO 20 MINUTES

BAKE: 48 TO 52 MINUTES

Vegetable oil spray
or shortening,
for greasing the pan

All-purpose flour or
unsweetened cocoa powder,
for dusting the pan

1 (15.25-ounce) package
chocolate cake mix

5 tablespoons (half a
3.9-ounce package)
chocolate instant
pudding mix

3 large eggs

⅔ cup vegetable oil

½ cup Kahlúa

½ cup water

½ cup vanilla Greek yogurt
(see Cook's Note)

2 cups (12 ounces) mini
semisweet chocolate chips
(see Cook's Note)

1 teaspoon confectioners'
sugar, for dusting

COOK'S NOTE:
Often Greek yogurt comes in
5.3-ounce cups, so use the
entire portion even though
it's a bit more than ½ cup.

When I wrote the first Cake Mix Doctor, *I created an entire chapter called "Cakes with Spirit." It seemed like some of the most popular cake recipes in the book all called for a cup of rum, Kahlúa, or amaretto, or they were named after drinks like Harvey Wallbanger or Fuzzy Navel! There is no doubt that boozy beverages do add a punchy flavor to just about any cake.*

1. Place a rack in the center of the oven and preheat the oven to 350°F. Grease and flour a 12-cup Heritage or standard Bundt pan. Set the pan aside.

2. In a large mixing bowl, stir together the cake mix and pudding mix. Add the eggs, oil, Kahlúa, water, and yogurt. Beat with an electric mixer on low speed until blended, about 30 seconds. Stop the machine and scrape down the sides of the bowl with a rubber spatula. Increase the mixer speed to medium and beat until the batter is smooth and fluffy, about 1 minute. Fold in the mini chocolate chips. Pour the batter into the prepared pan, smoothing the top with a rubber spatula.

3. Place the pan in the oven and bake until the cake springs back when gently pressed in the middle, 48 to 52 minutes.

4. Let the cake cool in the pan on a wire rack for 20 minutes. Run a long knife around the edges of the cake, shake the pan gently, then invert the cake onto a wire rack or cake plate. Let the cake cool for at least 20 minutes longer. Sift the confectioners' sugar on top. Slice and serve. Store, tightly covered, at room temperature for up to 5 days.

COOK'S NOTE:
Mini chocolate chips come in packages that range from 10 to 12 ounces. If you want to use the whole package, this recipe works with 1⅔ cups to 2 cups chips.

Tunnel of Fudge Cake

SERVES 12

PREP: 20 TO 25 MINUTES

BAKE: 43 TO 48 MINUTES

CHOCOLATE GANACHE FILLING AND TOPPING

1⅔ cups (10 ounces) semisweet chocolate chips

1 cup heavy cream

1 teaspoon vanilla extract

CAKE

Vegetable oil spray or shortening, for greasing the pan

All-purpose flour, for dusting the pan

½ cup finely chopped walnuts or pecans

1 (15.25-ounce) package chocolate cake mix

5 tablespoons (half a 3.9-ounce package) chocolate instant pudding mix

1 tablespoon unsweetened cocoa powder

3 large eggs

1 cup water

½ cup plain Greek yogurt or sour cream

½ cup vegetable oil

The original Tunnel of Fudge was a scratch cake using a Pillsbury dry frosting mix for the gooey fudge interior, but I've adapted the recipe to use a mix for the cake instead of the fudge filling. My go-to for the creamy texture and intense chocolate tunnel? Ganache, of course, which is perfect both as a filling and a topping.

1. Make the chocolate ganache filling and topping: Place the chocolate chips in a medium stainless-steel mixing bowl. Pour the cream into a small heavy saucepan and bring to a boil, stirring, over medium heat. Remove the cream from the heat and pour it over the chocolate. Using a wooden spoon, stir until the chocolate is melted. Stir in the vanilla. Pour about ⅔ cup of the mixture into a small bowl for use as the filling and refrigerate to firm up. Set aside the remaining ganache at room temperature for use as the topping.

2. Make the cake: Place a rack in the center of the oven and preheat the oven to 350°F. Grease and flour a 12-cup Bundt pan. Set the pan aside.

3. Scatter the walnuts on a small baking pan and place in the preheating oven until lightly toasted, 3 to 4 minutes. Set aside.

4. In a large mixing bowl, stir together the cake mix, pudding mix, and cocoa. Add the eggs, water, yogurt, and oil. Beat with an electric mixer on low speed until blended, about 30 seconds. Stop the machine and scrape down the sides of the bowl with a rubber spatula. Increase the mixer speed to medium and beat until the batter is smooth and fluffy, about 1 minute. Fold in the toasted walnuts. Remove the ganache from the refrigerator.

5. Pour 4 cups of the batter into the prepared pan, smoothing the top with a rubber spatula. With a soupspoon, dollop the ganache over the batter, staying away from the edges of the pan as much as possible. Ladle the remaining batter over the ganache, smoothing the top with the spatula.

6. Place the pan in the oven and bake until the cake springs back when gently pressed in the middle, 43 to 48 minutes.

7. Let the cake cool in the pan on a wire rack for 20 minutes. Run a long knife around the edges of the cake, shake the pan gently, then invert the cake onto a wire rack or cake plate. Let the cake cool for 10 minutes. Spoon the room-temperature ganache topping over the cake. If the ganache has firmed up, microwave it in 10-second intervals until it is pourable. Slice and serve. Store, lightly covered, at room temperature for up to a day or in the refrigerator for up to 5 days.

SERVES 16

PREP: 10 TO 15 MINUTES

BAKE: 45 TO 50 MINUTES

Vegetable oil spray
or shortening,
for greasing the pan

All-purpose flour,
for dusting the pan

1 (15.25-ounce) package
yellow or butter cake mix

1 cup all-purpose flour

½ cup granulated sugar

4 large eggs

1 cup sour cream

1 cup evaporated milk
or whole milk

½ cup vegetable oil

4 tablespoons (½ stick)
unsalted butter,
at room temperature

1 tablespoon vanilla extract
(see Cook's Note)

1 teaspoon confectioners'
sugar, for dusting

COOK'S NOTE:
This cake bakes best in a
tube pan because it is too
much batter for a Bundt.

Sour Cream Pound Cake

*Carol McMillion sent me this yummy recipe years ago, and
I've loved it with berries and peaches in the summertime
or hot fudge sauce once the weather is cool. You can always
count on sour cream to improve a cake mix, and this is
still the pound cake recipe that tastes likes scratch.*

1. Place a rack in the center of the oven and preheat the oven to 350°F. Grease and flour a 10-inch tube pan (see Cook's Note). Set the pan aside.

2. In a large mixing bowl, stir together the cake mix, flour, and granulated sugar. Add the eggs, sour cream, milk, oil, butter, and vanilla. Beat with an electric mixer on low speed until blended, about 30 seconds. Stop the machine and scrape down the sides of the bowl with a rubber spatula. Increase the mixer speed to medium and beat until the batter is smooth and fluffy, about 1 minute. Pour the batter into the prepared pan, smoothing the top with a rubber spatula.

3. Place the pan in the oven and bake until the cake springs back when gently pressed in the middle, 45 to 50 minutes.

4. Let the cake cool in the pan on a wire rack for 20 minutes. Run a long knife around the edges of the cake, shake the pan gently, and invert the cake once and then again so it rests right-side up on a wire rack or cake plate. Let the cake cool for at least 20 minutes longer. Dust confectioners' sugar over the top. Slice and serve. Store, tightly covered, at room temperature for up to 1 week.

COOK'S NOTE:
Vanilla is so expensive at this writing, so I understand if you
want to reduce the amount you add to this cake or find another
way to flavor it. The zest and juice of a lemon is an economical
option–1 teaspoon zest and up to 2 tablespoons juice.

Basic Buttermilk-Spice Cake

SERVES 12

PREP: 15 MINUTES

BAKE: 35 TO 40 MINUTES FOR A
12-CUP BUNDT PAN, 20 TO
25 MINUTES FOR 9-INCH
LAYERS, 25 TO 30 MINUTES
FOR A 13 × 9-INCH SHEET CAKE,
20 MINUTES FOR CUPCAKES

Vegetable oil spray
or shortening,
for greasing the pan

All-purpose flour,
for dusting the pan

1 (15.25-ounce) package
yellow or butter cake mix

4 tablespoons (half a
3.4-ounce package) vanilla
instant pudding mix

1 teaspoon
ground cinnamon

½ teaspoon ground allspice

¼ teaspoon ground nutmeg

¼ teaspoon ground ginger

3 large eggs

1 cup buttermilk,
preferably whole milk

¼ cup water

8 tablespoons (1 stick)
unsalted butter,
melted and cooled

Maple Caramel Drizzle
(page 372)

This cake might remind you of an old-fashioned doughnut, full of spice and so moist from buttermilk. It's a blueprint recipe to be poured into a Bundt pan, but also layer, cupcake, and sheet pans. Vary the spices to your taste, use milk or almond milk instead of buttermilk, and even applesauce in lieu of the eggs.

1. Place a rack in the center of the oven and preheat the oven to 350°F. Grease and flour a 12-cup Bundt pan. Set the pan aside.

2. In a large mixing bowl, stir together the cake mix, pudding mix, cinnamon, allspice, nutmeg, and ginger. Add the eggs, buttermilk, water, and melted butter. Beat with an electric mixer on low speed until blended, 30 seconds. Stop the machine and scrape down the sides of the bowl with a rubber spatula. Increase the mixer speed to medium and beat until the batter is smooth, about 1 minute. Pour the batter into the prepared Bundt pan, smoothing the top with a rubber spatula.

3. Place the pan in the oven and bake until the cake springs back when gently pressed in the middle, 35 to 40 minutes.

4. Let the cake cool in the pan on a wire rack for 20 minutes. Run a long knife around the edges of the cake, shake the pan gently, and invert the cake onto a wire rack or cake plate. Pour the glaze over the cake. Let the cake cool 20 minutes before slicing. Store, covered, at room temperature for up to 5 days.

How to Make a Blackberry Jam Cake

Make the batter for the Basic Buttermilk-Spice Cake, omitting the water and adding ¼ cup seedless blackberry jam instead. Bake in two greased and floured 9-inch round cake pans at 350°F for 23 to 27 minutes. To assemble, sandwich layers with 1 cup seedless blackberry jam. Pour ½ recipe Quick Caramel Frosting (page 364) over the top, letting it drip down the sides.

Chocolate-Layered Pistachio Cake

SERVES 12

PREP: 30 TO 35 MINUTES

BAKE: 42 TO 47 MINUTES

Vegetable oil spray
or shortening,
for greasing the pan

All-purpose flour,
for dusting the pan

½ cup finely chopped
unroasted pistachios

1 (15.25- or 16.25-ounce)
package white cake mix

4 tablespoons (half a
3.4-ounce package)
pistachio instant
pudding mix

3 large eggs

1 cup water

⅔ cup vegetable oil

1 tablespoon pistachio
syrup, preferably Monin
(optional)

1 teaspoon vanilla extract

½ cup chocolate syrup

⅓ cup (2 ounces) semisweet
chocolate chips or chopped
semisweet chocolate

I adore pistachio anything, and when you place it alongside chocolate, it's a match made in heaven. So for this recipe, I revisited the nostalgic pistachio Watergate Cake of the 1970s, named after the Watergate hearings when pistachio cake happened to be all the rage. But with a layer of added chocolate as well as chopped pistachios toasting in the bottom of the Bundt pan, this cake is improved and bakes miraculously into layers.

1. Place a rack in the center of the oven and preheat the oven to 350°F. Grease and flour a 12-cup Bundt pan. Scatter the pistachios in the bottom of the pan and set aside.

2. In a large mixing bowl, stir together the cake mix and pudding mix. Add the eggs, water, oil, pistachio syrup, and vanilla. Beat with an electric mixer on low speed until blended, about 30 seconds. Stop the machine and scrape down the sides of the bowl with a rubber spatula. Increase the mixer speed to medium and beat until the batter is smooth and fluffy, about 1 minute.

3. Place about one-third of the batter (about 1½ cups) in a small bowl and fold in the chocolate syrup. Place the chocolate chips in small microwave-safe bowl and microwave on high power until nearly melted, 20 to 30 seconds. Stir until the chocolate is completely melted. Cool for a few minutes, then fold the melted chocolate into the chocolate batter. Pour this batter into the pan over the pistachios. Gently spoon the pistachio batter on top, making sure the chocolate batter is completely covered.

4. Carefully place the pan in the oven and bake until the cake springs back when gently pressed in the middle and the sides just pull away from the pan, 42 to 47 minutes.

5. Let the cake cool in the pan on a wire rack for 20 minutes. Run a long knife around the edges of the cake, shake the pan gently, then invert the cake onto a wire rack or cake plate. Let the cake cool for at least 20 minutes longer before slicing. Store, tightly covered, at room temperature for up to 5 days.

Apple Cider Cake
with Cider Glaze

SERVES 12

PREP: 15 TO 20 MINUTES

BAKE: 43 TO 48 MINUTES

CAKE

Vegetable oil spray
or shortening,
for greasing the pan

All-purpose flour,
for dusting the pan

1 (15.25-ounce) package
yellow or butter cake mix

4 tablespoons (half a
3.4-ounce package) vanilla
instant pudding mix

1 teaspoon
ground cinnamon

3 large eggs

1 cup apple cider

⅔ cup vegetable oil

⅓ cup sour cream

1 teaspoon vanilla extract

APPLE CIDER GLAZE

2 tablespoons apple cider

1 cup confectioners' sugar

My friend Martha loves fresh apples, cider, and baking cakes. Each Christmas, her uncle brings her a gallon jug of apple cider from Fairmount Orchard in Signal Mountain, Tennessee; she freezes what her family doesn't drink to use in baking throughout the year. As we were testing this recipe in the summertime, she pulled out some of her beloved frozen cider to thaw for this cake, and I was most honored.

1. Make the cake: Place a rack in the center of the oven and preheat the oven to 350°F. Grease and flour a 12-cup Bundt pan. Set the pan aside.

2. In a large mixing bowl, stir together the cake mix, pudding mix, and cinnamon. Add the eggs, cider, oil, sour cream, and vanilla. Beat with an electric mixer on low speed until blended, about 30 seconds. Stop the machine and scrape down the sides of the bowl with a rubber spatula. Increase the mixer speed to medium and beat until the batter is smooth and fluffy, about 1 minute. Pour into the prepared pan, smoothing the top.

3. Place the pan in the oven and bake until the cake is golden brown and the top springs back when gently pressed in the middle, 43 to 48 minutes.

4. Transfer the pan to a wire rack to cool for 20 minutes.

5. Meanwhile, make the glaze: In a small bowl, whisk the cider into the confectioners' sugar until smooth and pourable.

6. Run a long knife around the edges of the cake, shake the pan gently, and invert the cake onto a wire rack or cake plate. Let the cake cool 10 minutes. Drizzle the cider glaze over the cake. Let for rest 10 to 15 minutes longer, then slice and serve. Store, lightly covered, at room temperature for up to 5 days.

COOK'S NOTE:
Freeze leftover cider in 1-cup portions in small plastic resealable bags and thaw at room temperature or in a saucepan over low heat.

Maple Nut Coffee Cake

SERVES 12

PREP: 20 TO 25 MINUTES

BAKE: 40 TO 45 MINUTES

BROWN SUGAR STREUSEL

⅓ cup (packed) light brown sugar

2 teaspoons ground cinnamon

½ cup finely chopped pecans or walnuts

CAKE

Vegetable oil spray or shortening, for greasing the pan

All-purpose flour, for dusting the pan

1 (15.25-ounce) package yellow or butter cake mix

4 tablespoons (half a 3.4-ounce package) vanilla instant pudding mix

3 large eggs

1 cup water or milk

⅔ cup vegetable oil

½ cup sour cream or Greek yogurt

1 teaspoon maple flavoring

1 teaspoon confectioners' sugar, for dusting

Several years ago reader Betty Minton of West Virginia wrote to tell me how much she loved one of my coffee cakes. And she went on to say she had tweaked the recipe with maple flavoring. Everyone loves it, she said, with a cup of coffee or glass of cold milk. I tried it and I loved it, too—especially warm! While I find this cake gorgeous baked in the Magnolia Bundt pan, you can use any 12-cup Bundt pan with this recipe.

1. Make the brown sugar streusel: In a small bowl, stir together the brown sugar, cinnamon, and nuts. Set aside.

2. Make the cake: Place a rack in the center of the oven and preheat the oven to 350°F. Grease and flour a 12-cup Magnolia or standard Bundt pan. Set the pan aside.

3. In a large mixing bowl, stir together the cake mix and pudding mix. Add the eggs, water, oil, sour cream, and maple flavoring. Beat with an electric mixer on low speed until blended, about 30 seconds. Stop the machine and scrape down the sides of the bowl with a rubber spatula. Increase the mixer speed to medium and beat until the batter is smooth and fluffy, about 1 minute. Pour one-third of the batter into the prepared pan, smoothing the top with a rubber spatula. Sprinkle with half of the streusel. Spoon another one-third of the batter on top and smooth with the spatula. Sprinkle the remaining streusel over the top. Spoon the rest of the batter over the streusel layer and smooth the top.

4. Place the pan in the oven and bake until the cake is golden brown and the top springs back when gently pressed in the middle, 40 to 45 minutes.

5. Let the cake cool in the pan on a wire rack for 20 minutes. Run a long knife around the edges of the cake, shake the pan gently, and invert the cake onto the wire rack or a cake plate. Let the cake cool for 20 minutes longer. Dust the confectioners' sugar over the top. Slice and serve. Store, lightly covered, at room temperature for up to 5 days.

COOK'S NOTE:
If desired, drizzle a maple
glaze over the cooled cake
instead of dusting with
sugar: Whisk 2 tablespoons
whole milk and ½ teaspoon
maple flavoring into
1 cup confectioners'
sugar until smooth.

The Best Sock-It-to-Me Cake

SERVES 12

PREP: 20 TO 25 MINUTES

BAKE: 45 TO 50 MINUTES

½ cup finely chopped walnuts or pecans

½ cup (packed) light brown sugar

1 tablespoon ground cinnamon

Vegetable oil spray or shortening, for greasing the pan

All-purpose flour, for dusting the pan

1 (15.25-ounce) package yellow or butter cake mix

4 tablespoons (half a 3.4-ounce package) vanilla instant pudding mix

3 large eggs

1 cup water

⅔ cup vegetable oil

½ cup sour cream

1 teaspoon vanilla extract

COOK'S NOTE:
For a quick glaze, whisk 1 to 2 tablespoons milk into ½ cup confectioners' sugar and drizzle over the cooled cake.

Swirled with cinnamon, brown sugar, and finely chopped pecans, this cake, which was born in the Duncan Hines test kitchen, has been baked so often across America that it may feel like your own. Through the years I have improved the original recipe by amping up the cinnamon and adding sour cream, making it even more moist.

1. Place a rack in the center of the oven and preheat the oven to 350°F.

2. Place the chopped nuts on a small baking sheet and toast while the oven preheats, 3 to 4 minutes. Transfer ¼ cup of the nuts to a small bowl and stir in the brown sugar and cinnamon. Set the nut filling aside.

3. Grease and flour a 12-cup Bundt pan. Sprinkle the remaining ¼ cup toasted nuts into the bottom of the pan. Set the pan aside.

4. In a large mixing bowl, stir together the cake mix and pudding mix. Add the eggs, water, oil, sour cream, and vanilla. Beat with an electric mixer on low speed until blended, about 30 seconds. Stop the machine and scrape down the sides of the bowl with a rubber spatula. Increase the mixer speed to medium and beat until the batter is smooth and fluffy, about 1 minute.

5. Pour two-thirds of the batter over the nuts in the prepared pan, smoothing the top with a rubber spatula (adding this much batter to the pan first will help suspend the nut filling). Sprinkle with two-thirds of the nut filling. Pour the remaining batter into the pan, then sprinkle with the remaining filling. Using a small spatula or dinner knife, gently swirl the filling into the batter, going one rotation around the pan.

6. Place the pan in the oven and bake until the cake is golden brown and the top springs back when gently pressed in the middle, 45 to 50 minutes.

7. Let the cake cool in the pan on a wire rack for 20 minutes. Run a long knife around the edges of the cake, shake the pan gently, and invert the cake onto a wire rack or cake plate. Let the cake cool for 20 minutes longer. Slice and serve. Store, lightly covered, at room temperature for up to 5 days.

SUGAR-FREE SOCK-IT-TO-ME CAKE: Make the batter for the Sock-It-to-Me-Cake, substituting a 16-ounce package of Pillsbury sugar-free yellow cake mix and a 1-ounce package of sugar-free vanilla instant pudding mix for those respective mixes. Omit the sour cream and replace with plain nonfat Greek yogurt. In the filling, omit the brown sugar and replace with ½ cup finely chopped apple. Note that the batter is very thick. It does not pour into the pan; instead, you must dollop large spoonfuls of it into the pan. Assemble and bake as directed, until the cake springs back when lightly pressed, 37 to 42 minutes.

Sherry–Poppy Seed Cake

SERVES 12

PREP: 15 TO 20 MINUTES

BAKE: 35 TO 40 MINUTES

Vegetable oil spray or shortening, for greasing the pan

All-purpose flour, for dusting the pan

1 (15.25- or 16.25-ounce) package white cake mix

4 tablespoons (half a 3.4-ounce package) vanilla instant pudding mix

3 large eggs

⅔ cup vegetable oil

½ cup vanilla Greek yogurt (one 5.3-ounce container)

½ cup medium-dry sherry, such as Amontillado

½ cup water

1½ tablespoons poppy seeds

The late Teresa Pregnall was known as the Charleston Cake Lady, a cook famous for her mail-order cakes. Teresa shared her sherry and poppy seed cake recipe with me because it started with a mix, and it's one I have treasured. Sherry is a fortified wine, and it ranges from dry to sweet, but for baking this cake choose a medium-dry and nutty Amontillado sherry from Spain. And never use cooking sherry, which is full of salt!

1. Place a rack in the center of the oven and preheat the oven to 350°F. Grease and flour a 12-cup Heritage or standard Bundt pan. Set the pan aside.

2. In a large mixing bowl, stir together the cake mix and pudding mix. Add the eggs, oil, yogurt, sherry, water, and poppy seeds. Beat with an electric mixer on low speed until blended, about 30 seconds. Stop the machine and scrape down the sides of the bowl with a rubber spatula. Increase the mixer speed to medium and beat until the batter is smooth and fluffy, about 1 minute. Pour the batter into the prepared pan and smooth the top with a rubber spatula.

3. Place the pan in the oven and bake until the cake is golden brown and the top springs back when gently pressed in the middle, 35 to 40 minutes.

4. Let the cake cool in the pan on a wire rack for 20 minutes. Run a long knife around the edges of the cake, shake the pan gently, and invert the cake onto a wire rack or cake plate. Let the cake cool 20 minutes longer before slicing. Store, tightly covered, at room temperature for up to 5 days.

My Bacardi Rum Cake

SERVES 12

PREP: 20 TO 25 MINUTES

BAKE: 45 TO 50 MINUTES

CAKE

Vegetable oil spray or shortening, for greasing the pan

All-purpose flour, for dusting the pan

¼ cup shredded coconut (sweetened or unsweetened)

¼ cup finely chopped pecans

1 (15.25-ounce) package yellow or butter cake mix

4 tablespoons (half a 3.4-ounce package) vanilla instant pudding mix

3 large eggs

⅔ cup vegetable oil

½ cup sour cream

½ cup dark or gold rum

½ cup water

GLAZE

4 tablespoons (½ stick) unsalted butter

2 tablespoons water

½ cup sugar

¼ cup dark or gold rum

This rum cake is based on the famous Bacardi Rum Cake— the recipe that, once upon a time, was printed on rum bottles and recipe cards. With that sort of history staring me in the face, I thought twice before deviating from the original cake mix–based recipe, and yet tastes and mixes have changed in four decades. In this modernized version, I fold in sour cream for richness and add shredded coconut along with pecans on the bottom of the Bundt pan. I also spice the glaze with just the right amount of rum— so you still know you're eating rum cake when you take a bite!

1. Make the cake: Place a rack in the center of the oven and preheat the oven to 350°F. Grease and flour a 12-cup Bundt pan. Sprinkle the coconut and pecans in the bottom of the pan and set the pan aside.

2. In a large mixing bowl, stir together the cake mix and pudding mix. Add the eggs, oil, sour cream, rum, and water. Beat with an electric mixer on low speed until blended, about 30 seconds. Stop the machine and scrape down the sides of the bowl with a rubber spatula. Increase the mixer speed to medium and beat until the batter is smooth and fluffy, about 1 minute. Pour the batter over the coconut and pecans in the prepared pan, smoothing the top with a rubber spatula.

3. Place the pan in the oven and bake until the cake springs back when gently pressed in the middle, 45 to 50 minutes.

4. Let the cake cool in the pan on a wire rack for 20 minutes. Run a long knife around the edges of the cake, shake the pan gently, and invert the cake onto a wire rack or cake plate. Let the cake cool for at least 20 minutes longer.

5. Make the glaze: While the cake cools, in a small saucepan, melt the butter over low heat. Add the water and sugar, increase the heat to medium, and stir until the mixture comes to a boil. Reduce the heat to low and simmer, stirring, until thickened, 4 to 5 minutes. Remove the pan from the heat and stir in the rum.

6. Poke holes all over the cake with a wooden skewer or chopstick. If the cake is still on the rack, slide a sheet of wax paper or parchment under the rack to catch the drippings. Slowly spoon the glaze over the cake, letting it soak into the holes. Reserve some of the glaze for serving, if desired. Let the cake rest for 1 hour before slicing. Serve with toasted coconut garnish and extra glaze, if desired. Store, tightly covered, at room temperature for up to 1 week.

Lemon and Sorghum Marble Spice Cake

SERVES 12

PREP: 25 TO 30 MINUTES

BAKE: 40 TO 45 MINUTES

CAKE

Vegetable oil spray or
shortening, for greasing
the pan

All-purpose flour,
for dusting the pan

1 (15.25-ounce) package
yellow or butter cake mix

4 tablespoons (half a
3.4-ounce package) vanilla
instant pudding mix

3 large eggs

1 cup buttermilk,
preferably whole milk

¼ cup water

8 tablespoons (1 stick)
unsalted butter,
melted and cooled

1 tablespoon
grated lemon zest

1 tablespoon
fresh lemon juice

⅓ cup sorghum or molasses

½ teaspoon ground
cinnamon

¼ teaspoon ground nutmeg

¼ teaspoon ground cloves

Here I've turned one of my favorite cakes from my book
American Cake *into a cake mix version. This marbled pound
cake is flavored not only with lemon but also spices and molasses,
or in this case, sorghum. Sorghum is a dark, amber sweet
syrup used like molasses across the South and Midwest and
brings a lot of flavor and color to cakes in which it is baked.*

1. Make the cake: Place a rack in the center of the oven and
    preheat the oven to 350°F. Grease and flour a 12-cup Bundt pan.
    Set the pan aside.

2. In a large mixing bowl, stir together the cake mix and pudding
    mix. Add the eggs, buttermilk, water, and melted butter. Beat
    with an electric mixer on low speed until blended, about
    30 seconds. Stop the machine and scrape down the sides of
    the bowl with a rubber spatula. Increase the mixer speed to
    medium and beat until the batter is smooth and fluffy, about
    1 minute. Pour half of the batter into a separate bowl and stir
    in the lemon zest and lemon juice to combine. To the batter
    remaining in the large bowl, stir in the sorghum, cinnamon,
    nutmeg, and cloves to combine.

3. Dollop alternating large spoonfuls of each batter to make one
    layer in the bottom of the prepared Bundt. Add alternating
    dollops again for the next layer. Continue until all the batter has
    been used. Using a small offset spatula or dinner knife, slowly
    swirl the batter in one rotation of the pan.

4. Place the pan in the oven and bake until the cake just begins
    to pull away from the sides of the pan and the top springs back
    when gently pressed in the middle, 40 to 45 minutes.

5. Transfer the pan to a wire rack to cool for 20 minutes.

½ cup confectioners' sugar

1 tablespoon fresh
lemon juice

1 tablespoon water,
or as needed

COOK'S NOTES:

You can substitute orange
zest and juice for the
lemon in this recipe.

And you can vary the
spices as you like, adding
allspice, cardamom, or
coriander instead.

6. Meanwhile, make the glaze: In a small bowl, whisk together
    the confectioners' sugar and lemon juice, adding water as
    needed to make a pourable glaze.

7. Run a long knife around the edges of the cake, shake the pan
    gently, and invert the cake onto a wire rack or cake plate.
    Pour the glaze over the cake and let the cake cool for another
    20 minutes before slicing. Store, lightly covered, at room
    temperature for up to 5 days.

Susan's Lemon Cake

SERVES 12

PREP: 15 TO 20 MINUTES

BAKE: 30 TO 35 MINUTES

Vegetable oil spray
or shortening,
for greasing the pan

All-purpose flour,
for dusting the pan

2 teaspoons grated
lemon zest

2 tablespoons fresh
lemon juice

1 to 1½ cups confectioners'
sugar, or as needed

1 (15.25-ounce) package
yellow cake mix

1 (3-ounce) package
lemon gelatin

3 large eggs

⅔ cup hot tap water

⅔ cup vegetable oil

I'll never forget the morning when a friend called, screaming into the phone for me to turn on the TV. Jamie Lee Curtis was on Rachael Ray's show holding up a copy of my book saying it was her favorite cookbook. I caught up with Jamie Lee later to thank her, and she said her absolute favorite cake was Susan's Lemon Cake, a cake even a novice baker like herself could make. The recipe originally came from my sister Susan, who, truth-be-told, fessed up that she got the recipe from her neighbor Sally Roy. Sort of the way all good recipes make their way to you, right?

1. Place a rack in the center of the oven and preheat the oven to 350°F. Grease and flour a 12-cup Bundt pan. Set the pan aside.

2. Place 1 teaspoon of the lemon zest and the lemon juice in a small bowl. Whisk in enough confectioners' sugar to create a pourable glaze. Thin with a little water if needed. Set the glaze aside.

3. In a large mixing bowl, stir together the cake mix, gelatin, and remaining 1 teaspoon lemon zest. Add the eggs, water, and oil. Beat with an electric mixer on low speed until blended, about 30 seconds. Stop the machine and scrape down the sides of the bowl with a rubber spatula. Increase the mixer speed to medium and beat until the batter is smooth, about 1 minute. Pour the batter into the prepared pan, smoothing the top with a rubber spatula.

4. Place the pan in the oven and bake until the cake is golden brown and the top springs back when gently pressed in the middle, 30 to 35 minutes.

5. Let the cake cool in the pan on a wire rack for 20 minutes. Run a long knife around the edges of the cake, shake the pan gently, and invert the cake onto a wire rack or cake plate. If you are using a rack, slide a piece of wax paper or parchment under the rack to catch drips. Pour the reserved glaze over the cake. Let the cake cool at least 20 minutes longer before slicing. Store, lightly covered, at room temperature for up to 5 days.

Melted Ice Cream Cake

SERVES 12

PREP: 10 TO 15 MINUTES

BAKE: 38 TO 43 MINUTES

1 pint premium ice cream (see Cook's Notes)

Vegetable oil spray or shortening, for greasing the pan

All-purpose flour, for dusting the pan

1 (15.25- or 16.25-ounce) package white cake mix

3 large eggs

Dark Chocolate Glaze (page 370) or 1 teaspoon confectioners' sugar

COOK'S NOTES:

Buy good ice cream for this cake. I use Ben & Jerry's Cherry Garcia ice cream, but choose the flavor you like.

If you're feeling fancy, fold 1 teaspoon vanilla extract and ½ cup mini semisweet chocolate chips into the batter before baking.

When I was interviewing a home economist from the Pillsbury test kitchen for my Cake Mix Doctor *book, she shared that you can make a cake from melted ice cream, cake mix, and eggs. A bit skeptical, I baked that cake, and then baked it again and again, each time trying a new flavor of ice cream. It is the most curious sort of cake, and I marvel that it works. If you have child scientists in your house, or if you have a pint of ice cream to play with, then bake this cake and see what I mean. And then bake it again . . .*

1. Place the ice cream in a shallow glass dish on the counter until melted (or melt it in the microwave). You need 2 cups melted.

2. Place a rack in the center of the oven and preheat the oven to 350°F. Grease and flour a 12-cup Heritage or standard Bundt pan. Set the pan aside.

3. In a large mixing bowl, combine the melted ice cream, cake mix, and eggs. Beat with an electric mixer on low speed until blended, about 30 seconds. Stop the machine and scrape down the sides of the bowl with a rubber spatula. Increase the mixer speed to medium and beat until the batter is smooth and fluffy, about 1 minute. Pour the batter into the prepared pan, smoothing the top with a rubber spatula.

4. Place the pan in the oven and bake until the cake springs back when gently pressed in the middle, 38 to 43 minutes.

5. Let the cake cool in the pan on a wire rack for 20 minutes. Run a long knife around the edges of the cake, shake the pan gently, and invert the cake onto a wire rack or cake plate. Let the cake cool for at least 20 minutes longer.

6. Spoon the glaze over the cake or sift confectioners' sugar on top. Slice and serve. Store, lightly covered, at room temperature for up to 5 days.

How to Melt Chocolate

Whether you melt chocolate on top of the stove or in the microwave, make sure you take it low and slow. First chop it. To melt in the microwave: Place the chopped chocolate in a glass dish and microwave uncovered on high power in 15- to 20-second intervals, removing and stirring after each interval, until the chocolate melts. As a general rule, 4 ounces of chopped unsweetened or semisweet chocolate takes about 1 minute total to melt. White chocolate takes slightly less time. To melt on the stovetop: Place the chopped chocolate in a saucepan over very low heat, and stir constantly with a wooden spoon so the chocolate does not stick or burn. When it looks nearly melted, remove from the heat and stir until completely melted.

Our Favorite Pumpkin Cake

SERVES 12

PREP: 15 TO 20 MINUTES

BAKE: 35 TO 40 MINUTES

CAKE

Vegetable oil spray or shortening, for greasing the pan

All-purpose flour, for dusting the pan

1 (15.25-ounce) package yellow or butter cake mix

4 tablespoons (half a 3.4-ounce package) vanilla instant pudding mix

2 teaspoons ground cinnamon

½ teaspoon ground nutmeg

½ teaspoon ground ginger

3 large eggs

1 cup canned unsweetened pumpkin puree

1 to 2 teaspoons grated orange zest

⅓ cup fresh orange juice

½ cup vegetable oil

HALLOWEEN GLAZE

2 tablespoons whole milk

1 heaping cup confectioners' sugar

2 teaspoons unsweetened cocoa powder

When my children were young the neighborhood families would gather for a chili party on Halloween night. Once the trick-or-treating was done and everyone had their fill of chili and fixings, the kids dove into their sacks of candy. We adults, though, dove into this pumpkin cake. It's nice to have a quick seasonal dessert like this one up your sleeve.

1. Make the cake: Place a rack in the center of the oven and preheat the oven to 350°F. Grease and flour a 12-cup Bundt pan. Set the pan aside.

2. Add the cake mix, pudding mix, cinnamon, nutmeg, ginger, eggs, pumpkin, orange zest, orange juice, and oil to a large mixing bowl. Beat with an electric mixer on low speed until blended, about 30 seconds. Stop the machine and scrape down the sides of the bowl with a rubber spatula. Increase the mixer speed to medium and beat until the batter is smooth and fluffy, about 1 minute. Pour the batter into the prepared pan, smoothing the top with a rubber spatula.

3. Place the pan in the oven and bake until the cake springs back when gently pressed in the middle, 35 to 40 minutes.

4. Let the cake cool in the pan on a wire rack for 20 minutes. Run a long knife around the edges of the cake, shake the pan gently, and invert the cake onto a wire rack or cake plate. Let cool for another 20 minutes.

5. Meanwhile, make the glaze: In a small bowl, whisk the milk into the confectioners' sugar until smooth and pourable. Pour half of the glaze into a measuring cup. To the remaining glaze in the bowl, whisk in the cocoa powder. Add a drop or two of milk as needed to make the glazes pourable. Drizzle the white glaze over the cake and let it set for 10 minutes. Then drizzle the chocolate (black) glaze over the white. Let it set for 10 more minutes before slicing. Store, lightly covered, at room temperature for up to 5 days.

Pumpkin Icebox Cake

Here's how to turn Our Favorite Pumpkin Cake into a holiday showstopper: Slice the cake horizontally into 4 equal layers: First slice it horizontally through the middle into two equal halves (a top and a bottom half) and then slice the bottom half horizontally through the middle and repeat with the top half. Then sandwich the layers with Sweetened Whipped Cream (page 366) or Homemade Cool Whip (page 368) and confectioners' sugar. You can decorate with the berries from whole berry cranberry sauce or pomegranate seeds. Chill until serving.

7Up Pound Cake

SERVES 12

PREP: 10 TO 15 MINUTES

BAKE: 40 TO 45 MINUTES

Vegetable oil spray
or shortening,
for greasing the pan

All-purpose flour,
for dusting the pan

1 (15.25-ounce) package
yellow cake mix

4 tablespoons
(half a 3.4-ounce package)
lemon instant pudding mix

3 large eggs

¾ cup 7Up or other
lemon-lime soda

⅔ cup vegetable oil

½ cup sour cream

1 teaspoon confectioners'
sugar, for dusting (optional)

Did you know that the "up" in 7Up was originally thanks to lithium? Yes! Invented in 1929, 7Up's original name was "Bib-Label Lithiated Lemon-Lime Soda" and it contained lithium citrate, used in treating manic disorders but banned in 1948. Needless to say, thanks to the stock market crash and the Great Depression, sales of 7Up were strong in the 1930s, and as fate would have it, it made its way into cake recipes. This is a great cake—simple, moist, reliable, lemony. And while the soda doesn't contain lithium anymore, its sparkle is always at home in pound cake!

1. Place a rack in the center of the oven and preheat the oven to 350°F. Grease and flour a 10-inch tube pan. Set the pan aside.

2. In a large mixing bowl, stir together the cake mix and pudding mix. Add the eggs, 7Up, oil, and sour cream. Beat with an electric mixer on low speed until blended, about 30 seconds. Stop the machine and scrape down the sides of the bowl with a rubber spatula. Increase the mixer speed to medium and beat until the batter is smooth and fluffy, about 1 minute. Pour the batter into the prepared pan, smoothing the top with a rubber spatula.

3. Place the pan in the oven and bake until the cake is golden brown and the top springs back when gently pressed in the middle, 40 to 45 minutes.

4. Let the cake cool in the pan on a wire rack for 20 minutes. Run a long knife around the edges of the cake, shake the pan gently, and invert the cake once and then again so it rests right-side up on a wire rack or cake plate. Let the cake cool at least another 20 minutes. If desired, dust the top with confectioners' sugar before slicing. Store, tightly covered, at room temperature for up to 5 days.

Fab Five-Flavor Pound Cake

CAKE

Vegetable oil spray or shortening, for greasing the pan

All-purpose flour, for dusting the pan

1 (15.25- or 16.25-ounce) package white cake mix

4 tablespoons (half a 3.4-ounce package) vanilla instant pudding mix

3 large eggs

8 tablespoons (1 stick) unsalted butter, at room temperature

1 cup buttermilk, preferably whole milk

¼ cup water

2 teaspoons vanilla extract

1½ teaspoons ground cinnamon

1 teaspoon ground turmeric

½ teaspoon ground nutmeg

¼ teaspoon ground cardamom

GLAZE (OPTIONAL)

1 to 2 tablespoons whole milk or half-and-half

1 cup confectioners' sugar

One of the most popular cakes that begins with a cake mix is the "five-flavor" variation, which contains five extracts—vanilla, butter, rum, coconut, and lemon—that together create an unusual flavor, which admittedly is not my favorite. I started thinking how this is my chance to create a more fab five-flavor cake, so I reached for five flavors that work together for me: vanilla, cinnamon, nutmeg, cardamom, and turmeric. What are your five favorite flavors?

1. Make the cake: Place a rack in the center of the oven and preheat the oven to 350°F. Grease and flour a 10-inch tube pan. Set the pan aside.

2. In a large mixing bowl, stir together the cake mix and pudding mix. Add the eggs, butter, buttermilk, water, and vanilla. Beat with an electric mixer on low speed until blended, about 30 seconds. Stop the machine and scrape down the sides of the bowl with a rubber spatula. Increase the mixer speed to medium and beat until the batter is smooth and fluffy, about 1 minute. Fold in the cinnamon, turmeric, nutmeg, and cardamom. Pour the batter into the prepared pan, smoothing the top with a rubber spatula.

3. Place the pan in the oven and bake until the cake springs back when gently pressed in the middle, 35 to 40 minutes.

4. Transfer the pan to a wire rack to cool for 20 minutes.

5. Meanwhile, make the glaze (if using): In a small bowl, whisk the milk into the confectioners' sugar until smooth and pourable.

6. Run a long knife around the edges of the cake, shake the pan gently, and invert the cake once and then again so it rests right-side up on a wire rack or cake plate. Pour the glaze over the top of the cake, letting it trickle down the sides. Let the cake cool for another 20 minutes before slicing. Store, lightly covered, at room temperature for up to 5 days.

Chocolate Chip Tahini Loaf

Vegetable oil spray or
shortening, for greasing
the pan

All-purpose flour,
for dusting the pan

1 (15.25-ounce) package
yellow or butter cake mix

4 tablespoons (half a
3.4-ounce package) vanilla
instant pudding mix

3 large eggs

1 cup plain almond milk,
preferably unsweetened,
or whole milk

¾ cup tahini (see Cook's
Note)

¼ cup vegetable oil

1 teaspoon vanilla extract

1⅔ cups (10 ounces)
mini semisweet chocolate
chips or chopped semisweet
chocolate

1 teaspoon confectioners'
sugar, for dusting (optional)

COOK'S NOTE:
Just as with natural peanut
butter, you should always
stir tahini well before using.

*Tahini is a paste made from roasted and ground sesame seeds.
Most popular for being the essential ingredient in hummus and
a staple of Middle Eastern and Mediterranean cooking, tahini
can be used like peanut butter in baking to impart a nutty sesame
flavor to cakes, breads, and cookies; and just like peanut butter,
it is a good friend to chocolate. In this loaf, tahini brings not
only flavor but a warm color, rich texture, and a savory quality
that makes even this chocolate chip cake taste less sweet.*

1. Place a rack in the center of the oven and preheat the oven to
    350°F. Grease and flour a 10 × 5-inch loaf pan. (See Baking in a
    9-Inch Loaf Pan on page 171 if you want to bake in a 9-inch pan
    instead.) Set the pan aside.

2. In a large mixing bowl, stir together the cake mix and pudding
    mix. Add the eggs, milk, tahini, oil, and vanilla. Beat with an
    electric mixer on low speed until blended, about 30 seconds.
    Stop the machine and scrape down the sides of the bowl with
    a rubber spatula. Increase the mixer speed to medium and
    beat until the batter is smooth and fluffy, about 1 minute.
    Fold in the chocolate chips. Pour the batter into the prepared
    pan, smoothing the top with a rubber spatula.

3. Place the pan in the oven and bake until the cake springs back
    when gently pressed in the middle, 50 to 55 minutes.

4. Let the cake cool in the pan on a wire rack for 20 minutes.
    Run a dinner knife around the edges of the cake, shake the pan
    gently, and carefully unmold the loaf right-side up. Let the cake
    cool for another 20 minutes. If desired, dust with confectioners'
    sugar before slicing. Store, tightly covered, at room temperature
    for up to 5 days.

SERVES 12

PREP: 15 TO 20 MINUTES

BAKE: 50 TO 55 MINUTES

Vegetable oil spray or
shortening, for greasing
the pan

All-purpose flour,
for dusting the pan

2 very ripe medium bananas
(see Cook's Note)

1 (15.25-ounce) package
chocolate cake mix

3 large eggs

1 cup full-fat or light
canned coconut milk

¼ cup vegetable oil

¼ teaspoon
ground cinnamon

½ cup mini semisweet
chocolate chips

¼ cup unsweetened
shredded coconut

COOK'S NOTE:
Store unpeeled ripe bananas
(the blacker the peel, the
sweeter the fruit) in a plastic
bag in the fridge or freezer
until you have time to bake.

Coconut, Banana, Chocolate Loaf

*This recipe was born of a few overripe bananas. It helped that
my pantry was stocked and I had been craving chocolate, too!
Because bananas hydrate dry ingredients, they keep the cake
nice and moist, meaning you need to add little oil in this recipe.
Veganize this cake by using ¾ cup unsweetened applesauce
instead of the eggs and vegan chocolate chips, if you like.*

1. Place a rack in the center of the oven and preheat the oven to
   350°F. Grease and flour a 10 × 5-inch loaf pan. (If you don't have
   a 10-inch pan, see Baking in a 9-Inch Loaf Pan, opposite.)
   Set the pan aside.

2. Place the bananas in a large mixing bowl and mash with a fork
   or potato masher to yield 1 cup banana puree. Remove excess
   puree from the bowl. Add the cake mix, eggs, coconut milk, oil,
   and cinnamon. Beat with an electric mixer on low speed until
   blended, about 30 seconds. Stop the machine and scrape down
   the sides of the bowl with a rubber spatula. Increase the mixer
   speed to medium and beat until the batter is smooth and fluffy,
   about 1 minute. Fold in the chocolate chips. Pour the batter into
   the prepared pan, smoothing the top with a rubber spatula.
   Scatter the coconut over the top.

3. Place the pan in the oven and bake until the cake springs back
   when gently pressed in the middle and the coconut is golden
   brown, 50 to 55 minutes.

4. Let the cake cool in the pan on a wire rack for 20 minutes.
   Run a dinner knife around the edges of the cake, shake the
   pan gently, and carefully unmold the loaf right-side up.
   Let the cake cool 20 minutes longer, then slice and serve.
   Store, tightly covered, at room temperature for up to 1 week.

If you don't own a 10-inch loaf pan, you can bake this recipe and the other loaves in this chapter in one 9 x 5-inch loaf (two-thirds full of batter) plus a smaller 5½ x 3-inch loaf (or two muffins). The 9-inch loaf bakes in 40 to 45 minutes and the smaller loaf in about 25 minutes. Muffins bake in about 20 minutes. Or, you can bake two 9-inch loaves—one for you and one for a friend—by filling the pans a little more than halfway full and baking them for 30 to 35 minutes.

Chocolate Nutella Loaf

SERVES 12

PREP: 10 TO 15 MINUTES

BAKE: 1 HOUR 7 MINUTES
TO 1 HOUR 12 MINUTES

Vegetable oil spray or
shortening, for greasing
the pan

All-purpose flour,
for dusting the pan

1 (15.25-ounce) package
chocolate cake mix

1 cup Nutella
(chocolate-hazelnut spread)

3 large eggs

¾ cup full-fat or light
canned coconut milk

½ cup vegetable oil

½ cup (3 ounces) mini
semisweet chocolate chips
(optional)

COOK'S NOTES:

To veganize this cake,
use ¾ cup unsweetened
applesauce instead
of the eggs.

For fancy days, scatter ¼ cup
chopped blanched hazelnuts
on top before baking.

*We thought this deep, dark chocolate loaf was fabulous
freshly baked. And then we tasted it the next day, and the
next. It's one of those magical cakes that becomes more moist
and more delicious over time as the chocolate and hazelnut
flavors of Nutella develop. It's our new cake for breakfast!*

1. Place a rack in the center of the oven and preheat the oven to
   350°F. Grease and flour a 10 × 5-inch loaf pan. (If you don't have
   a 10-inch pan, see Baking in a 9-Inch Loaf Pan, page 171.)
   Set the pan aside.

2. In a large mixing bowl, combine the cake mix, Nutella, eggs,
   coconut milk, and oil. Beat with an electric mixer on low speed
   until blended, about 30 seconds. Stop the machine and scrape
   down the sides of the bowl with a rubber spatula. Increase the
   mixer speed to medium and beat until the batter is smooth and
   fluffy, about 1 minute. Fold in the chocolate chips, if desired.
   Pour the batter into the prepared pan, smoothing the top with
   a rubber spatula.

3. Place the pan in the oven and bake until the cake springs back
   when gently pressed in the middle, 1 hour 7 minutes to 1 hour
   12 minutes.

4. Let the cake cool in the pan on a wire rack for 20 minutes.
   Run a dinner knife around the edges of the cake, shake the pan
   gently, and carefully unmold the loaf right-side up. Let the cake
   cool for 20 minutes longer, then slice and serve. Store, tightly
   covered, at room temperature for up to 5 days.

Ginger-Pear Loaf
with Vanilla Drizzle

SERVES 12

PREP: 20 TO 25 MINUTES

BAKE: 55 MINUTES TO 1 HOUR

Vegetable oil spray or shortening, for greasing the pan

All-purpose flour, for dusting the pan

1 (15.25-ounce) package yellow or butter cake mix

1 cup ¼-inch cubes Bartlett or other semi-firm, flavorful pear (from 1 large peeled pear)

4 tablespoons (half a 3.4-ounce package) vanilla instant pudding mix

1 teaspoon ground ginger

1 teaspoon ground cinnamon

¼ teaspoon ground nutmeg

3 large eggs

1 cup buttermilk

⅔ cup vegetable oil

Vanilla Drizzle (page 373)

COOK'S NOTE:
No pears? Use 1 cup of chopped Jonathan, McIntosh, or other cooking apples.

The nice thing about baking with pears is that you don't have to wait for them to get ripe before you fold them into a cake batter. Which makes this recipe perfect for those pears that aren't quite ripe enough yet for eating out of hand. I love how ginger and pears marry so well together, and after storing a day this cake gets even more delicious.

1. Place a rack in the center of the oven and preheat the oven to 350°F. Grease and flour a 10 × 5-inch loaf pan. (If you don't have a 10-inch pan, see Baking in a 9-Inch Loaf Pan, page 171.) Set the pan aside.

2. Place the cake mix in a large mixing bowl. Remove 1 tablespoon of the mix to a small bowl and toss with the pears and set aside.

3. Add the pudding mix, ginger, cinnamon, and nutmeg to the large bowl and stir to combine. Add the eggs, buttermilk, and oil. Beat with an electric mixer on low speed until blended, about 30 seconds. Stop the machine and scrape down the sides of the bowl with a rubber spatula. Increase the mixer speed to medium and beat until the batter is smooth and fluffy, about 1 minute. Fold in the reserved pears. Pour the batter into the prepared pan, smoothing the top with a rubber spatula.

4. Place the pan in the oven and bake until the cake is deeply golden brown and the top springs back when gently pressed in the middle, 55 minutes to 1 hour.

5. Let the cake cool in the pan on a wire rack for 20 minutes. Run a dinner knife around the edges of the cake, shake the pan gently, and carefully unmold the loaf right-side up. Drizzle the glaze over the top of the cake. Let the cake cool for 30 minutes longer before slicing. Store, tightly covered, at room temperature for up to 5 days.

Rosemary-Lemon Syrup Loaf

SERVES 12

PREP: 40 TO 45 MINUTES

BAKE: 50 TO 55 MINUTES

ROSEMARY-LEMON SYRUP

1 heaping teaspoon grated lemon zest

½ cup water

¼ cup fresh lemon juice

¾ cup sugar

1 sprig fresh rosemary (see Cook's Note)

CAKE

Vegetable oil spray or shortening, for greasing the pan

All-purpose flour, for dusting the pan

1 (15.25-ounce) package yellow cake mix

¼ cup all-purpose flour

¼ cup sugar

3 large eggs

1 cup whole milk

8 tablespoons (1 stick) unsalted butter, at room temperature

You might think of rosemary as the pungent herb that partners well with garlic. But the herb of remembrance is also a sophisticated addition to cakes and pastries, especially alongside lemon. In this recipe you simmer a syrup of lemon juice, sugar, water, and a sprig of rosemary before making the cake. Some syrup is added to the batter and the rest is poured onto the cake as it cools.

1. Make the rosemary-lemon syrup: In a small saucepan, combine the lemon zest, water, lemon juice, sugar, and rosemary. Cook, stirring frequently, over medium-low heat until the sugar dissolves and the mixture is syrupy and reduced to ¾ cup, 25 to 30 minutes. Set aside to cool. Discard the rosemary sprig.

2. Make the cake: Place a rack in the center of the oven and preheat the oven to 350°F. Grease and flour a 10 × 5-inch loaf pan. (If you don't have a 10-inch pan, see Baking in a 9-Inch Loaf Pan, page 171.) Set the pan aside.

3. In a large mixing bowl, stir together the cake mix, flour, and sugar. Add the eggs, milk, butter, and ¼ cup of the rosemary-lemon syrup. Beat with an electric mixer on low speed until blended, about 30 seconds. Stop the machine and scrape down the sides of the bowl with a rubber spatula. Increase the mixer speed to medium and beat until the batter is smooth and fluffy, about 1 minute. Pour the batter into the prepared pan, smoothing the top with a rubber spatula.

4. Place the pan in the oven and bake until the cake springs back when gently pressed in the middle, 50 to 55 minutes.

5. Let the cake cool in the pan on a wire rack for 20 minutes. Run a dinner knife around the edges of the cake, shake the pan gently, and carefully unmold the loaf right-side up. With a wooden skewer, poke holes all over the top of the loaf. Spoon the remaining ½ cup rosemary-lemon syrup over the cake, letting it soak in. Let the cake cool for 1 hour longer before slicing. Store, tightly covered, at room temperature for up to 5 days.

COOK'S NOTE:
No rosemary? Substitute
½ packed cup fresh
basil leaves.

Blood Orange Loaf
with Campari Glaze

SERVES 12

PREP: 20 TO 25 MINUTES

BAKE: 48 TO 53 MINUTES

CAKE

Vegetable oil spray or shortening, for greasing the pan

All-purpose flour, for dusting the pan

1 (15.25-ounce) package yellow or butter cake mix

3 large eggs

¾ cup sour cream

⅔ cup light olive oil

¼ cup blood orange juice (see Cook's Notes)

2 tablespoons Campari

SWEET ORANGE SPRINKLE

⅓ cup (packed) light brown sugar

⅓ cup finely chopped almonds

1 teaspoon grated blood orange zest (see Cook's Notes)

The crimson Italian aperitif known as Campari has bitter, herbal, and citrus flavors that are fun to incorporate in cocktails and baking, too. Campari's natural flavor partner is orange, and the two come together in this moist and flavor-packed loaf.

1. Make the cake: Place a rack in the center of the oven and preheat the oven to 350°F. Grease and flour a 10 × 5-inch loaf pan. (If you don't have a 10-inch pan, see Baking in a 9-Inch Loaf Pan, page 171.) Set the pan aside.

2. In a large mixing bowl, combine the cake mix, eggs, sour cream, olive oil, orange juice, and Campari. Beat with an electric mixer on low speed until blended, about 30 seconds. Stop the machine and scrape down the sides of the bowl with a rubber spatula. Increase the mixer speed to medium and beat until the batter is smooth and fluffy, about 1 minute. Set the batter aside.

3. Make the sweet orange sprinkle: In a small bowl, stir together the brown sugar, almonds, and orange zest.

4. Pour one-third of the batter into the prepared loaf pan, smoothing the top with a rubber spatula. Scatter one-third of the sprinkle over. Pour another third of the batter on top, smoothing it with the spatula. Scatter with another third of the sprinkle. Pour the last of the batter on top, smoothing it with the spatula. Top with the last of the sprinkle.

5. Place the pan in the oven and bake until the cake is golden brown and the top springs back when gently pressed in the middle, 48 to 53 minutes.

6. Transfer the pan to a wire rack to cool for 20 minutes.

7. Meanwhile, make the Campari glaze: In a small bowl, whisk the Campari and orange juice into the confectioners' sugar until smooth.

CAMPARI GLAZE

1 tablespoon Campari

1 tablespoon orange juice
(see Cook's Notes)

1 cup confectioners' sugar

COOK'S NOTES:
My favorite oranges for baking are blood oranges, navel, and Cara Cara.

If you have more blood orange juice than the amount you need for the cake, use it in the glaze; otherwise use carton orange juice.

If you don't have any fresh oranges but you do have carton orange juice, you can omit the zest in the sprinkle and use carton OJ in the cake and glaze.

8. Run a dinner knife around the edges of the cake, shake the pan gently, and carefully unmold the loaf right-side up. Drizzle the glaze over the top of the cake. Let the cake cool for 30 minutes before slicing. Store, lightly covered, at room temperature for up to 5 days.

CAKE

Vegetable oil spray or
shortening, for greasing
the pan

All-purpose flour,
for dusting the pan

Grated zest and juice
of 1 small lime

Water, as needed

1 (15.25- or 16.25-ounce)
package white cake mix

4 tablespoons (half a
3.4-ounce package) vanilla
instant pudding mix

3 large eggs

½ cup sour cream

½ cup vegetable oil

2 tablespoons rum
(see Cook's Notes)

1½ cups fresh raspberries
(see Cook's Notes)

LIME DRIZZLE

Grated zest and juice
of 1 small lime

½ cup confectioners' sugar

Fresh Raspberry Mojito Loaf

This loaf might remind you of a mojito, the Cuban rum drink, but minus the fresh mint. Lime juice goes into the batter as well as the drizzle. But the real stars are the fresh raspberries. Slice and serve at brunch, garnished with mint!

1. Make the cake: Place a rack in the center of the oven and preheat the oven to 350°F. Grease and flour a 10 × 5-inch loaf pan. (If you don't have a 10-inch pan, see Baking in a 9-Inch Loaf Pan, page 171.) Set the pan aside.

2. Place the lime zest in a large mixing bowl. Place the juice in a measuring cup and add water to reach ¾ cup.

3. Add the cake mix and pudding mix to the bowl with the lime zest and stir to combine. Add the lime juice mixture, eggs, sour cream, oil, and rum. Beat with an electric mixer on low speed until blended, about 30 seconds. Stop the machine and scrape down the sides of the bowl with a rubber spatula. Increase the mixer speed to medium and beat until the batter is smooth and fluffy, about 1 minute.

4. Pour one-third of the batter into the prepared pan, smoothing the top with a rubber spatula. Scatter on one-third (½ cup) of the raspberries. Spoon another one-third of the batter over the raspberries and smooth the top with a rubber spatula. Add another one-third of the berries, followed by the last of the batter. Spread smoothly, then scatter the final third of the raspberries over the top.

5. Place the pan in the oven and bake until the cake springs back when gently pressed in the middle, 58 minutes to 1 hour 2 minutes.

6. Transfer the pan to a wire rack to cool for 20 minutes.

COOK'S NOTES:

Use whatever rum you have on hand—white, gold, or dark—or substitute water for the rum.

When baking with fresh berries such as raspberries, blackberries, or blueberries, drain them very well on paper towels after rinsing to make sure they are dry.

7. Meanwhile, make the lime drizzle: In a small bowl, stir together the lime zest and confectioners' sugar. Stir in enough of the lime juice to make a pourable glaze.

8. Run a dinner knife around the edges of the cake, shake the pan gently, and carefully unmold the loaf, right-side up. our the glaze over the top. Let the cake cool for 30 minutes before slicing. Store, lightly covered, at room temperature for up to 3 days.

Earl Grey Tea Loaf

SERVES 12

PREP: 20 TO 25 MINUTES,
PLUS 1 HOUR STEEPING TIME

BAKE: 50 TO 55 MINUTES

2 Earl Grey tea bags

1 cup boiling water

Vegetable oil spray or shortening, for greasing the pan

All-purpose flour, for dusting the pan

1 (15.25-ounce) package yellow or butter cake mix

¼ cup all-purpose flour

¼ cup sugar

3 large eggs

⅓ cup whole milk, warmed

12 tablespoons (1½ sticks) unsalted butter, at room temperature

Vanilla Drizzle (page 373)

Earl Grey is my favorite tea, a classic English black tea flavored with bergamot, a member of the citrus family. I was curious how a tea would taste in a tea cake, so I brewed a strong cup of Earl Grey and used this as the liquid in a very basic butter cake. The flavor really came through and makes me think you could bake with your favorite tea, too.

1. Place the tea bags in the boiling water and let them steep for at least 1 hour.

2. Place a rack in the center of the oven and preheat the oven to 350°F. Grease and flour a 10 × 5-inch loaf pan. (If you don't have a 10-inch pan, see Baking in a 9-Inch Loaf Pan, page 171.) Set the pan aside.

3. In a large mixing bowl, stir together the cake mix, flour, and sugar. Add the tea (remove the tea bags), eggs, milk, and butter. Beat with an electric mixer on low speed until blended, about 30 seconds. Stop the machine and scrape down the sides of the bowl with a rubber spatula. Increase the mixer speed to medium and beat until the batter is smooth and fluffy, about 1 minute. Pour the batter into the prepared pan, smoothing the top with a rubber spatula.

4. Place the pan in the oven and bake until the cake is deeply golden brown and the top springs back when gently pressed in the middle, 50 to 55 minutes.

5. Let the cake cool in the pan on a wire rack for 20 minutes. Run a dinner knife around the edges of the cake, shake the pan gently, and carefully unmold the loaf right-side up. Drizzle the glaze over the cake. Let the cake cool for 30 minutes longer before slicing. Store, lightly covered, at room temperature for up to 5 days.

Pumpkin and Fresh Cranberry Loaf

SERVES 12

PREP: 35 TO 40 MINUTES

BAKE: 58 MINUTES TO 1 HOUR
2 MINUTES

2 cups fresh cranberries

Vegetable oil spray or
shortening, for greasing
the pan

All-purpose flour,
for dusting the pan

1 (15.25-ounce) package
yellow or butter cake mix

4 tablespoons (half a
3.4-ounce package) vanilla
instant pudding mix

2 teaspoons ground
cinnamon

½ teaspoon ground ginger

½ teaspoon ground nutmeg

1 teaspoon grated
orange zest

⅓ cup fresh orange juice

3 large eggs

1 cup canned unsweetened
pumpkin puree

½ cup vegetable oil

Two seasonal flavors align in this bright and happy loaf cake—pumpkin and cranberries. Cranberries are a late fall and winter seasonal crop, so make sure you stash some in the freezer to get you through baking the rest of the year (you can also find them frozen in many supermarkets); if using frozen berries, set them on paper towels to thaw and dry before using. This recipe makes really nice muffins, too, which bake at 375°F in about 20 minutes.

1. Coarsely chop the cranberries to yield about 1½ cups. Set aside.

2. Place a rack in the center of the oven and preheat the oven to 350°F. Grease and flour a 10 × 5-inch loaf pan. (If you don't have a 10-inch pan, see Baking in a 9-Inch Loaf Pan, page 171.) Set the pan aside.

3. In a large mixing bowl, stir together the cake mix, pudding mix, cinnamon, ginger, and nutmeg. Add the orange zest, orange juice, eggs, pumpkin puree, and oil. Beat with an electric mixer on low speed until blended, about 30 seconds. Stop the machine and scrape down the sides of the bowl with a rubber spatula. Increase the mixer speed to medium and beat until the batter is smooth and fluffy, about 1 minute. Fold in half of the chopped cranberries. Pour the batter into the prepared pan, smoothing the top with a rubber spatula. Scatter the rest of the cranberries evenly on top.

4. Place the pan in the oven and bake until the cake springs back when gently pressed in the middle, 58 minutes to 1 hour 2 minutes.

5. Let the cake cool in the pan on a wire rack for 20 minutes. Run a dinner knife around the edges of the cake, shake the pan gently, and carefully unmold the loaf right-side up. Let the cake cool for 30 minutes, then slice and serve. Store, tightly covered, at room temperature for up to 5 days.

Chocolate Praline Cake
(page 198)

Skillets and Springforms

I love the rustic beauty of cakes that come out of a cast-iron skillet and the simple elegance of those from a springform pan. They are unexpected and unusual, as comfortable after a cozy family meal as they are sliced for company. Two pans that have proved to be indispensable in baking these cakes are the 12-inch cast-iron skillet and the 9-inch springform.

Pineapple Upside-Down Cake

SERVES 12

PREP: 15 TO 20 MINUTES

BAKE: 32 TO 37 MINUTES FOR
A 12-INCH SKILLET OR 43 TO
48 MINUTES FOR A 13 × 9-INCH
PAN (SEE COOK'S NOTE)

1 (20-ounce) can juice-
packed pineapple rings

14 tablespoons unsalted
butter, at room temperature

¼ cup pineapple or
apricot preserves

½ cup (packed)
light brown sugar

1 (15.25-ounce) package
yellow or butter cake mix

4 tablespoons (half a
3.4-ounce package) vanilla
instant pudding mix

3 large eggs

1 cup whole milk, warmed

¼ cup vegetable oil

1 teaspoon vanilla extract

COOK'S NOTE:

If you bake this cake in a
13 × 9-inch pan, use
pineapple chunks instead
of rings because it makes
cutting easier. Instead of
melting butter right in the
pan, you will melt the butter
separately and then pour
it into the baking pan.

The cast-iron skillet was the most widely used pan a hundred years ago, and Dole pineapple's recipe contest of the 1920s put this cake on the map. Since then, it's been a perennial favorite for so many reasons—it totes to potlucks right in the skillet, doesn't need refrigeration, and it tastes so good warm from the oven. Here is a blueprint recipe that you can tweak as you see fit, adding spices and flavorings and whatever canned fruit you have in the cupboard.

1. Place a rack in the center of the oven and preheat the oven to 350°F.

2. Open the can of pineapple and pour it into a sieve set over a small bowl to catch the juice. Set the pineapple rings and juice aside separately.

3. In a 12-inch cast-iron skillet, melt 6 tablespoons of the butter over low heat. Stir in the preserves and remove from the heat. Sprinkle the brown sugar over the melted butter and stir to combine. Arrange the reserved pineapple rings on top, placing 7 rings around the perimeter of the skillet and 1 in the center. If there is another ring, cut in half and place these halves around the center ring. Set the skillet aside.

4. In a large mixing bowl, stir together the cake mix and pudding mix. Add the eggs, milk, oil, vanilla, ⅓ cup of the reserved pineapple juice, and the remaining 8 tablespoons butter. Beat with an electric mixer on low speed until blended, about 30 seconds. Stop the machine and scrape down the sides of the bowl with a rubber spatula. Increase the mixer speed to medium and beat until the batter is smooth, about 1 minute. Pour the batter evenly over the pineapple and transfer the skillet to the oven.

5. Bake until the cake is golden brown and the top springs back when gently pressed in the middle, 32 to 37 minutes. Place the skillet on a wire rack and let the cake cool for 2 minutes. Run a

dinner knife around the edges of the cake and give the pan a good shake to loosen the cake. Place a large serving plate over the skillet and carefully invert the cake, fruit-side up, onto the plate. Slice and serve warm. Store, lightly covered, at room temperature for up to 3 days.

Pumpkin Skillet Crumble

SERVES 12

PREP: 15 TO 20 MINUTES

BAKE: 45 TO 50 MINUTES

1 (15.25-ounce) package
yellow or butter cake mix

1 cup (packed)
light brown sugar

2 teaspoons
ground cinnamon

16 tablespoons (2 sticks)
cold unsalted butter,
cut into tablespoons

½ cup chopped pecans
or walnuts

3 large eggs

1 (15-ounce) can
unsweetened pumpkin puree

1 (5-ounce) can
evaporated milk

½ teaspoon maple extract
(optional)

Sweetened Whipped Cream
(page 366)

The original version of this recipe has been a favorite for twenty years. It's a nice change from pumpkin pie, plus it's portable, and so easy. All that is still true with this new recipe. But now the crust is crispier, the crumble more decadent, and the pumpkin filling creamier.

1. Place a rack in the center of the oven and preheat the oven to 350°F.

2. For the crumble, place 1 cup of the cake mix in a food processor or a large mixing bowl. Add ⅔ cup of the brown sugar, 1 teaspoon of the cinnamon, and 8 tablespoons (1 stick) of the chilled butter. Pulse or beat until the mixture comes together into a ball, 1 to 2 minutes. Fold in the pecans. Remove to a medium bowl and set the crumble aside.

3. For the crust, place the remaining cake mix in the food processor or mixing bowl—no need to wash it—and add ½ teaspoon of the cinnamon, the remaining 8 tablespoons (1 stick) butter, and 1 of the eggs. Pulse or beat until the mixture is smooth, about 1 minute. It should have the consistency of thick frosting. Using a metal icing spatula, spread this crust mixture into the bottom and ½ inch up the sides of a 12-inch cast-iron skillet. Set aside.

4. For the filling, place the pumpkin, evaporated milk, maple extract (if using) and the remaining 2 eggs, ⅓ cup brown sugar, and ½ teaspoon cinnamon in the food processor or mixing bowl. Pulse or beat until smooth, about 30 seconds. Pour the filling into the crust. With your fingers, break the crumble into pieces and scatter it over the pumpkin filling, nearly covering the top.

5. Place the skillet in the oven and bake until golden brown and it jiggles slightly when you shake the pan, 45 to 50 minutes.

6. Serve warm with whipped cream. Remove leftover cake from the skillet and store, covered, in the refrigerator for up to 3 days. You can reheat the cake in a metal pie or cake pan in a 300°F oven for 10 to 15 minutes.

Caramelized Bananas Foster Skillet Cake

SERVES 12

PREP: 15 TO 20 MINUTES

BAKE: 28 TO 33 MINUTES

8 tablespoons (1 stick) unsalted butter

½ cup (packed) light brown sugar

½ teaspoon ground cinnamon

¼ cup plus 1 tablespoon light rum

3 firm-ripe medium bananas

1 (15.25-ounce) package yellow or butter cake mix

3 large eggs

1 (8-ounce) can juice-packed crushed pineapple, undrained

1 cup full-fat or light canned coconut milk

¼ cup vegetable oil

You just might think you're in New Orleans when you take a bite of this cake, what with the classic Bananas Foster flavors of bananas, brown sugar, and rum. But sorry to disappoint, you are at home in your kitchen using up ripe bananas in the fruit bowl and rum from your bar cart. Enjoy!

1. Place a rack in the center of the oven and preheat the oven to 350°F.

2. In a 12-inch cast-iron skillet, melt 6 tablespoons of the butter over low heat. Stir in the brown sugar, cinnamon, and ¼ cup rum. Remove from the heat. Continue to stir the mixture until combined, about 30 seconds; don't worry if it separates a bit. Peel the bananas and slice them lengthwise into ½-inch-thick slices. Arrange the banana slices in a spiral in the pan. Set the skillet aside.

3. In a large mixing bowl, combine the cake mix, eggs, and pineapple. In a small saucepan, combine the coconut milk and the remaining 2 tablespoons butter and warm over low heat, just until the butter softens and the milk is no longer cold, about 2 minutes. Add to the mixing bowl along with the oil and remaining 1 tablespoon rum. Beat with an electric mixer on low speed until blended, about 30 seconds. Stop the machine and scrape down the sides of the bowl with a rubber spatula. Increase the mixer speed to medium and beat until the batter is smooth, about 1 minute. Pour the batter evenly over the bananas and transfer the skillet to the oven.

4. Bake until the cake is golden brown and the top springs back when gently pressed in the middle, 28 to 33 minutes.

5. Place the skillet on a wire rack and let the cake cool for 2 minutes. Run a dinner knife around the edges of the cake and give the pan a good shake to loosen the cake. Invert a large serving plate on top of the skillet and carefully flip the skillet and plate so the cake rests fruit-side up. Slice and serve warm. Store, lightly covered, at room temperature for up to 3 days.

Blueberry Cornmeal Skillet Cake

SERVES 12

PREP: 15 TO 20 MINUTES

BAKE: 30 TO 35 MINUTES

8 tablespoons (1 stick)
unsalted butter

⅓ cup blueberry preserves
or orange marmalade

2 tablespoons
fresh orange juice

1 (15.25-ounce) package
yellow cake mix

½ cup finely ground
yellow cornmeal

3 large eggs

1 cup buttermilk,
preferably whole milk

¼ cup water

Grated zest of 1 orange

2 cups fresh blueberries

A riff on one of my favorite scratch skillet cakes, this easy recipe stars cornmeal and blueberries. I've added both orange juice and zest as well as blueberry preserves and fresh blueberries. And you can use this method for a blackberry or raspberry cake, too— use whatever berries are in season. Flip it out onto a cake plate and slice or serve it warm right from the skillet.

1. Place a rack in the center of the oven and preheat the oven to 350°F.

2. In a 12-inch cast-iron skillet, melt the butter over low heat, 1 to 2 minutes. Pour the butter into a small bowl and set aside. Do not wipe out the skillet.

3. Warm the preserves and orange juice in the skillet over low heat, spreading them out in an even layer. Set the skillet aside.

4. In a large mixing bowl, stir together the cake mix and cornmeal. Add the eggs, buttermilk, water, and reserved melted butter. Beat with an electric mixer on low speed until blended, about 30 seconds. Stop the machine and scrape down the sides of the bowl with a rubber spatula. Increase the mixer speed to medium and beat until the batter is smooth, about 1 minute. Fold in the orange zest and blueberries. Pour the batter evenly over the preserves in the pan and transfer the skillet to the oven.

5. Bake until the cake is golden brown and the top springs back when gently pressed in the middle, 30 to 35 minutes.

6. Place the skillet on a wire rack and let the cake cool for 2 minutes. Run a dinner knife around the edges of the cake and give the pan a good shake to loosen the cake. Invert a serving plate on top of the skillet and carefully flip the skillet and plate so the preserves are on top. Slice and serve warm. Store, lightly covered, at room temperature for up to 3 days.

Lemon, Caramel, Peach Skillet Cake

SERVES 12

PREP: 15 TO 20 MINUTES

BAKE: 35 TO 40 MINUTES

6 peaches (1½ pounds; see Cook's Note)

20 tablespoons (2½ sticks) unsalted butter

Pinch of salt

1 cup (packed) light brown sugar

¼ cup heavy cream

1 teaspoon grated lemon zest

1 (15.25-ounce) package yellow or butter cake mix

3 large eggs

2 tablespoons fresh lemon juice

1 cup whole milk

2 teaspoons vanilla extract

COOK'S NOTE:
You can use all peaches or a mix of peaches and plums in this recipe.

It's just so easy to let the skillet do all the work, from making the caramel on the bottom of the pan to cooking peaches to baking a cake. All you do is turn out this cake with its glorious crown of peaches and whip some cream to dollop on top. What's not gobbled up for dessert becomes tomorrow morning's coffee cake.

1. Place a rack in the center of the oven and preheat the oven to 350°F.

2. Peel the peaches, cut in half, and remove the pits. Cut into ⅓-inch-thick slices. (You need about 36 peach slices.) Set the peaches aside.

3. In a 12-inch cast-iron skillet, melt 8 tablespoons (1 stick) of the butter over low heat. Sprinkle with the salt. Stir in the brown sugar, cream, and lemon zest. Cook, stirring, until the mixture begins to bubble up, then remove from the heat. Arrange the peach slices on top of the caramel in the skillet. Set the skillet aside.

4. In a large mixing bowl, combine the cake mix and eggs and set aside. Add 1 tablespoon of the lemon juice to the milk and let it rest for 5 minutes to give the lemon juice a chance to curdle the milk. Sprinkle the rest of the lemon juice over the peaches in the skillet.

5. In a small saucepan, warm the remaining 12 tablespoons (1½ sticks) butter over low heat until softened but not completely melted, about 2 minutes. Add the warmed butter, lemon juice/milk mixture, and vanilla to the mixing bowl. Beat with an electric mixer on low speed until blended, about 30 seconds. Stop the machine and scrape down the sides of the bowl with a rubber spatula. Increase the mixer speed to medium and beat until the batter is smooth, about 1 minute. Pour the batter evenly over the peaches and transfer the skillet to the oven.

6. Bake until the cake is golden brown and the top springs back when gently pressed in the middle, 35 to 40 minutes.

7. Place the skillet on a rack and let the cake cool for 2 minutes. Run a dinner knife around the edges of the cake and give the pan a good shake to loosen the cake. Invert a large serving plate on top of the skillet and carefully flip the skillet and plate so the cake rests fruit-side up. Slice and serve warm. Store, lightly covered, at room temperature for up to 3 days.

Skillet Care— How to Clean Your Cast-Iron Skillet After Baking a Cake

To clean up sticky bits that remain in a cast-iron skillet after you turn out a cake, add ½ inch of water to the skillet and set the pan over medium heat. With a silicone spatula, loosen the bits that stick to the bottom and sides of the pan. Discard and then run hot water into the pan and scrub gently with a sponge or cast-iron scrubber. No soap needed. Pat the skillet dry and place the pan back over low heat for a few minutes to dry it out. Rub with a little light vegetable oil, then put the pan away.

Apple Slice Skillet Cake

SERVES 12

PREP: 20 TO 25 MINUTES

BAKE: 35 TO 40 MINUTES

10 tablespoons (1¼ sticks) unsalted butter

4 large tart apples, preferably Granny Smiths, peeled and cut into ¼-inch-thick slices (5 to 6 cups)

½ cup (packed) light brown sugar

1 teaspoon ground cinnamon

½ teaspoon ground nutmeg

¼ teaspoon ground allspice or ginger

1 cup whole milk

⅓ cup apple cider or water

1 (15.25-ounce) package yellow or butter cake mix

3 large eggs

¼ cup vegetable oil

½ teaspoon maple extract

Years back Cake Mix Doctor *reader Diana Crawford sent me an apple cake recipe with maple flavoring, spices, and fresh apple slices simply called Apple Slice Cake. I always felt that cake was screaming for the cast-iron skillet to do its magic and caramelize the apple slices and spices on the bottom of the pan. So here it is!*

1. Place a rack in the center of the oven and preheat the oven to 350°F.

2. In a 12-inch cast-iron skillet, melt 6 tablespoons of the butter over low heat. Add the apple slices and cook, stirring, until the apples begin to soften, about 5 minutes. Remove from the heat. Sprinkle the brown sugar, cinnamon, nutmeg, and allspice over the apples and stir to combine. Spread the apples out evenly to cover the bottom of the skillet. Set the skillet aside.

3. In a small saucepan, combine the milk, cider, and the remaining 4 tablespoons butter. Cook over low heat just until the milk is warm and the butter is softened but not quite melted, about 2 minutes. Remove from the heat and set aside to cool slightly.

4. In a large mixing bowl, combine the milk/butter mixture, cake mix, eggs, oil, and maple extract. Beat with an electric mixer on low speed until blended, about 30 seconds. Stop the machine and scrape down the sides of the bowl with a rubber spatula. Increase the mixer speed to medium and beat until the batter is smooth, about 1 minute. Pour the batter evenly over the apples and transfer the skillet to the oven.

5. Bake until the cake is deeply golden brown and the top springs back when gently pressed in the middle, 35 to 40 minutes.

6. Place the skillet on a wire rack and let the cake cool for 2 minutes. Run a dinner knife around the edges of the cake and give the pan a good shake to loosen the cake. Invert a large serving plate on top of the skillet and carefully flip the skillet and plate so the cake rests fruit-side up. Slice and serve warm. Store, lightly covered, at room temperature for up to 3 days.

Roasted Strawberry Upside-Down Cake

SERVES 12

PREP: 15 TO 20 MINUTES

BAKE: 35 TO 40 MINUTES

16 ounces fresh strawberries

½ cup (packed) light brown sugar

2 tablespoons honey

1 tablespoon balsamic glaze

1 teaspoon vegetable oil or light olive oil

1 (15.25-ounce) package yellow or butter cake mix

¼ cup all-purpose flour

¼ cup granulated sugar

3 large eggs

1¼ cups whole milk or full-fat canned coconut milk, warmed slightly

12 tablespoons (1½ sticks) unsalted butter, at room temperature

Fresh local strawberries that come into season in the spring should be eaten out of hand. But for those big, flavorless strawberries available all year? Toss them in the skillet, roast to bring out their jammy sweetness, and pour a cake batter right on top!

1. Rinse the strawberries and pat dry. Remove their caps and slice lengthwise in half, or in thirds if very large. Place in a medium bowl and add the brown sugar, honey, and balsamic glaze. Stir until the strawberries are well coated. Set aside for 10 minutes.

2. Place a rack in the center of the oven and preheat the oven to 350°F.

3. In a 12-inch cast-iron skillet, heat the oil over medium-low heat. Turn the strawberry mixture into the skillet and bring to a simmer, stirring constantly, until just bubbling about 2 minutes. Remove the skillet from the heat.

4. In a large mixing bowl, stir together the cake mix, flour, and granulated sugar. Add the eggs, milk, and butter. Beat with an electric mixer on low speed until blended, about 30 seconds. Stop the machine and scrape down the sides of the bowl with a rubber spatula. Increase the mixer speed to medium and beat until the batter is smooth, about 1 minute. Pour the batter evenly over the strawberries and transfer the skillet to the oven.

5. Bake until the cake is golden brown and the top springs back when gently pressed in the middle, 35 to 40 minutes.

6. Place the skillet on a wire rack and let the cake cool for 2 minutes. Run a dinner knife around the edges of the cake and give the pan a good shake to loosen the cake. Invert a serving plate on top of the skillet and carefully flip the skillet and plate so the cake rests fruit-side up. Slice and serve warm. Store, lightly covered, at room temperature for up to 3 days.

Chocolate Triple-Berry Cake

CAKE

Vegetable oil spray,
for misting the pan

8 ounces frozen
unsweetened berries (a mix
of raspberries, blackberries,
and blueberries), thawed

1 (15.25-ounce) package
chocolate cake mix

5 tablespoons (half a
3.9-ounce package)
chocolate instant
pudding mix

3 large eggs

¾ cup sour cream

½ cup vegetable oil

1 cup (6 ounces)
semisweet chocolate chips

ASSEMBLY

Small-Batch Chocolate
Ganache Topping (page 362)

1 cup fresh berries (a mix
of raspberries, blackberries,
and blueberries) or
kumquats

1 teaspoon granulated or
confectioners' sugar, for
coating

One of my favorite cake recipes called for a puree of thawed frozen raspberries, but you can seldom find those berries anymore. What you can find is a mixture of frozen berries for smoothies. So I thawed and whizzed them in the food processor, pressed the puree through a sieve to remove the seeds, and folded them into the batter. You get a moist and slightly floral chocolate cake thanks to those berries.

1. Make the cake: Place a rack in the center of the oven and preheat the oven to 350°F. Mist the bottom and sides of a 9-inch springform pan with oil and set the pan aside.

2. Pulse the thawed berries and their juices in a food processor and puree, about 15 pulses. Place a fine-mesh sieve over a large mixing bowl and turn the contents of the food processor into the sieve. With a rubber spatula, press the berries through the sieve and into the bowl. Use the spatula to scrape the puree off the bottom of the sieve and into the bowl.

3. Add the cake mix, pudding mix, eggs, sour cream, and oil to the mixing bowl. Beat with an electric mixer on low speed until blended, about 30 seconds. Stop the machine and scrape down the sides of the bowl with a rubber spatula. Increase the mixer speed to medium and beat until the batter is smooth and fluffy, about 1 minute. Fold in the chocolate chips. Pour the batter into the prepared pan, smoothing the top with a rubber spatula.

4. Place the pan in the oven and bake until the cake springs back when gently pressed in the middle, 48 to 52 minutes.

5. Let the cake cool in the pan on a wire rack for 10 to 15 minutes. Run a dinner knife around the edge and unsnap and remove the sides of the pan. Allow to cool completely, 30 minutes longer.

6. Assemble the cake: Carefully run a long knife under the cake to remove it from the base of the pan. Place the cake on a plate and spread with ganache. Garnish with berries or kumquats rolled in sugar, if desired. Slice and serve.

Vegan Chocolate Tangerine Cake

SERVES 12

PREP: 20 TO 25 MINUTES

BAKE: 35 TO 40 MINUTES

CAKE

Vegetable oil spray, for misting the pan

⅔ cup aquafaba (see Cook's Note, page 196), drained from a 15-ounce can of chickpeas

¼ teaspoon cream of tartar

1 (15.25-ounce) package chocolate cake mix

2 tablespoons unsweetened cocoa powder

¾ cup water

½ cup tahini

¼ cup tangerine juice (2 to 3 tangerines)

¼ cup vegetable oil

1 teaspoon vanilla extract

ASSEMBLY

Vegan Chocolate Buttercream (page 353)

Peel or zest from 2 scrubbed tangerines

Thinking that vegan cakes face similar challenges to cakes baked at high altitude, I applied the mile-high principles of cake baking to this recipe. Rule number one: Reduce the size of the pan. A springform supports this cake and helps it rise evenly. Rule two: Bake a little hotter, which helps high-altitude and vegan cakes set their shape quickly. You'll love the combination of chocolate and tangerine! Use the juice of the tangerines in the cake, and decorate the top with the tangerine peel.

1. Make the cake: Place a rack in the center of the oven and preheat the oven to 375°F. Mist the bottom and sides of a 9-inch springform pan with oil and set the pan aside.

2. In a medium bowl (or food processor), combine the aquafaba and cream of tartar. Beat with an electric mixer (or process) on high speed until stiff peaks form, about 2 minutes. Set the bowl aside (or scrape the whipped aquafaba from the processor into a medium bowl and set aside).

3. In a large mixing bowl (or in the food processor), stir together the cake mix, cocoa, water, tahini, tangerine juice, oil, and vanilla. With the same beaters (or blade) used to whip the aquafaba—no need to wash them—beat on low speed (or process) until blended, about 30 seconds. Stop the machine and scrape down the sides of the bowl with a rubber spatula. Increase the mixer speed to medium and beat until the batter is smooth, about 1 minute, or if using the processor, process until smooth, 30 to 45 seconds. Scrape the whipped aquafaba on top of the batter (or turn the chocolate batter onto the whipped aquafaba if using the food processor). Fold the aquafaba into the batter until the mixture is well combined but still light. Pour the batter into the prepared pan, smoothing the top with the rubber spatula.

CONTINUED

4. Place the pan in the oven and bake until the cake springs back when gently pressed in the middle, 35 to 40 minutes.

5. Let the cake cool in the pan on a wire rack for 20 minutes. Run a long knife around the edges of the cake and unsnap and remove the sides of the pan. Let the cake cool completely, 20 minutes longer.

6. Assemble the cake: Carefully run a long knife under the cake to remove it from the base of the pan. Place the cake on a serving plate and spread the frosting on top and around the sides of the cake. Garnish with the tangerine peel or zest. Slice and serve. Store, lightly covered, at room temperature for up to 3 days.

How to Tell When a Chocolate Springform Cake Is Done

It won't turn "golden brown," but you can jiggle the pan. The cake itself should be set and the top should spring back when you press it lightly with your finger. And if all else fails, a wooden skewer inserted in the cake should come out clean.

Two Egg Replacers—Aquafaba and Applesauce

To calculate how much aquafaba you need to replace eggs in a recipe, count on 3 tablespoons of the bean water to whip for each large egg in a recipe. It amounts to about ⅔ cup total in the Vegan Chocolate Tangerine Cake, which is how much liquid you usually will find in a can of chickpeas. After you whip the aquafaba with a little cream of tartar at high speed to stiff peaks, you then fold it into the recipe as you would beaten egg whites. Unsweetened applesauce can also be used as an egg replacer. Use about ¼ cup applesauce for each egg, which would be a total of ¾ cup in the Vegan Chocolate Tangerine Cake recipe.

Chocolate Praline Cake

SERVES 12 TO 16

PREP: 25 TO 30 MINUTES

BAKE: 50 TO 55 MINUTES

Vegetable oil spray,
for misting the pan

PRALINE

8 tablespoons (1 stick)
unsalted butter

Pinch of salt

¼ cup heavy cream

1 cup (packed)
light brown sugar

1 cup coarsely chopped
(¼-inch pieces) pecans

CAKE

1 (15.25-ounce) package
chocolate cake mix

1 tablespoon unsweetened
cocoa powder

2 large eggs

¾ cup water

⅔ cup sour cream

½ cup vegetable oil

Originally a layer cake with whipped cream filling and praline on top, this new version is still rich and dense but requires no stacking or fussing. All the praline goes into the bottom of the pan and after inverting winds up on top—brilliant! To keep the praline intact, you place the pan in the freezer to chill while you make the batter. This is a fabulous do-ahead cake for a weekend dinner party—pile on whipped cream just before serving.

1. Place a rack in the center of the oven and preheat the oven to 350°F. Mist the bottom of a 9-inch springform pan with oil. Line the bottom with a round of parchment paper and mist the parchment and sides of the pan. Wrap aluminum foil around the bottom edge of the pan so the praline layer doesn't leak out while cooking.

2. Make the praline: In a small saucepan, combine the butter, salt, cream, and brown sugar. Cook over low heat, stirring, until the butter has melted and the mixture begins to boil, about 3 minutes. Pour the mixture in the prepared pan. Sprinkle the pecans over the top. Place the pan in the freezer while you prepare the cake batter.

3. Make the cake: In a large mixing bowl, combine the cake mix, cocoa, eggs, water, sour cream, and oil. Beat with an electric mixer on low speed until blended, about 30 seconds. Stop the machine and scrape down the sides of the bowl with a rubber spatula. Increase the mixer speed to medium and beat until thick and smooth, about 1 minute. Remove the pan from the freezer and set it on a sheet pan. Pour the batter over the praline layer, smoothing it out with a rubber spatula.

4. Place the sheet pan in the oven and bake until the cake springs back when gently pressed in the middle, 50 to 55 minutes.

5. Let the cake cool in the springform on a wire rack for 10 to 15 minutes. Run a dinner knife around the edge and unsnap and

remove the sides of the springform pan. Allow the cake to cool completely, about 30 minutes longer.

6. Invert the cake onto a cake plate, praline-side up. Carefully remove the base of the pan and the parchment. Cover the top with plastic wrap until time to serve. Store in the refrigerator for up to 3 days.

Gluten-Free Chocolate Swirled Apricot Cake

SERVES 8 TO 12

PREP: 20 TO 25 MINUTES

BAKE: 45 TO 50 MINUTES

CAKE

Vegetable oil spray, for misting the pan

6 ounces dried apricots, coarsely chopped

½ cup orange juice, plus more as needed

1 (15-ounce) package gluten-free yellow cake mix

4 tablespoons (half a 3.4-ounce package) vanilla instant pudding mix

3 large eggs

8 tablespoons (1 stick) unsalted butter, at room temperature

2 teaspoons vanilla extract

¼ teaspoon almond extract

⅓ cup (2 ounces) semisweet chocolate chips

APRICOT GLAZE (OPTIONAL)

1 cup confectioners' sugar

2 to 3 teaspoons water

Yes, a swirl of chocolate runs through this single layer cake, but in the end the flavor is all about the apricots. You get that clear taste not from canned or fresh apricots, but dried. Keep them in your pantry and you are ready to make this cake whether you are gluten-free or not.

1. Make the cake: Place a rack in the center of the oven and preheat the oven to 350°F. Mist the bottom and sides of a 9-inch springform pan with oil and set the pan aside.

2. In a small saucepan, combine the apricots and orange juice. Cover and bring to a simmer over medium heat. Reduce the heat to low and simmer until all the juice has been absorbed by the apricots, 12 to 15 minutes. Be careful not to scorch the fruit.

3. Transfer the mixture to a food processor and process until pureed but still with some tiny flecks of apricot, about 1 minute. Set aside 1 tablespoon of the puree for the glaze, if desired. Pour the remaining puree into a large glass measuring cup and add orange juice to make 1¼ cups. Pour into a large mixing bowl.

4. Add the cake mix, pudding mix, eggs, butter, vanilla, and almond extract to the mixing bowl. Beat with an electric mixer on low speed until blended, about 30 seconds. Stop the machine and scrape down the sides of the bowl with a rubber spatula. Increase the mixer speed to medium and beat until the batter is smooth and fluffy, about 1 minute. Measure out ⅔ cup of the batter and place in a small bowl. Set both bowls of batter aside.

5. Place the chocolate chips in a small microwave-safe bowl and microwave on high power until nearly melted, 30 to 40 seconds. Stir until the chocolate is completely melted. Set aside to cool for 3 to 4 minutes.

CONTINUED

Gluten-free cake mixes do
not rise as much as regular
cake mixes, so this is a
shorter cake baked in the
9-inch springform. You can
bake a taller cake by using
an 8-inch springform or a
deep layer pan. If so, bake
for 55 minutes to 1 hour.

6. Pour the large bowl of batter into the prepared pan, smoothing the top with a rubber spatula. Stir the cooled melted chocolate into the ⅔ cup batter. Drop the chocolate batter by teaspoonfuls on top of the plain batter and swirl it in with a dinner knife.

7. Place the pan in the oven and bake until the cake springs back when gently pressed in the middle, 45 to 50 minutes.

8. Let the cake cool in the pan on a wire rack for 10 to 15 minutes. Run a dinner knife around the edge and unsnap and remove the sides of the springform. Allow the cake to cool completely, about 30 minutes longer.

9. Meanwhile, if desired, make the apricot glaze: In a small bowl, whisk the reserved 1 tablespoon apricot puree into the confectioners' sugar. Whisk in enough water to make the glaze pourable.

10. To assemble the cake, carefully run a long knife under the cake to remove it from the base of the pan. Transfer the cake to a serving plate. If you made a glaze, pour it over the cake. Let rest for 10 minutes before slicing. Store, lightly covered, at room temperature for up to 3 days.

Strawberry-Lemon Tres Leches Cake

SERVES 12

PREP: 20 TO 25 MINUTES

BAKE: 45 TO 50 MINUTES

CHILL: 2 HOURS

CAKE

Vegetable oil spray, for misting the pan

1 (15.25- or 16.25-ounce) package white cake mix

1 (3-ounce) package strawberry gelatin

3 large eggs

⅔ cup water

⅔ cup vegetable oil

1 teaspoon grated lemon zest (optional)

MILK SYRUP

1 (12-ounce) can evaporated milk

⅔ cup sweetened condensed milk (half a 7-ounce can; see Cook's Note)

½ cup heavy cream

1 teaspoon vanilla extract

Pastel de tres leches *means "three milk cake" because of the soaking syrup made of whole milk, evaporated milk, and sweetened condensed milk that gets spooned over the cake to make it extra moist. Tres leches cake dates back centuries to Spain and Portugal where an egg-cream mixture was poured over day-old cake to moisten it and make it more palatable. Since the focus of tres leches is not so much the cake itself, but the milk syrup, it makes sense to start with a mix. And definitely use a springform pan as the cake bakes in the pan and stays in the pan in the fridge to soak up the syrup, making prep and cleanup a snap.*

1. Make the cake: Place a rack in the center of the oven and preheat the oven to 350°F. Mist the bottom and sides of a 9-inch springform pan with oil and set the pan aside.

2. In a large mixing bowl, stir together the cake mix and gelatin. Add the eggs, water, oil, and lemon zest (if using). Beat with an electric mixer on low speed until blended, about 30 seconds. Stop the machine and scrape down the sides of the bowl with a rubber spatula. Increase the mixer speed to medium and beat until the batter is smooth and fluffy, about 1 minute. Pour the batter into the prepared pan, smoothing the top with a rubber spatula.

3. Place the pan in the oven and bake until the cake springs back when gently pressed in the middle, 45 to 50 minutes.

4. Let the cake cool in the pan on a wire rack for 20 minutes. Run a knife around the edge of the cake and unsnap and remove the sides of the pan. Let the cake cool to room temperature, about 1 hour.

5. Make the milk syrup: Meanwhile, in a medium bowl, stir together the evaporated milk, sweetened condensed milk, cream, and vanilla. Place the bowl in the refrigerator to chill while the cake cools.

RECIPE AND INGREDIENTS CONTINUED

Sweetened Whipped Cream
(page 366)

1 cup whole strawberries

Strands of lemon zest

Lemon and kumquat slices
(optional)

COOK'S NOTE:

With the smaller cake mixes
I had to reduce the amount
of milk syrup, leaving you
with a half can of unused
sweetened condensed
milk. Save it to melt with
unsweetened chocolate for
a quick fudge sauce, which
is great with the Melted Ice
Cream Cake (page 162).

6. To soak the cake, snap the sides of the springform back around the cake. Poke 10 to 12 holes in the cake with a chopstick or the blunt end of a wooden skewer. Place the springform pan on a small baking sheet or in a larger cake pan. Slowly ladle the milk syrup over the cake, allowing plenty of time for the syrup to soak in, 4 to 5 minutes. Cover the springform pan with plastic wrap and chill in the fridge for at least 2 hours and preferably overnight. (A little syrup may leak out.)

7. Assemble the cake: Remove the plastic wrap and unsnap and remove the sides of the pan. Transfer the cake (on the pan base) to a serving plate. Spread the whipped cream over the cake and decorate with the strawberries, lemon zest, and citrus slices (if using). Slice and serve. Store, tightly covered, in the refrigerator for up to 3 days.

How to Make Chocolate Espresso Tres Leches Cake

Use a chocolate cake mix and 2 tablespoons unsweetened cocoa powder instead of the white mix and strawberry gelatin. Use 1¼ cups coconut milk, ½ cup vegetable oil, 1 shot (4 teaspoons) espresso, and 1 teaspoon vanilla in addition to 3 eggs. For the Milk Syrup, use ⅔ cup dulce de leche instead of sweetened condensed milk. Follow the directions for the Strawberry-Lemon Tres Leches Cake. Garnish with semisweet chocolate shavings.

"Cinnabon" Cake

SERVES 12

PREP: 30 TO 35 MINUTES

BAKE: 42 TO 47 MINUTES

CAKE

Vegetable oil spray,
for misting the pan

1 (15.25-ounce) package
yellow or butter cake mix

3 large eggs

1 cup sour cream

1 teaspoon grated lemon zest

1 tablespoon
fresh lemon juice

½ cup vegetable oil

1 teaspoon vanilla extract

CINNAMON SWIRL

½ cup (packed)
dark brown sugar

¼ cup finely chopped
walnuts or pecans

¼ cup chopped raisins

1 tablespoon ground
cinnamon

GLAZE

1 cup confectioners' sugar

Pinch of ground cinnamon

1 to 2 tablespoons whole milk

If you are the person who walks into the mall and follows the scent of cinnamon to the cinnamon bun stand, then this is the cake for you. It is a sour cream coffee cake laced with dark brown sugar, raisins, nuts, and a ton of cinnamon. While the cake is still warm, I pour over the glaze so it seeps in. This cake not only tastes like that famous cinnamon roll, but it looks like it, too.

1. Make the cake: Place a rack in the center of the oven and preheat the oven to 350°F. Mist the bottom and sides of a 9-inch springform pan with oil and set the pan aside.

2. In a large mixing bowl, combine the cake mix, eggs, sour cream, lemon zest, lemon juice, oil, and vanilla. Beat with an electric mixer on low speed until blended, about 30 seconds. Stop the machine and scrape down the sides of the bowl with a rubber spatula. Increase the mixer speed to medium and beat until the batter is smooth, about 1 minute. It will be thick. Spoon half of the batter into the prepared pan and spread it evenly with a rubber spatula.

3. Make the cinnamon swirl: In a small bowl, stir together the brown sugar, nuts, raisins, and cinnamon. Scatter half of the mixture over the batter. Spoon the rest of the batter over the top, smoothing the top with a rubber spatula. Scatter the rest of the mixture over it. Swirl the cinnamon mixture into the batter with a dinner knife.

4. Place the pan in the oven and bake until the cake is golden brown and the top springs back when gently pressed in the middle, 42 to 47 minutes. If it browns too quickly, cover the top with foil until it tests done.

5. Let the cake cool in the pan on a wire rack for 10 minutes. Run a dinner knife around the edge and unsnap and remove the sides of the springform.

6. Make the glaze: In a small bowl, whisk together the confectioners' sugar and cinnamon. Whisk in enough milk so the glaze is pourable.

7. Carefully run a long knife under the cake to remove it from the base of the pan. Transfer the cake to a serving plate. Pour the glaze over the warm cake, spreading it to the edges with the spatula. Let it rest for 30 minutes, then slice and serve. Store, lightly covered, at room temperature for up to 3 days.

Italian Cream Cake

SERVES 12

PREP: 30 TO 35 MINUTES

BAKE: 50 TO 55 MINUTES

Vegetable oil spray,
for misting the pan

1 cup (1½ ounces)
sweetened shredded coconut

⅓ cup plus 2 tablespoons
finely chopped pecans

1 (15.25- or 16.25-ounce)
package white cake mix

4 tablespoons (half a
3.4-ounce package) vanilla
instant pudding mix

3 large eggs

1 cup whole milk

10 tablespoons (1¼ sticks)
unsalted butter,
melted and cooled

1½ teaspoons
vanilla extract

½ teaspoon coconut extract

Small-Batch Cream Cheese
Frosting (page 357)

COOK'S NOTES:
Chopping the coconut makes
the cake less crumbly.

Toasting the nuts brings out
their flavor and balances
the sweetness in the cake.

Italian cream cake comes in different forms. It can be filled with ricotta and candied fruit like an Italian bakery cannoli, or packed with coconut and pecans. It is this latter, and possibly Southern version, that I know best. And I love this cake's new look—one beautiful layer, lightly frosted and garnished with pecans and coconut.

1. Place a rack in the center of the oven and preheat the oven to 350°F. Mist the bottom and sides of a 9-inch springform pan with oil and set the pan aside.

2. Finely chop ½ cup of the shredded coconut with a heavy knife and set aside for the cake. Place the remaining ½ cup coconut on a small baking sheet and toast in the preheating oven until lightly browned, 5 to 7 minutes. Set aside for the garnish.

3. Place the chopped pecans on the baking sheet and toast in the preheating oven until lightly browned, 3 to 4 minutes. Set aside ⅓ cup of the pecans for the cake and 2 tablespoons for the garnish.

4. In a large mixing bowl, stir together the cake mix and pudding mix. Add the eggs, milk, melted butter, vanilla, and coconut extract. Beat with an electric mixer on low speed until blended, about 30 seconds. Stop the machine and scrape down the sides of the bowl with a rubber spatula. Increase the mixer speed to medium and beat until the batter is smooth and fluffy, about 1 minute. Fold in the reserved ½ cup finely chopped untoasted coconut and ⅓ cup toasted pecans. Pour the batter into the prepared pan, smoothing the top with a rubber spatula.

5. Place the pan in the oven and bake until the cake is lightly browned and the top springs back when gently pressed in the middle, 50 to 55 minutes.

6. Let the cake cool in the pan on a wire rack for 20 minutes. Run a knife around the edges of the pan and unlock and remove the sides of the springform. Carefully run a long sharp knife under the cake to separate it from the base of the pan, then transfer it to a cake plate to cool for 20 minutes longer.

7. To assemble the cake, spread the frosting over the top (if desired, frost the sides as well). Sprinkle the reserved ½ cup toasted coconut and 2 tablespoons toasted pecans over the top. Store, lightly covered, at room temperature for up to 3 days.

COOK'S NOTE:
Make your own half-and-half
by mixing ½ cup heavy cream
with ½ cup whole milk.

Eggnog Cake
with Bourbon Cream

SERVES 12

PREP: 20 TO 25 MINUTES

BAKE: 50 TO 55 MINUTES

CAKE

Vegetable oil spray, for misting the pan

1 (15.25-ounce) package yellow or butter cake mix

4 tablespoons (half a 3.4-ounce package) vanilla instant pudding mix

½ teaspoon ground nutmeg

3 large eggs

1 cup half-and-half (see Cook's Note)

3 ounces bourbon (6 tablespoons)

8 tablespoons (1 stick) unsalted butter, melted and cooled

1 teaspoon vanilla extract

ASSEMBLY

Bourbon Whipped Cream (page 366)

¼ teaspoon ground nutmeg, for dusting (optional)

Every Christmas my husband makes his family's recipe for eggnog, a potent nutmeg-dusted libation full of eggs, sugar, cream, and "nog" (whiskey!). With this holiday drink as my muse, I created an eggnog cake that says eggnog, pure and simple. The batter smells like eggnog, tastes like eggnog, and the cake with a bourbon-infused whipped cream on top screams eggnog!

1. Make the cake: Place a rack in the center of the oven and preheat the oven to 350°F. Mist the bottom and sides of a 9-inch springform pan with oil and set the pan aside.

2. In a large mixing bowl, stir together the cake mix, pudding mix, and nutmeg. Add the eggs, half-and-half, bourbon, melted butter, and vanilla. Beat with an electric mixer on low speed until blended, about 30 seconds. Stop the machine and scrape down the sides of the bowl with a rubber spatula. Increase the mixer speed to medium and beat until the batter is smooth and fluffy, about 1 minute. Pour the batter into the prepared pan, smoothing the top with a rubber spatula.

3. Place the pan in the oven and bake until the cake is lightly browned and the top springs back when gently pressed in the middle, 50 to 55 minutes.

4. Let the cake cool in the pan on a wire rack for 10 minutes. Run a dinner knife around the edge and unsnap and remove the sides of the springform.

5. Assemble the cake: Carefully run a long knife under the cake to remove it from the base of the pan. Place the cake on a cake plate and spoon the bourbon whipped cream on top. Dust with a little nutmeg, if desired, then slice and serve. Store in the fridge for up to 3 days. (Or store the ungarnished cake, lightly covered, at room temperature for up to 5 days.)

Orange-Pistachio Cake

with Fresh Ginger Glaze

SERVES 12

PREP: 25 TO 30 MINUTES

BAKE: 42 TO 47 MINUTES

CAKE

Vegetable oil spray, for misting the pan

1 cup pistachios, preferably unsalted

1 (15.25- or 16.25-ounce) package white cake mix

4 tablespoons (half a 3.4-ounce package) vanilla instant pudding mix

3 large eggs

1 cup whole milk, warmed

¼ cup vegetable oil or light olive oil

8 tablespoons (1 stick) unsalted butter, melted and cooled

1 teaspoon grated orange zest

¼ cup fresh orange juice

When my children were younger we always had oranges on hand. We munched on them, cooked with them, relied on them. Pistachios in the shell were on hand, too, and were a favorite snack because shelling kept those little hands busy! Our palates today welcome these fresh and bold flavors, and together in this simple yet lovely cake, the freshness of orange meets the earthy nuttiness of the pistachio and the spice of fresh ginger—all staples in my modern pantry.

1. Make the cake: Place a rack in the center of the oven and preheat the oven to 350°F. Mist the bottom and sides of a 9-inch springform pan with oil and set the pan aside.

2. Pulse the pistachios in a food processor until roughly chopped and the size of peas, 10 to 12 pulses. Set aside half of the chopped pistachios for topping the cake. Continue to pulse the remaining pistachios until finely ground, like cornmeal, 10 to 12 more pulses. Transfer the ground pistachios to a large mixing bowl (or you can mix the batter in the food processor). Set aside.

3. Place the cake mix and pudding mix in the large bowl with the ground pistachios and stir to combine. Add the eggs, milk, oil, melted butter, orange zest, and orange juice. Beat with an electric mixer on low speed until blended, about 30 seconds. Stop the machine and scrape down the sides of the bowl with a rubber spatula. Increase the mixer speed to medium and beat until the batter is smooth and fluffy, about 1 minute. Pour the batter into the prepared pan, smoothing the top with a rubber spatula. Scatter the reserved chopped pistachios over the top.

4. Place the pan in the oven and bake until the cake is golden brown and the top springs back when gently pressed in the middle, 42 to 47 minutes.

FRESH GINGER GLAZE

2 tablespoons unsalted butter, at room temperature

2 ounces cream cheese, at room temperature

1 cup confectioners' sugar

1 heaping teaspoon finely grated fresh ginger

1 teaspoon grated orange zest

1 tablespoon fresh orange juice, plus more if needed

COOK'S NOTE:
If you can find them, try the sweet pinkish-orange Cara Cara oranges.

5. Let the cake cool in the pan on a wire rack for 10 minutes. Run a dinner knife around the edge and unsnap and remove the sides of the springform.

6. Make the fresh ginger glaze: In a medium mixing bowl, combine the butter and cream cheese and beat with an electric mixer on low speed until smooth, about 30 seconds. Blend in the confectioners' sugar, ginger, orange zest, and orange juice to create a loose glaze.

7. To assemble the cake, carefully run a long knife under the cake to remove it from the base of the pan. Transfer the cake to a serving plate. Pour the glaze over the top of the cake, letting the glaze dribble down the sides. Slice and serve. Store, lightly covered, in the refrigerator for up to 3 days.

Warm Chocolate Cookie Dough Cake

SERVES 12

PREP: 15 TO 20 MINUTES

FREEZE: 1 HOUR

BAKE: 55 MINUTES TO 1 HOUR

1 (16-ounce) package chocolate chip cookie dough (see Cook's Note)

Vegetable oil spray, for misting the pan

1 (15.25-ounce) package yellow or butter cake mix

4 tablespoons (half a 3.4-ounce package) vanilla instant pudding mix

3 large eggs

1 cup full-fat or light canned coconut milk

⅔ cup vegetable oil

2 teaspoons vanilla extract

1 cup (6 ounces) mini semisweet chocolate chips

½ cup chopped walnuts or pecans (optional)

Vanilla ice cream, for serving

COOK'S NOTE:
For this cake and any cake in which you don't fully cook the cookie dough, be sure to use store-bought cookie dough that is ultrapasteurized.

Readers have asked me how to turn the cookie dough cupcake from my cupcake book into a larger cake. Here it is and even better with some new additions like using canned coconut milk.

1. Open the package of cookie dough and slice it into 20 to 24 chunks 1 inch thick. Place the cookie pieces on a freezer-safe pie plate and freeze until firm, about 1 hour.

2. Place a rack in the center of the oven and preheat the oven to 350°F. Mist the bottom and sides of a 9-inch springform pan with oil and set the pan aside.

3. In a large mixing bowl, stir together the cake mix and pudding mix. Add the eggs, coconut milk, oil, and vanilla. Beat with an electric mixer on low speed until blended, about 30 seconds. Stop the machine and scrape down the sides of the bowl with a rubber spatula. Increase the mixer speed to medium and beat until the batter is smooth and fluffy, about 1 minute. Fold in the chocolate chips. Pour the batter into the prepared pan, smoothing the top with a rubber spatula.

4. Place the pan in the oven and bake the cake for 25 minutes. Remove the cookie dough pieces from the freezer. Open the oven door and, working quickly, carefully place the pieces onto the cake, keeping them away from the center (if cookie dough pieces pile up in the center, it takes longer for the cake to bake, and then the cookie dough is cooked through rather than ooey-gooey). Scatter the top with nuts, if desired.

5. Continue to bake until the center springs back when gently pressed in the middle, 30 to 35 minutes longer.

6. Let the cake cool in the pan on a wire rack for 15 minutes. Run a knife around the edge and unsnap and remove the sides of the springform. Slice and serve warm with ice cream. Store, lightly covered, at room temperature for up to 3 days.

Sour Cream Chocolate Chip Cheesecake

SERVES 12 TO 16

PREP: 30 TO 35 MINUTES

BAKE: 1 HOUR 21 MINUTES
TO 1 HOUR 27 MINUTES

CHILL: 2 TO 3 HOURS

1 teaspoon unsalted butter,
at room temperature,
for greasing the pan

CRUST

½ cup sliced almonds

8 tablespoons (1 stick)
unsalted butter,
melted and cooled

1 (15.25-ounce) package
yellow or butter cake mix

1 large egg white

FILLING

2 (8-ounce) packages cream
cheese, at room temperature

1 (14-ounce) can sweetened
condensed milk

1 large egg yolk

3 large eggs

½ cup sour cream

1½ teaspoons vanilla
extract

½ teaspoon almond extract

1 cup (6 ounces) plus
2 tablespoons mini
semisweet chocolate chips

Before I wrote The Cake Mix Doctor *I had no idea you could make something as glorious as a cheesecake with a cake mix. For this book, I wanted to take cheesecake up a notch . . . or two. So we baked it in the traditional springform pan to create the look of a New York-style cheesecake. This recipe is a keeper. It's delicious with the chocolate chips streaking through the cake or without if you like plain and simple cheesecake.*

1. Place a rack in the center of the oven and another rack in the lowest position. Place 3 cups water in a 13 × 9-inch pan and place the pan with water on the lower oven rack. Preheat the oven to 350°F. Grease the bottom and sides of a 9-inch springform pan with the softened butter. Line the bottom of the pan with a round of parchment paper. Wrap the bottom and 2 inches up the sides of the pan with aluminum foil to prevent leaks. Set the pan aside.

2. Make the crust: Place the almonds on a small baking sheet and toast in the oven until lightly browned, 4 to 5 minutes. Remove the almonds to a plate to cool for 6 to 8 minutes. When cool, pulse the almonds in a food processor until they look like coarse meal, about 15 pulses or 30 seconds. Add the melted butter and pulse to combine. Measure out ¼ cup of the cake mix and set it aside for the filling. Add the remaining cake mix and the egg white to the almonds and butter in the processor and pulse until combined but still crumbly, about 45 seconds. Press the mixture over the bottom and 2 inches up the sides of the prepared pan. Set the pan aside.

3. Make the filling: In a large mixing bowl, combine the cream cheese and condensed milk. Beat with an electric mixer on

RECIPE AND INGREDIENTS CONTINUED

low speed until just combined, about 30 seconds. Increase the speed to medium and beat for 1 minute longer to thoroughly cream the mixture. Stop the machine and add the egg yolk and whole eggs and beat on medium speed until blended, about 10 seconds. Scrape down the sides of the bowl with a rubber spatula. Add the reserved ¼ cup cake mix, the sour cream, vanilla, and almond extract. Beat on medium speed until blended and creamy, about 1 minute. Do not overbeat. Fold in 1 cup of the chocolate chips. Pour the filling into the crust, spreading it evenly with a rubber spatula. Sprinkle the remaining 2 tablespoons chocolate chips over the top.

4. Carefully place the pan on the middle rack in the oven. Bake for 15 minutes.

5. Meanwhile, make the topping: In a small bowl, stir together the sour cream and brown sugar. Set aside.

6. After 15 minutes of baking, reduce the oven temperature to 325°F without opening the oven door. Continue to bake until the cheesecake is mostly firm and just a bit jiggly and the temperature of the center registers 150°F on an instant-read thermometer, 58 minutes to 1 hour 2 minutes longer. Remove the cheesecake from the oven and immediately spread the topping over. Return the cheesecake to the oven and bake until the topping barely sets, 8 to 10 minutes.

7. Let the cheesecake cool on a wire rack for 1 hour. Run a dinner knife around the edges of the pan and unsnap and remove the sides of the springform. Lift the cheesecake and parchment off the bottom of the pan onto a serving plate. Cover lightly in plastic wrap and store in the fridge until ready to serve. (Cheesecakes slice best if allowed to chill for 2 to 3 hours.) Store for up to 1 week. You can freeze leftover pieces, wrapped in parchment and foil, for up to 1 month.

COOK'S NOTE:

When you remove the cheesecake from the oven to cool, make sure there are no sudden changes in temperature. Even a slight change, such as a cold kitchen counter, can trigger cracks.

Pumpkin Gingersnap Cheesecake

SERVES 12 TO 16

PREP: 30 TO 35 MINUTES

BAKE: 1 HOUR 13 MINUTES TO
1 HOUR 30 MINUTES

CHILL: 2 TO 3 HOURS

1 teaspoon unsalted butter,
at room temperature,
for greasing the pan

CRUST

½ cup chopped pecans

1 ounce crystallized
or candied ginger,
finely chopped (about
a scant ¼ cup)

1 (15.25-ounce) package
yellow or butter cake mix

8 tablespoons (1 stick)
unsalted butter,
melted and cooled

2 tablespoons molasses

Tired of pumpkin pie? Bake this cheesecake, a favorite of both my husband and the husband of my friend and kitchen co-conspirator Martha. The crust tastes of gingersnaps because of the molasses and crystallized ginger, which packs a bigger punch than your usual spice rack ginger. Maybe that's why the guys like it so much. To me, best of all, it can be baked ahead, frozen, and thawed for Thanksgiving or any feast.

1. Place a rack in the center of the oven and another rack in the lowest position. Pour 3 cups water into a 13 × 9-inch pan and place the pan on the lower oven rack. Preheat the oven to 325°F. Grease the bottom and sides of a 9-inch springform pan with the softened butter. Line the bottom of the pan with a round of parchment paper. Wrap the bottom and 2 inches up the sides of the pan with aluminum foil to prevent leaks. Set the pan aside.

2. Make the crust: Place the pecans on a small baking sheet and toast in the oven until lightly browned, 4 to 5 minutes. Remove to a plate to cool for 6 to 8 minutes. When cool, pulse in a food processor until they look like coarse meal, 15 to 20 seconds. Add the chopped ginger and pulse to combine. Measure out ½ cup of the cake mix and set it aside for the filling. Place the remainder of the cake mix, the melted butter, and molasses in the processor with the pecans and ginger and pulse until combined but still crumbly, about 45 seconds. Press the mixture into the bottom and 2 inches up the sides of the prepared pan. Set the pan aside.

3. Make the filling: In a large mixing bowl, combine the cream cheese and condensed milk. Beat with an electric mixer on low speed until just combined, about 30 seconds. Increase the speed to medium and beat for 1 minute longer to thoroughly cream the mixture. Stop the machine and add the eggs and beat on medium speed until blended, about 10 seconds. Scrape down the sides of the bowl with a rubber spatula. Add the reserved ½ cup cake mix, the pumpkin puree, sour cream, brown sugar, cinnamon, ginger, nutmeg, and vanilla. Beat on medium speed until blended

FILLING

2 (8-ounce) packages cream cheese, at room temperature

1 (14-ounce) can sweetened condensed milk

3 large eggs

1 cup canned unsweetened pumpkin puree

⅓ cup sour cream

¼ cup (packed) dark brown sugar

1½ teaspoons ground cinnamon

1 teaspoon ground ginger

½ teaspoon ground nutmeg

1 teaspoon vanilla extract

TOPPING

⅓ cup sour cream

4 teaspoons maple syrup

and creamy, about 1 minute. Do not overbeat. Pour the filling into the crust, spreading it evenly with a rubber spatula.

4. Carefully place the pan on the middle oven rack and bake until the cheesecake is mostly firm but still jiggles in the center when you shake the pan, and it registers 150°F on an instant-read thermometer, 1 hour 5 minutes to 1 hour 20 minutes.

5. Meanwhile, make the topping: In a small bowl, stir together the sour cream and maple syrup. Set aside.

6. Remove the cheesecake from the oven and immediately spread the topping over the top. Return the cheesecake to the oven and bake until the topping barely sets, 8 to 10 minutes.

7. Let the cheesecake cool on a wire rack for 1 hour. Run a knife around the edges of the pan and unsnap and remove the sides of the springform. Lift the cheesecake and parchment off the bottom of the pan and onto a serving plate. Cover lightly in plastic wrap and store in the fridge until ready to serve. (Cheesecakes slice best if allowed to chill for several hours.) Store in the refrigerator for up to 1 week. You can freeze leftover pieces, wrapped in parchment and foil, for up to 1 month.

How to Make a Meyer Lemon Cheesecake

Follow the directions for the Sour Cream Chocolate Chip Cheesecake, page 215. Make the crust. For the filling, omit the almond extract. Zest and juice 3 Meyer lemons, and add 1 tablespoon zest and ½ cup juice to the filling. Omit the chocolate chips. Pour the filling over the unbaked crust. Bake at 325°F until mostly firm, 75 to 80 minutes. Make the topping using white granulated sugar. Spread it over the cheesecake and bake until set, 8 to 10 minutes more. Cool, then arrange fresh raspberries and pomegranate seeds on top of the cake. Slice and serve.

Black- and Blueberry Buckle
(page 243)

Snack Cakes and Slabs

I've always thought a perfect kitchen is where dishes wash themselves. But until this happens, thank goodness for cakes that are baked and served from the same pan—from snacking cakes to large slabs. This chapter is full of such cakes, baked in a 13 × 9-inch pan, 8- or 9-inch square pan, and often in a larger half sheet pan. You can even frost the cake right in these pans!

GLAZE (OPTIONAL)

1 tablespoon milk or orange juice, or as needed

¾ cup confectioners' sugar

½ teaspoon vanilla extract

COOK'S NOTE:
Use all one type of berry
or a combination for
visual fun and interesting
flavor. If the blackberries
are large, cut them
in half. Pick peaches
that aren't too juicy.

Basic Sour Cream Coffee Cake

SERVES 12 TO 16

PREP: 15 TO 20 MINUTES

BAKE: 35 TO 40 MINUTES

CAKE

Vegetable oil spray,
for misting the pan

1 (15.25-ounce) package
yellow or butter cake mix

⅓ cup all-purpose flour

¼ cup granulated sugar

3 large eggs

1 cup sour cream

⅔ cup vegetable oil

1 teaspoon vanilla extract
or grated lemon or orange
zest, or ½ teaspoon
almond extract

TOPPING

2 tablespoons cold
unsalted butter

½ cup finely chopped
pecans, walnuts, or almonds

½ cup (packed) light
or dark brown sugar

1 tablespoon
ground cinnamon

1 to 1½ cups blueberries,
blackberries (halved if
large), raspberries, or
chopped peaches, plums, or
cranberries (see Cook's Note)

Life seems too short to bake only one kind of coffee cake, so here is a blueprint recipe for changing it up as much as you like! From adding berries or peaches when the weather is warm to plums in the fall and cranberries in the winter, this is your recipe to bake and take to potlucks and breakfast meetings or the new neighbor down the street.

1. Make the cake: Place a rack in the center of the oven and preheat the oven to 350°F. Mist a 13 × 9-inch metal cake pan with oil and set the pan aside.

2. In a large mixing bowl, stir together the cake mix, flour, and granulated sugar. Add the eggs, sour cream, oil, and flavoring of choice. Beat with an electric mixer on low speed until blended, about 30 seconds. Stop the machine and scrape down the sides of the bowl with a rubber spatula. Increase the mixer speed to medium and beat until the batter is smooth, about 1 minute. Pour the batter into the prepared pan, smoothing the top with a rubber spatula, and set the pan aside.

3. Make the topping: Cut the butter into smaller pieces and place in a medium bowl. Add the nuts, brown sugar, and cinnamon. Cut the butter into the mixture using two dinner knives or a pastry cutter until it resembles coarse meal. Sprinkle the topping evenly over the batter. Scatter the fruit over the topping.

4. Place the pan in the oven and bake until the cake is golden brown and the top springs back when gently pressed in the middle, 35 to 40 minutes.

5. Let the cake cool in the pan on a wire rack for 20 minutes.

6. Meanwhile, make the glaze (opposite), if desired: In a small bowl, whisk the milk into the confectioners' sugar until pourable. Whisk in the vanilla.

7. Pour the glaze over the cake. Let the cake rest for 20 minutes longer before slicing. Store, lightly covered, at room temperature for up to 3 days.

Chocolate Mayo Slab Cake

SERVES 16 TO 24

PREP: 20 TO 25 MINUTES

BAKE: 19 TO 24 MINUTES

CAKE

Vegetable oil spray,
 for misting the pan

1 (15.25-ounce) package
chocolate cake mix

5 tablespoons (half a
3.9-ounce package)
chocolate instant
pudding mix

2 large eggs

1 cup mayonnaise

1 cup water

¼ cup honey

1 teaspoon vanilla extract

ASSEMBLY

Chocolate Pan Frosting
(page 361), warm

1 teaspoon unsweetened
cocoa powder, for dusting

It's no secret that I love food history and am fascinated by cake origin stories—like how in the World War II rationing years, mayonnaise was used instead of butter in baking. It might sound odd to think of adding mayonnaise to a cake batter, but anyone raised during the Depression knew this trick as "making do." I like to think of it as "making delicious"—think of mayonnaise as an enriching buttermilk/ sour cream hybrid added to your batter. Here is a new way to present chocolate mayonnaise cake today, with chocolate pan frosting.

1. Make the cake: Place a rack in the center of the oven and preheat the oven to 350°F. Mist an 18 × 13-inch half-sheet pan (rimmed baking sheet) with oil. Line the pan with parchment or wax paper. Set the pan aside.

2. In a large mixing bowl, stir together the cake mix and pudding mix. Add the eggs, mayonnaise, water, honey, and vanilla. Beat with an electric mixer on low speed until blended, about 30 seconds. Stop the machine and scrape down the sides of the bowl with a rubber spatula. Increase the mixer speed to medium and beat until the batter is smooth, about 1 minute. Pour the batter into the prepared pan, smoothing the top with a rubber spatula.

3. Place the pan in the oven and bake until the cake springs back when gently pressed in the middle, 19 to 24 minutes.

4. Transfer the pan to a wire rack. Pour the warm frosting over the top of the cake, smoothing it out quickly with a long metal spatula and spreading it nearly to the edges of the cake. Let the cake rest at least 30 minutes, then dust with cocoa. Slice and serve. Store, lightly covered, at room temperature for up to 4 days.

Lazy Daisy Cake

SERVES 12 TO 16

PREP: 20 TO 25 MINUTES

BAKE: 28 TO 32 MINUTES

CAKE

Vegetable oil spray,
for misting the pan

1 (15.25-ounce) package
yellow or butter cake mix

4 tablespoons (half a
3.4-ounce package) vanilla
instant pudding mix

3 large eggs

1 cup buttermilk,
preferably whole milk

¼ cup water

8 tablespoons (1 stick)
unsalted butter,
at room temperature

2 teaspoons vanilla extract

TOPPING

8 tablespoons (1 stick)
unsalted butter

1 cup (packed)
light brown sugar

⅓ cup heavy cream

1½ to 2 cups unsweetened
or sweetened shredded
coconut

1 teaspoon vanilla extract

Pinch of salt

Maybe it's the quirky name or the topping of coconut, brown sugar, and cream that crisps on top of the cake under the broiler, or the ease of the cake since everything is mixed in one bowl—they're all good reasons to love the Lazy Daisy.

1. Make the cake: Place a rack in the center of the oven and preheat the oven to 350°F. Mist a 13 × 9-inch metal baking pan with oil and set the pan aside.

2. In a large mixing bowl, combine the cake mix, pudding mix, eggs, buttermilk, water, butter, and vanilla. Beat with an electric mixer on low speed until blended, about 30 seconds. Stop the machine and scrape down the sides of the bowl with a rubber spatula. Increase the mixer speed to medium and beat until the batter is smooth, about 1 minute. Pour the batter into the prepared pan, smoothing the top with a rubber spatula.

3. Place the pan in the oven and bake until the cake is golden brown and the top springs back when gently pressed in the middle, 28 to 32 minutes. Transfer the cake to a wire rack.

4. Preheat the broiler to high and carefully position a rack 4 to 6 inches from the heat.

5. Meanwhile, make the topping: In a medium saucepan, melt the butter over medium heat, about 1 minute. Stir in the brown sugar and cream, let the mixture come to a boil, and cook until slightly thickened, about 2 minutes. Remove the pan from the heat and stir in the coconut, vanilla, and salt.

6. Pour the topping over the warm cake, spreading it out to the edges. Broil the topping, leaving the door ajar or the oven light on, until the topping bubbles up and the coconut caramelizes, 30 seconds to 3 minutes, depending on your broiler.

7. Remove the cake from the oven and let it rest for 15 minutes before slicing. Serve warm. Store, lightly covered, at room temperature for 1 day, then in the refrigerator for up to 4 days. Reheat, if desired, uncovered, in a low oven until warm.

COOK'S NOTE:
To toast the chopped pecans
for the icing, place them on
a small baking pan in the
preheating oven until they
take on a little color, 4 to
5 minutes. Set the pecans aside
until ready to make the icing.

Texas Sheet Cake

CAKE

Vegetable oil spray, for misting the pan

1 (15.25-ounce) package chocolate cake mix

1 tablespoon unsweetened cocoa powder

2 large eggs

1⅓ cups buttermilk, preferably whole milk

12 tablespoons (1½ sticks) unsalted butter, melted and cooled

1 teaspoon vanilla extract

1 teaspoon ground cinnamon

SHEET CAKE ICING

8 tablespoons (1 stick) unsalted butter

¼ teaspoon salt

¼ cup unsweetened cocoa powder

⅓ cup whole milk

3¾ cups confectioners' sugar

1 teaspoon vanilla extract

¾ to 1 cup chopped toasted pecans (see Cook's Note)

While the mention of "sheet pan" brings to mind the large, shallow, rimmed pans used in restaurant kitchens, the original meaning of this term was any long pan made from a sheet of metal. In Texas, the sheet pan is equated to the "sheet cake," made of buttermilk and chocolate and baked in a 13 × 9-inch pan. This cake is cloaked in a fabulous chocolate icing where pecans are folded in before pouring it over the warm cake.

1. Make the cake: Place a rack in the center of the oven and preheat the oven to 350°F (see Cook's Note). Mist a 13 × 9-inch metal baking pan with oil and set the pan aside.

2. In a large mixing bowl, stir together the cake mix and cocoa. Add the eggs, buttermilk, melted butter, vanilla, and cinnamon. Beat with an electric mixer on low speed until blended, about 30 seconds. Stop the machine and scrape down the sides of the bowl with a rubber spatula. Increase the mixer speed to medium and beat until the batter is smooth, about 1 minute. Pour the batter into the prepared pan, smoothing the top with a rubber spatula.

3. Place the pan in the oven and bake until the cake springs back when gently pressed in the middle, 23 to 28 minutes.

4. Meanwhile, make the sheet cake icing: In a medium saucepan, melt the butter over low heat, 2 to 3 minutes. Stir in the salt, cocoa, and milk. Cook, stirring, until the mixture just begins to come to a boil, about 2 minutes. Remove from the heat. Place the confectioners' sugar in a large bowl and pour the hot cocoa mixture over it. Stir until smooth. Fold in the vanilla and pecans.

5. When the cake is done, transfer the pan to a wire rack. Pour the warm icing over the top of the cake, smoothing it out quickly with a long metal spatula. Let the cake rest at least 30 minutes before slicing and serving. Store, lightly covered, at room temperature for up to 4 days.

SERVES 12 TO 16

PREP: 45 TO 50 MINUTES

BAKE: 33 TO 37 MINUTES

CAKE

Vegetable oil spray,
for misting the pan

¾ cup (4½ ounces)
semisweet chocolate chips

1 (15.25-ounce) package
yellow or butter cake mix

4 tablespoons
(half a 3.4-ounce package)
vanilla instant pudding mix

3 large eggs

1 cup whole milk

10 tablespoons (1¼ sticks)
unsalted butter,
at room temperature

1 teaspoon vanilla extract

ESPRESSO SYRUP

⅔ cup Marsala wine
or cream sherry

¼ cup brewed espresso

⅓ cup sugar

Chocolate Marbled Tiramisu

Nancy Copeland of Virginia shared this recipe with me a while back, and it is one of my favorites. I have moved Nancy's recipe to a long pan and cranked up the flavors with brewed espresso instead of instant granules. Use either Marsala wine—the sweet fortified wine originating in Sicily—or a cream sherry. Tiramisu translates from Italian as "pick me up"; after one bite of this cake, you'll see it's true to its name.

1. Make the cake: Place a rack in the center of the oven and preheat the oven to 350°F. Mist a 13 × 9-inch metal cake pan with oil and set the pan aside.

2. Place the chocolate chips in a small microwave-safe bowl and microwave on high power until nearly melted, 30 to 40 seconds. Stir until the chocolate is completely melted. Set aside.

3. In a large mixing bowl, stir together the cake mix and pudding mix. Add the eggs, milk, butter, and vanilla. Beat with an electric mixer on low speed until blended, about 30 seconds. Stop the machine and scrape down the sides of the bowl with a rubber spatula. Increase the mixer speed to medium and beat until the batter is smooth, about 1 minute. Measure out 1½ cups of the batter and place in a small bowl. Stir in the reserved melted chocolate. Pour the remaining batter into the prepared pan, smoothing the top with a rubber spatula. Dollop several tablespoons of the chocolate batter on top of the plain batter and swirl with a dinner knife or small metal spatula to marbleize.

4. Place the pan in the oven and bake until the cake springs back when gently pressed in the middle, 33 to 37 minutes.

5. Let the cake cool in the pan on a wire rack for 15 minutes. Run a knife around the sides of the pan. Invert the cake once onto the rack, then invert again so the cake is right-side up. Allow to cool to room temperature.

TOPPING

1½ cups heavy cream

⅓ cup sugar

8 ounces mascarpone cheese

1 tablespoon Marsala wine or cream sherry

GARNISH

Unsweetened cocoa powder

½ cup semisweet chocolate shavings (optional)

COOK'S NOTE:
For easy cleanup of this cake, line the oil-misted pan with parchment paper. Lift the cake from the pan to the rack using the parchment paper.

6. Meanwhile, make the espresso syrup: Pour the Marsala into a glass measuring cup. Measure out 1 teaspoon of the espresso and set it aside for the topping. Add the remaining espresso to the Marsala, stir to combine, and microwave on high power until warmed through, about 1 minute. Stir in the sugar until dissolved. Set aside.

7. Make the topping: Place a large bowl and mixer beaters in the freezer to chill for several minutes. Pour the cream into the chilled bowl and beat on high speed, adding the sugar in thirds, until soft peaks form, about 3 minutes. Continue beating and when stiff peaks form, stop the machine and add one-third of the mascarpone. Reduce the mixer speed to medium and continue to beat, adding the remaining two-thirds of the mascarpone. Fold in the Marsala and the reserved 1 teaspoon espresso until just blended. Place the topping in the fridge while you assemble the cake.

8. When the cake has cooled completely, transfer it to a serving platter. Poke about 50 holes in the top with a large wooden skewer or chopstick. Using a soupspoon, ladle the syrup over the surface of the cake, then brush it lightly into the holes using a pastry brush. Be patient, as you need to use all the syrup.

9. When all the syrup has soaked into the cake, remove the topping from the fridge and spread it evenly over the top of the cake. Garnish with sifted cocoa and/or chocolate shavings. Cover the cake and place in the fridge until time to slice and serve. Store, tightly covered, in the refrigerator for up to 3 days.

Buttermilk Yellow Cake
with Martha's Chocolate Fudge Icing

SERVES 12 TO 16

PREP: 30 TO 35 MINUTES

BAKE: 25 TO 30 MINUTES

Vegetable oil spray,
for misting the pan

1 (15.25-ounce) package
yellow or butter cake mix

4 tablespoons (half a
3.4-ounce package) vanilla
instant pudding mix

3 large eggs

1¼ cups buttermilk,
preferably whole milk

12 tablespoons (1½ sticks)
unsalted butter,
melted and cooled

2 teaspoons vanilla extract

½ teaspoon almond extract
(optional)

Martha's Chocolate Fudge
Icing (page 373), warm

Sprinkles, for decorating
(optional)

Here's the cake that pleases both sides of the aisle, a cake of compromise, perhaps, but also true to its convictions. Yellow cake lovers will be smitten with the moist, springy texture. They'll appreciate the vanilla and hint of almond. And chocolate lovers will adore the warm and cozy pan frosting that you pour over the cake right in the pan. It tastes like fudge . . . except better!

1. Place a rack in the center of the oven and preheat the oven to 350°F. Mist a 13 × 9-inch metal baking pan with oil and set the pan aside.

2. In a large mixing bowl, stir together the cake mix and pudding mix. Add the eggs, buttermilk, butter, vanilla, and almond extract, if using. Beat with an electric mixer on low speed until blended, about 30 seconds. Stop the machine and scrape down the sides of the bowl with a rubber spatula. Increase the mixer speed to medium and beat until the batter is smooth, about 1 minute. Pour the batter into the prepared pan, smoothing the top with a rubber spatula.

3. Place the pan in the oven and bake until the cake is golden brown and the top springs back when gently pressed in the middle, 25 to 30 minutes.

4. Transfer the pan to a wire rack. Pour the warm frosting over the top of the cake, smoothing it out quickly with a long metal spatula. If decorating with sprinkles, add them now. Let the cake rest at least 30 minutes before slicing and serving from the pan. Store, lightly covered, at room temperature for up to 4 days.

The BTSC (Better Than Sex Cake)

CAKE

Vegetable oil spray, for misting the pan

1 cup (6 ounces) mini semisweet chocolate chips

1 (15.25-ounce) package chocolate cake mix

5 tablespoons (half a 3.9-ounce package) chocolate instant pudding mix

2 large eggs

1 cup water

½ cup sour cream

½ cup vegetable oil

CARAMEL SAUCE

4 tablespoons (½ stick) unsalted butter

¼ cup (packed) light brown sugar

2 tablespoons granulated sugar

¼ cup heavy cream

½ teaspoon vanilla extract

Pinch of salt

The 1980s were quite a decade in American baking and beguiled us with the chocolate-packed Neiman Marcus cookie, Robert Redford cake (and other chocolate confections named after movie stars), and zany cakes like this one that continue to be baked today. The original calls for caramel ice cream topping and a tub of Cool Whip. I took it as a challenge to not only modernize the recipe with an updated name (the BTSC), but to also refresh it with a homemade caramel sauce, real whipped cream, and a simple yet decadent chocolate cake. The entire layered confection can go into the fridge for serving later, which is a good reason to love this cake. And now I do!

1. Make the cake: Place a rack in the center of the oven and preheat the oven to 350°F. Mist a 13 × 9-inch metal baking pan with oil and set the pan aside.

2. Place the chocolate chips in a microwave-safe bowl and microwave on high power until nearly melted, 30 to 40 seconds. Stir until the chocolate is completely melted. Set aside to cool for 10 minutes.

3. In a large mixing bowl, stir together the cake mix and pudding mix. Add the melted chocolate, eggs, water, sour cream, and oil. Beat with an electric mixer on low speed until blended, about 30 seconds. Stop the machine and scrape down the sides of the bowl with a rubber spatula. Increase the mixer speed to medium and beat until the batter is smooth, about 1 minute. Pour the batter into the prepared pan, smoothing the top with a rubber spatula.

4. Place the pan in the oven and bake until the cake springs back when gently pressed in the middle, 35 to 40 minutes.

5. Meanwhile, make the caramel sauce: In a small saucepan, combine the butter, brown sugar, granulated sugar, cream,

RECIPE AND INGREDIENTS CONTINUED

WHIPPED CREAM TOPPING

1 cup heavy cream

2 tablespoons confectioners' sugar

GARNISH

½ cup (3 ounces) mini semisweet chocolate chips

¼ cup (2 ounces) English toffee bits

vanilla, and salt. Bring to a boil over medium heat, stirring, and let the mixture boil for 1 minute. Remove from the heat and set aside.

6. Transfer the cake pan to a wire rack. Poke 50 to 60 holes in the cake with a wooden skewer or chopstick. Spoon the caramel sauce over the cake, letting it seep into the holes. Set aside to cool while you whip the cream.

7. Make the whipped cream topping: Chill a large mixing bowl and mixer beaters in the freezer for several minutes. When they're cold, pour the cream into the bowl and add the confectioners' sugar. Beat on high speed until stiff peaks form, 3 to 4 minutes.

8. Spread the whipped cream topping evenly over the cake. Sprinkle the top with the chocolate chips and toffee bits. Slice and serve, or cover the pan with plastic wrap until time to serve. Store, tightly covered, in the refrigerator for up to 4 days.

How to Make Perfect Sour Cream Chocolate Cake

Make the BTSC batter, but increase the eggs to 3 and substitute strong brewed coffee for the water, if desired. Bake in a greased and floured 9-inch springform pan at 350°F for 48 to 52 minutes. Remove from the pan, cool, then cut in half horizontally. Fill with ½ recipe Whipped Cream Topping and spread the top generously with Chocolate Pan Frosting (page 361). Chill before serving.

The Pineapple Dump Cake

SERVES 12

PREP: 5 TO 10 MINUTES

BAKE: 40 TO 45 MINUTES

1 (20-ounce) can juice-packed crushed pineapple, undrained

24 fresh Bing cherries (6 ounces), halved and pitted (about 1 cup), or 1 cup drained canned or thawed frozen sour cherries

1 (15.25-ounce) package yellow or butter cake mix

½ teaspoon ground cinnamon

1 cup finely chopped pecans

½ cup unsweetened shredded coconut

16 tablespoons (2 sticks) unsalted butter, cut into tablespoons

Vanilla ice cream, for serving

This dump cake is more like a fruit crisp than a cake, and it's destined for a bowl and scoop of vanilla ice cream. Served warm, it's super comforting, and I don't think it matters if it's technically a cake or a crisp! To modernize the recipe a bit, I've omitted the customary cherry pie filling and used fresh cherries instead.

1. Place a rack in the center of the oven and preheat the oven to 350°F.

2. Pour the pineapple and juice into an ungreased 13 × 9-inch metal baking pan and spread it out evenly with a rubber spatula. Scatter the cherry halves on top. Spoon the cake mix evenly over the cherries and sprinkle the cinnamon over the top. Scatter on the pecans and coconut. Distribute the butter pats evenly over the top.

3. Place the pan in the oven and bake until the cake is golden brown and the top springs back when gently pressed in the middle, 40 to 45 minutes.

4. Let the cake cool in the pan on a wire rack for 10 minutes. Spoon warm cake into bowls and serve topped with vanilla ice cream. Store, tightly covered, in the refrigerator for up to 5 days. To reheat, uncover, and heat in a 300°F oven until warm.

Peanut Butter and Jelly Snack Cake

SERVES 12 TO 16

PREP: 15 TO 20 MINUTES

BAKE: 28 TO 32 MINUTES

Vegetable oil spray,
for misting the pan

1 (15.25-ounce) package
yellow or butter cake mix

¼ cup all-purpose flour

2 large eggs

1¼ cups (10 ounces)
full-fat canned coconut milk
or whole milk

½ cup creamy or chunky
peanut butter

⅓ cup vegetable oil

½ cup strawberry, plum,
or blackberry preserves,
or grape jelly

1 teaspoon confectioners'
sugar, for dusting (optional)

Everything needed for this cake is likely already in your pantry, which is its appeal. Well, that plus the nostalgic and wonderful peanut butter and jelly flavor combination. This is the type of cake that's made for life's spur-of-the-moment celebrations, whenever you feel like baking cake. And who doesn't like peanut butter and jelly?

1. Place a rack in the center of the oven and preheat the oven to 350°F. Mist a 13 × 9-inch metal baking pan with oil and set the pan aside.

2. In a large mixing bowl, stir together the cake mix and flour. Add the eggs, coconut milk, peanut butter, and oil. Beat with an electric mixer on low speed until blended, about 30 seconds. Stop the machine and scrape down the sides of the bowl with a rubber spatula. Increase the mixer speed to medium and beat until the batter is smooth, about 1 minute. Pour the batter into the prepared pan, smoothing the top with a rubber spatula. Dollop the preserves by teaspoonfuls on top and swirl into the batter with a dinner knife.

3. Place the pan in the oven and bake until the cake is golden brown and the top springs back when gently pressed in the middle, 28 to 32 minutes.

4. Let the cake cool in the pan on a wire rack for 20 to 25 minutes before serving. If desired, dust the top with confectioners' sugar when the cake is cool to the touch. Store, lightly covered, at room temperature for up to 5 days.

Roasted Sweet Potato Snack Cake

SERVES 12

PREP: 1 HOUR 5 MINUTES
TO 1 HOUR 10 MINUTES

BAKE: 25 TO 30 MINUTES

3 medium sweet potatoes
(1 pound; see Cook's Note)

Vegetable oil spray, for
misting the sweet potatoes
and the pan

1 tablespoon ground
cinnamon

½ teaspoon ground allspice

½ teaspoon ground
cardamom

½ teaspoon ground ginger

½ teaspoon ground nutmeg

1 (15.25-ounce) package
yellow or butter cake mix

2 large eggs

⅔ cup light olive oil

⅓ cup orange juice,
buttermilk, or water

1 teaspoon confectioners'
sugar, or Small-Batch Cream
Cheese Frosting (page 357)

This sweet potato cake is everything we crave today—fewer pans to wash up, more spice and bold flavors, and cakes that actually feel like they're kind of even good for us. It came about by accident as I was making my usual pumpkin cake and substituted some leftover roasted sweet potatoes in the fridge. Success! A moist and flavorful cake. Now, I prefer to begin with the warm sweet potato mash, seasoned with lots of spice.

1. Place a rack in the center of the oven and preheat the oven to 400°F. Wash the sweet potatoes and pat dry with paper towels. Quarter lengthwise and place cut-side up on a baking sheet. Mist the sweet potatoes with oil. Transfer to the oven and roast until tender when pricked with a fork, 30 to 35 minutes. Remove from the oven but leave the oven on and reduce the temperature to 350°F.

2. Meanwhile, mist a 13 × 9-inch metal baking pan with oil and set the pan aside.

3. Let the sweet potatoes cool slightly, about 10 minutes, and spoon the flesh into a large mixing bowl. Discard the skins. Mash several times with a potato masher to yield about 1 cup. (If there is more than a cup, reserve for another use.) Add the cinnamon, allspice, cardamom, ginger, and nutmeg. Mash until nearly smooth.

4. Add the cake mix, eggs, oil, and orange juice to the bowl and beat with an electric mixer on low speed until blended, about 30 seconds. Stop the machine and scrape down the sides of the bowl with a rubber spatula. Increase the mixer speed to medium and beat until the batter is smooth, about 1 minute. Pour the batter into the prepared pan, smoothing the top with a rubber spatula.

5. Place the pan in the oven and bake until the cake is deeply golden brown and the top springs back when gently pressed in the middle, 25 to 30 minutes.

6. Let the cake cool in the pan on a wire rack for 20 to 25 minutes before serving. If desired, dust the top with confectioners' sugar or spread with the frosting when the cake is cool to the touch. Store, lightly covered, at room temperature for up to 5 days.

Costco Sheet Cake Reimagined

SERVES 24 TO 36

PREP: 40 TO 45 MINUTES

BAKE: 53 TO 57 MINUTES

CAKE

Vegetable oil spray,
for misting the pan

All-purpose flour,
for dusting the pan

1 (15.25-ounce) package
butter cake mix

1 (15.25- or 16.25-ounce)
package white cake mix

5 large eggs

2 cups full-fat or light
canned coconut milk

⅔ cup vegetable oil

2 teaspoons vanilla extract

½ teaspoon almond extract

FILLING

2 (3.9-ounce) packages
white chocolate instant
pudding mix

3 cups half-and-half,
chilled

During the early days of the pandemic in 2020, Costco stopped selling white sheet cakes. When you can't gather with fifty of your best friends, do you really need a sheet cake? Obviously many folks thought so because they complained about it. And people with a hankering for the cake started baking their own—myself included. Except I didn't want to make one as large as Costco does, so I came up with a version for a 13 × 9-inch pan. I filled it with the custardy filling people drool about online and smothered it in a refreshed bakery-style vanilla buttercream made lighter with plant butter. Necessity is the mother of invention!

1. Make the cake: Place a rack in the center of the oven and preheat the oven to 350°F. Mist a 13 × 9-inch metal baking pan with oil, dust the pan with flour, shaking out the excess, and set the pan aside.

2. In a large mixing bowl, combine the butter cake mix, white cake mix, eggs, coconut milk, oil, vanilla, and almond extract. Beat with an electric mixer on low speed until blended, about 30 seconds. Stop the machine and scrape down the sides of the bowl with a rubber spatula. Increase the mixer speed to medium and beat until the batter is smooth, about 1 minute. Pour the batter into the prepared pan, smoothing the top with a rubber spatula.

3. Place the pan in the oven and bake until the cake springs back when gently pressed in the middle, 53 to 57 minutes.

4. Let the cake cool in the pan on a wire rack for 15 minutes. Run a knife around the edges of the pan and invert the cake onto the rack. Then invert again so the cake rests right-side up on the rack.

5. Make the filling: Pour both pudding mixes into a large mixing bowl and whisk in the cold half-and-half until well combined, about 2 minutes. Place the bowl in the refrigerator to chill.

FROSTING

10 tablespoons (1¼ sticks) unsalted butter, at room temperature

10 tablespoons (1¼ sticks) plant butter

2 teaspoons vanilla extract

7 cups confectioners' sugar

4 to 5 tablespoons whole milk

¼ teaspoon salt

GARNISH (OPTIONAL)

Tubes of icing, to pipe messages on the cake

Edible flower petals

COOK'S NOTE:

To cut the sheet cake evenly in half horizontally, measure with a ruler to find the center point. Then mark the center point with toothpicks all around the sides of the cake where you will cut partway through the cake on all sides. Remove the toothpicks, and then slice all the way through to the other side.

6. Make the frosting: In a large mixing bowl, beat the butter and plant butter with an electric mixer on low speed until creamy. Add the vanilla and half of the confectioners' sugar and blend to just combine. Add half of the milk and blend to combine. Add the remaining confectioners' sugar as needed to thicken the frosting, the rest of the milk, and the salt and blend on low speed until creamy. Increase the mixer speed to medium and beat until light and smooth, about 1 minute.

7. When the cake has cooled, trim any browned edges and the domed top. For easy slicing and handling, freeze the cake for 1 hour to firm. (If you don't have the time you can skip this step.) With a long serrated knife, carefully slice the cake in half horizontally into two layers (see Cook's Note). Carefully set aside the top layer. Transfer the bottom layer to a long serving plate. Remove the filling from the refrigerator.

8. Spoon about 1 cup of the frosting into a pastry bag fitted with a large round tip about ⅞ inch in diameter. Pipe a rope of frosting around the inside edges of the bottom layer. This serves as a dam, preventing the filling from escaping from the middle of the cake. Spoon the filling into the center of the dam, spreading it with a small rubber spatula in an even layer. Top with the other cake layer. Carefully spread a thin layer of frosting—a "crumb coat" (see page 35)—over the top and sides of the cake. Place the cake in the refrigerator to set, about 20 minutes.

9. Remove the cake from the fridge. Frost the top and sides with the rest of the frosting. If desired, reserve some of the frosting to pipe onto the cake with the pastry bag. Using a star tip, pipe a rope of frosting around the top edges of the cake. Or just frost with a long metal spatula and decorate the top with a birthday message, edible flowers, or candles. Store in the fridge until time to serve, or up to 5 days.

Black- and Blueberry Buckle

SERVES 12

PREP: 10 TO 15 MINUTES

BAKE: 45 TO 50 MINUTES

Vegetable oil spray,
for misting the pan

TOPPING

⅓ cup sugar

¼ cup all-purpose flour

½ teaspoon
ground cinnamon

2 tablespoons cold
unsalted butter

CAKE

1 (15.25-ounce) package
yellow or butter cake mix

4 tablespoons (half a
3.4-ounce package) vanilla
instant pudding mix

2 large eggs

1 cup full-fat or light canned
coconut milk

10 tablespoons (1¼ sticks)
unsalted butter,
at room temperature

2 teaspoons vanilla extract

1 cup blueberries

1 cup blackberries

I once called coffee cakes the stretchy pants of the cake world. They transition from breakfast to lunch to dinner without a change of clothes and are as welcome warm from the oven at the beginning of the day as they are reheated after dinner with a scoop of ice cream. If you bake this rich and buttery coffee cake and see the way the blueberries and blackberries cause the cake to sink and buckle into delicious valleys, you'll understand how it got its name.

1. Place a rack in the center of the oven and preheat the oven to 350°F. Mist a 9-inch square metal cake pan with oil; set aside.

2. Make the topping: In a small bowl, whisk together the sugar, flour, and cinnamon. Cut the butter into ½-inch pieces and work it into the sugar mixture using a pastry cutter or two dinner knives until the topping looks like small peas. Place in the refrigerator to keep cool.

3. Make the cake: In a large mixing bowl, stir together the cake mix and pudding mix. Add the eggs, coconut milk, butter, and vanilla. Beat with an electric mixer on low speed until blended, about 30 seconds. Stop the machine and scrape down the sides of the bowl with a rubber spatula. Increase the mixer speed to medium and beat until the batter is smooth, about 1 minute. Fold in the blueberries. Pour the batter into the prepared pan, smoothing the top with a rubber spatula.

4. Scatter the blackberries on top of the batter; cut the larger ones in half first. Remove the topping from the refrigerator and sprinkle it on top, all the way to the edges of the pan.

5. Place the pan in the oven and bake until the cake is golden brown and the top springs back when gently pressed in the middle, 45 to 50 minutes.

6. Let the cake cool in the pan on a wire rack for 20 minutes. Store, lightly covered, at room temperature for up to 3 days.

Vegan Cinnamon Applesauce Cake

SERVES 8 TO 12

PREP: 20 TO 25 MINUTES

BAKE: 45 TO 50 MINUTES

CAKE

Vegetable oil spray,
for misting the pan

1 (15.25-ounce) package
yellow cake mix

½ teaspoon ground
cinnamon

¼ teaspoon ground allspice

¼ teaspoon ground ginger

¼ teaspoon ground nutmeg

1 cup unsweetened
applesauce

¾ cup orange juice

8 tablespoons (1 stick)
plant butter, such as
Country Crock (with avocado
oil), at room temperature

CINNAMON "BUTTERCREAM"

2 tablespoons plant butter

¾ cup confectioners' sugar

1 tablespoon full-fat or
light canned coconut milk
or unsweetened plain
almond milk

¼ teaspoon ground
cinnamon

All that's required for this aromatic autumn cake are spices, some OJ, a cup of applesauce, a stick of plant-based butter, and a yellow cake mix. The cinnamon "buttercream" frosting spread over the cake while it's still in the pan is even simpler. For vegan bakers, applesauce substitutes beautifully for the eggs. And feel free to change up the spices for others in your pantry—I like coriander, cloves, or cardamom.

1. Make the cake: Place a rack in the center of the oven and preheat the oven to 350°F. Mist an 8-inch square metal baking pan with oil and set the pan aside.

2. In a large mixing bowl, stir together the cake mix, cinnamon, allspice, ginger, and nutmeg. Add the applesauce, orange juice, and butter. Beat with an electric mixer on low speed until blended, about 30 seconds. Stop the machine and scrape down the sides of the bowl with a rubber spatula. Increase the mixer speed to medium and beat until the batter is smooth, about 1 minute. Pour the batter into the prepared pan, smoothing the top with a rubber spatula.

3. Place the pan in the oven and bake until the cake is lightly golden brown and the top springs back when gently pressed in the middle, 45 to 50 minutes. (The cake may dip a little in the center because of the lack of eggs, but this will be covered by the frosting.)

4. Let the cake cool in the pan on a wire rack for 10 minutes.

5. Meanwhile, make the cinnamon "buttercream": In a medium mixing bowl, beat the butter with an electric mixer on low speed (or with a wooden spoon) until creamy, then continue to beat while you add the confectioners' sugar, coconut milk, and cinnamon.

6. Spread the frosting over the cake in the pan. Let rest for 20 minutes, then slice and serve. Store, lightly covered, at room temperature for up to 3 days.

Sour Cream–Peach Kuchen

SERVES 12

PREP: 25 TO 30 MINUTES

BAKE: 50 TO 56 MINUTES

1 (15.25-ounce) package yellow or butter cake mix

2 large eggs

10 tablespoons (1¼ sticks) unsalted butter, melted and cooled

2 (29-ounce) cans juice-packed sliced peaches, well drained (see Cook's Note)

½ cup plus 1 tablespoon granulated sugar

1¼ teaspoons ground cinnamon

1⅓ cups sour cream

COOK'S NOTE:
If you can't find two of the big cans of peaches, use four 15-ounce cans. You will have a few more ounces of peaches in the kuchen, but that's not a bad thing!

Just because fresh peaches aren't in season doesn't mean you can't fork into a warm peach kuchen. This quick spin-off of the German kuchen—a cross between cake and pie with a creamy custard—looks to the pantry for inspiration. Canned peaches taste like a burst of summertime, which is just what's needed when it's cold and wintry outside.

1. Place a rack in the center of the oven and preheat the oven to 375°F.

2. Measure out 2 tablespoons of the cake mix and set aside. Separate one of the eggs and place the white in a large mixing bowl. Set the egg yolk aside for the topping.

3. Add the rest of the cake mix and the melted butter to the egg white in the mixing bowl. Beat with an electric mixer on low speed until well blended, about 1 minute.

4. Scrape the mixture into a 13 × 9-inch metal cake pan and, with your fingers, press the crust mixture over the bottom of the pan and about 1 inch up the sides.

5. Place the pan in the oven and bake the crust until the edges are lightly brown, 15 to 17 minutes. Remove the pan from the oven but leave the oven on.

6. Press down on the crust with a spatula or smaller metal pan to flatten it. Arrange the peach slices evenly over the top. In a small bowl, combine ¼ cup of the sugar, 1 teaspoon of the cinnamon, and 1 tablespoon of the reserved cake mix. Sprinkle this mixture over the peaches.

7. Return the pan to the oven and bake until the peaches are partially cooked, 15 to 17 minutes.

8. Meanwhile, for the topping, place the sour cream, ¼ cup of the granulated sugar, the reserved egg yolk, and remaining

How to Make a Rhubarb and Spice Kuchen

When you can find fresh rhubarb at a local farmers' market or in your garden, turn it into a kuchen. Follow the same directions as the Sour Cream–Peach Kuchen, except:

1. Substitute 1½ pounds fresh rhubarb, trimmed and cut into 1-inch pieces.

2. Increase the butter to 12 tablespoons.

3. Increase the sugar to 1 cup plus 1 tablespoon. Sprinkle ½ cup of the sugar over the rhubarb and ½ cup goes into the sour cream filling. (The 1 tablespoon is sprinkled over the topping.)

4. The rhubarb takes the same time as the peach kuchen for the initial and final bake, but only 10 to 12 minutes in the oven to soften and partially cook the rhubarb before you pour over the topping and return it to the oven.

whole egg and 1 tablespoon reserved cake mix in a large mixing bowl. Beat with an electric mixer on medium speed until well blended, 30 to 45 seconds.

9. Remove the pan from the oven and pour the topping over the peaches. Sprinkle with the remaining 1 tablespoon sugar and ¼ teaspoon cinnamon.

10. Return the pan to the oven and bake until the crust is golden brown and the topping has set, 20 to 22 minutes.

11. Slice and serve warm. Store, lightly covered, at room temperature for 1 day. Or, store in the refrigerator for up to 5 days. Reheat in a 300°F oven for 15 to 20 minutes.

FRESH PEACH KUCHEN: Use 4 to 5 cups sliced, peeled fresh peaches. Drain the peaches well on paper towels before arranging over the batter. Combine ⅓ cup flour (instead of 1 tablespoon cake mix), ½ cup sugar, and 1 teaspoon cinnamon to sprinkle over the peaches (the flour thickens the extra juice naturally found in fresh peaches). You can keep that 1 tablespoon cake mix in the crust mixture.

Rhubarb and Spice Kuchen
(recipe at left)

Easy Fruit Slab Pie

SERVES 16 TO 24

PREP: 15 TO 20 MINUTES

BAKE: 25 TO 30 MINUTES

1 (15.25-ounce) package yellow or butter cake mix

12 tablespoons (6 ounces) unsalted butter, melted and cooled

1 egg white

1 cup (8 ounces) whole-milk ricotta cheese

2 egg yolks

¼ cup lemon curd, homemade (see page 365) or store-bought

3 cups soft fresh fruit, such as blueberries, raspberries, blackberries, or sliced bananas, peaches, plums, kiwi, or pineapple

½ cup apricot preserves, warmed

Whipped cream or ice cream, for serving

Part cake and part fruit tart, this dessert elevates fruit that's in your pantry or fruit bowl into a last-minute dessert for company. Here the cake mix becomes a soft crust on which rests a lemon curd/ricotta filling followed by sliced fruit—bananas, kiwi, peaches, plums, whatever you've got—that gets baked together to create a wonderfully fragrant patchwork of fruit. And to give it that glistening French tart look, finish with a brushstroke of warmed apricot preserves.

1. Place a rack in the center of the oven and preheat the oven to 350°F.

2. For the crust, in a large mixing bowl, combine the cake mix, melted butter, and egg white. Beat with an electric mixer on low speed until well blended, about 1 minute. Scrape the mixture into an 18 × 13-inch half-sheet pan (rimmed baking sheet) and, with your fingers, press the crust mixture into the bottom of the pan to cover. Set the pan aside.

3. For the filling, in a small bowl, stir together the ricotta, egg yolks, and lemon curd until well blended. Pour over the crust and spread it evenly to the edges using a rubber spatula. Arrange the fruit in vertical lines on top of the filling, or scatter the fruit randomly over the top.

4. Place the pan in the oven and bake until the crust is golden brown, 25 to 30 minutes.

5. Transfer the pan to a wire rack and immediately brush the fruit with the warmed apricot preserves. Let the cake cool for 1 hour before serving. Slice and serve with whipped cream or ice cream. Store, lightly covered, at room temperature for up to 2 days.

CAKE

Vegetable oil spray,
for misting the pan

1 (15.25-ounce) package
yellow or butter cake mix

4 tablespoons (half a
3.4-ounce package) vanilla
instant pudding mix

1½ teaspoons ground ginger

½ teaspoon ground cinnamon

¼ teaspoon ground nutmeg

3 large eggs

1 cup whole milk

½ cup molasses

10 tablespoons (1¼ sticks)
unsalted butter,
at room temperature

1 teaspoon grated lemon zest

LEMON BUTTERCREAM FROSTING

2 tablespoons unsalted
butter, at room temperature

½ cup confectioners' sugar

½ to 1 teaspoon grated
lemon zest

2 teaspoons fresh
lemon juice

Gingerbread Slab Cake
with Lemon and Buttermilk Stripes

There's no better cake to usher in December than gingerbread. One whiff of it baking and all of a sudden you're in the mood to deck the halls and spike the eggnog! And while we think of gingerbread as unadorned and cozy, if you bake it in the right pan and glaze it just so, you can turn it into impressive party fare.

1. Make the cake: Place a rack in the center of the oven and preheat the oven to 350°F. Mist an 18 × 13-inch half-sheet pan (rimmed baking sheet) with oil. Line the pan with parchment or wax paper. Set the pan aside.

2. In a large mixing bowl, stir together the cake mix, pudding mix, ginger, cinnamon, and nutmeg. Add the eggs, milk, molasses, butter, and lemon zest. Beat with an electric mixer on low speed until blended, about 30 seconds. Stop the machine and scrape down the sides of the bowl with a rubber spatula. Increase the mixer speed to medium and beat until the batter is smooth, about 1 minute. Pour the batter into the prepared pan, smoothing the top with a rubber spatula.

3. Place the pan in the oven and bake until the cake springs back when gently pressed in the middle, 20 to 25 minutes.

4. Meanwhile, make the lemon buttercream frosting: Place the butter, confectioners' sugar, lemon zest, and lemon juice in a medium bowl and beat with an electric mixer on low speed until creamy, 15 to 20 seconds. Increase the mixer speed to medium and beat until light, about 30 seconds.

RECIPE AND INGREDIENTS CONTINUED

BUTTERMILK GLAZE

¼ cup granulated sugar

2½ tablespoons buttermilk, preferably whole milk

1 tablespoon unsalted butter

1 teaspoon corn syrup

Dash of salt

½ teaspoon vanilla extract

Lemon zest, for garnish (optional)

COOK'S NOTE:
Shortcut this recipe and make just one frosting or glaze—simply double the amount of frosting or glaze so you have enough to cover the entire slab cake.

5. Make the buttermilk glaze: In a small saucepan, combine the granulated sugar, buttermilk, butter, corn syrup, and salt. Bring to a boil over medium heat, then reduce the heat to low and simmer until the mixture is smooth and thickened, about 2 minutes. Stir in the vanilla and set aside.

6. Let the cake cool in the pan on a wire rack for 30 minutes. If desired, turn the cake out onto a platter or board and remove the parchment paper. Spread the lemon frosting in stripes over the top of the cake. Fill in the space between the stripes with the buttermilk glaze. Sprinkle lemon zest over the top, if desired. Let the cake rest for 20 minutes before slicing and serving. Store, lightly covered, at room temperature for up to 3 days.

Zucchini Chocolate Chip Slab Cake

SERVES 16 TO 24

PREP: 25 TO 30 MINUTES

BAKE: 20 TO 25 MINUTES

Vegetable oil spray,
for misting the pan

1 (15.25-ounce) package
yellow or butter cake mix

4 tablespoons (half a
3.4-ounce package) vanilla
instant pudding mix

3 large eggs

1 cup full-fat or light
canned coconut milk

½ cup vegetable oil

1 teaspoon ground cinnamon

2 cups (packed) shredded
zucchini (1 medium-large
zucchini, about 8 ounces)

1 cup (6 ounces) mini
semisweet chocolate chips

Milk Chocolate Buttercream
(page 355)

COOK'S NOTE:

There is just a thin coating
of frosting on this cake. If
you want more frosting,
double the recipe.

August is invariably zucchini month at our house. If the weather has been hot and steamy enough, the garden cranks out more zucchini than we know what to do with. As a result, I bake with it . . . of course!

1. Place a rack in the center of the oven and preheat the oven to 350°F. Mist an 18 × 13-inch half-sheet pan (rimmed baking sheet) with oil. Line the pan with parchment or wax paper. Set the pan aside.

2. In a large mixing bowl, stir together the cake mix and pudding mix. Add the eggs, coconut milk, oil, and cinnamon. Beat with an electric mixer on low speed until blended, about 30 seconds. Stop the machine and scrape down the sides of the bowl with a rubber spatula. Increase the mixer speed to medium and beat until the batter is smooth, about 1 minute. Fold in the zucchini and chocolate chips. Pour the batter into the prepared pan, smoothing the top with a rubber spatula.

3. Place the pan in the oven and bake until the cake springs back when gently pressed in the middle, 20 to 25 minutes.

4. Let the cake cool in the pan on a wire rack for 30 minutes. Spread the frosting over the top of the cake, nearly to the edges. Let the cake rest 20 minutes longer before slicing and serving. Store, lightly covered, at room temperature for up to 4 days.

Birthday Cake for 50

SERVES 50

PREP: 30 TO 35 MINUTES

BAKE: 30 TO 35 MINUTES

Vegetable oil spray,
for misting the pan

2 (15.25-ounce) packages
yellow or butter cake mix

1 (3.4-ounce) package
vanilla instant pudding mix

6 large eggs

2 cups whole milk

16 tablespoons (2 sticks)
unsalted butter, melted
and cooled

½ cup vegetable oil

1 tablespoon vanilla extract

1 teaspoon almond extract
(optional)

Big-Batch Chocolate Pan
Frosting (page 361) or
Double White Chocolate
Glaze (page 370), warm

Sprinkles, for garnish
(optional)

COOK'S NOTE:
If you want to frost half
with chocolate and half
with white chocolate,
make half the amount of
each frosting called for.

It might be easy to place a bakery order for a cake to feed a crowd, but it is so much cheaper to make it at home—and more fun, too! This recipe fits beautifully in a half-sheet pan with at least 1 to 1¼-inch sides. Even with the cost of the double recipe you are still coming out ahead—spending 10 to 15 cents per serving. And you top it with a homemade poured icing, either dark chocolate or white, or both.

1. Place a rack in the center of the oven and preheat the oven to 350°F. Mist an 18 × 13-inch half-sheet pan (rimmed baking sheet) with oil. Line the pan with parchment or wax paper. Set the pan aside.

2. In a large mixing bowl, stir together the cake mix and pudding mix. Add the eggs, milk, melted butter, oil, vanilla, and almond extract (if using). Beat with an electric mixer on low speed until blended, about 30 seconds. Stop the machine and scrape down the sides of the bowl with a rubber spatula. Increase the mixer speed to medium and beat until the batter is smooth, about 1 minute. Pour the batter into the prepared pan, smoothing the top with a rubber spatula.

3. Place the pan in the oven and bake until the cake is golden brown and the top springs back when gently pressed in the middle, 30 to 35 minutes.

4. Transfer the pan to a wire rack.

5. Pour the warm frosting over the top of the cake, smoothing it out quickly with a long metal spatula. (If you want to decorate the cake with sprinkles, do so now, so they stick to the cake.) Let the cake rest for 30 minutes before slicing and serving. Store, lightly covered, at room temperature for up to 3 days.

Chocolate Marbled Birthday Cake for 50

Create some drama by marbling the cake. Melt 1½ cups (about 9 ounces) chocolate chips and stir the melted chocolate into 3 cups of the cake batter. Pour the plain batter into the sheet pan and drop the chocolate batter by tablespoonfuls over the top. With a dinner knife, swirl in the chocolate batter. The baking time may be slightly longer, about 35 minutes.

How to Cut the Cake to Make at Least 50 Squares

With a long side of the pan facing you, make 8 equidistant marks with a knife to create 9 rows of cake. Turn the pan so a short side is facing you and make 5 equidistant marks with the knife to create 6 rows of cake. Slice into 54 squares using the marks as your guide.

Big American Flag Cake

SERVES 20 TO 24

PREP: 40 TO 45 MINUTES

BAKE: 20 TO 25 MINUTES

CAKE

Vegetable oil spray,
for misting the pan

1 (15.25- or 16.25-ounce)
package white cake mix

4 tablespoons (half a
3.4-ounce package) vanilla
instant pudding mix

3 large eggs

1 cup whole milk or full-fat
canned coconut milk

8 tablespoons (1 stick)
unsalted butter, melted
and cooled

2 teaspoons vanilla extract

ASSEMBLY

Cream Cheese Frosting
(page 356)

1 pint blueberries

2 quarts strawberries

2 pints raspberries

Confectioners' sugar,
for dusting (optional)

My research into American cake history taught me that the most patriotic cakes were those that symbolized something. Such as the eighteenth-century election cakes of dried fruit that would feed an entire town when people traveled to vote. Or the dark chocolate blackout cakes that stood for mandated blackouts to protect naval yards from wartime attack. There really isn't any mention of a cake decorated to look like the American flag, yet in the last few decades this is the cake most baked for July Fourth barbecues, the one that pairs so well with fireworks, fried chicken, and summertime.

1. Make the cake: Place a rack in the center of the oven and preheat the oven to 350°F. Mist an 18 × 13-inch half-sheet pan (rimmed baking sheet) with oil. Line the pan with parchment or wax paper. Set the pan aside.

2. In a large mixing bowl, stir together the cake mix and pudding mix. Add the eggs, milk, melted butter, and vanilla. Beat with an electric mixer on low speed until blended, about 30 seconds. Stop the machine and scrape down the sides of the bowl with a rubber spatula. Increase the mixer speed to medium and beat until the batter is smooth, about 1 minute. Pour the batter into the prepared pan, smoothing the top with a rubber spatula.

3. Place the pan in the oven and bake until the cake springs back when gently pressed in the middle, 20 to 25 minutes.

4. Let the cake cool in the pan on a wire rack for 15 to 20 minutes.

5. Assemble the cake: Run a dinner knife around the edge of the pan and invert the cake onto a long platter or board. Remove the parchment paper. Frost the cake on top and sides of the cake with smooth strokes.

6. Select 50 blueberries of about equal size, preferably small, for the stars. Cap the strawberries and slice lengthwise into

CONTINUED

¼-inch-thick slices, or in half, depending on size. Slice the raspberries in half.

7. With a long side of the pan facing you, use a ruler to mark off a 6 × 4½-inch rectangle in the top left corner of the cake. In this rectangle, place 5 rows of 10 blueberries for the 50 stars on the American flag. Down the right edge of the cake, make 12 equidistant marks (a little less than 1 inch apart) to help you create the 13 stripes of the flag. Lightly run the knife across the cake to delineate these stripes. Starting at the top of the cake make a red stripe in the first row by covering it in strawberries and/or raspberries, placed cut-side down. Leave the next stripe white (empty) from the frosting. Cover the third stripe with red berries. Repeat this pattern across the cake until you have 7 horizontal red berry stripes and 6 white frosting stripes. These 13 stripes symbolize the 13 original American colonies.

8. Once the cake is decorated, you can serve at once, or cover it with plastic wrap and refrigerate until ready to serve, preferably within 3 hours. Store, lightly covered, in the refrigerator for up to 3 days.

Brown Butter Banana Pudding Slab Cake

SERVES 16 TO 24

PREP: 35 TO 40 MINUTES

BAKE: 16 TO 20 MINUTES FOR
THE CAKE, 12 TO 15 MINUTES
FOR THE MERINGUE

CAKE

Vegetable oil spray,
for misting the pan

1 (15.25-ounce) package
yellow or butter cake mix

1 large egg

3 egg yolks

1 cup full-fat or light
canned coconut milk

⅓ cup vegetable oil

1 teaspoon vanilla extract

PUDDING

4 tablespoons (½ stick)
unsalted butter

1 (3.4-ounce) package
vanilla instant pudding

2 cups full-fat canned
coconut milk or whole milk,
chilled

2 teaspoons vanilla extract

3 cups sliced bananas
(2 large or 3 medium
bananas)

As much as this recipe was a reader favorite in my first book, I was happy to introduce it to the flavor of browned butter. Banana puddin'— as it's called in the South—is revered, so even if this is a quick version, it needs good flavor as well as a topping of lightly browned soft meringue. This variation is a bit different and a lot more fun, served in a long slab cake. But if you prefer, you can bake the cake in a deeper 13 × 9-inch pan; note that it will take 10 to 15 minutes longer to bake.

1. Make the cake: Place a rack in the center of the oven and preheat the oven to 350°F. Mist an 18 × 13-inch half-sheet pan (rimmed baking sheet) with oil. Line the pan with parchment or wax paper. Set the pan aside.

2. In a large mixing bowl, combine the cake mix, whole egg, egg yolks, coconut milk, oil, and vanilla. Beat with an electric mixer on low speed until blended, about 30 seconds. Stop the machine and scrape down the sides of the bowl with a rubber spatula. Increase the mixer speed to medium and beat until the batter is smooth, about 1 minute. Pour the batter into the prepared pan, smoothing the top with a rubber spatula.

3. Place the pan in the oven and bake until the cake is golden brown and the top springs back when gently pressed in the middle, 16 to 20 minutes.

4. Meanwhile, make the pudding: In a small saucepan, melt the butter over medium-low heat, then cook until nut-brown in color, about 8 minutes. Do not let it burn. Pour the butter through a fine-mesh sieve (to remove any solids) into a small glass bowl. Set aside to cool.

5. While the butter cools, place the pudding mix in a medium bowl and whisk in the cold coconut milk until smooth.

RECIPE AND INGREDIENTS CONTINUED

MERINGUE TOPPING

6 large egg whites

½ cup sugar

COOK'S NOTE:
In a hurry? Skip the step about browning the butter and just melt it.

6. Whisk the cooled brown butter and vanilla into the pudding. Fold in the sliced bananas. Refrigerate the pudding mixture until ready to use.

7. Transfer the cake to a wire rack to cool for 25 to 30 minutes. Leave the oven on.

8. Meanwhile, make the meringue: Place the egg whites in a large, clean mixing bowl. Beat on high speed with an electric mixer until soft peaks form, 1 to 2 minutes. Gradually add the sugar, beating until stiff peaks form, 2 to 3 minutes.

9. To assemble the cake, spoon the banana pudding on top of the cooled cake, spreading the mixture to the edges with a rubber spatula. Using the rubber spatula, dollop the meringue on top of the pudding and spread it out so that it nearly covers the top, leaving the edges exposed so you can see the pudding underneath.

10. Place the pan in the oven and bake until the meringue is lightly browned, 12 to 15 minutes. Serve warm. Store, lightly covered, in the refrigerator for up to 3 days.

Chocolate-Covered Cherry Cake

SERVES 12 TO 16

PREP: 20 TO 25 MINUTES

BAKE: 28 TO 32 MINUTES

Vegetable oil spray,
for misting the pan

1 (15.25-ounce) package
chocolate cake mix

1 (21-ounce) can
cherry pie filling

2 large eggs

1 teaspoon almond extract

Chocolate Pan Frosting
(page 361), warm

In 1974 a recipe pairing chocolate cake mix and a can of cherry pie filling won the Pillsbury Bake-Off and would go down in baking history as the cake with just four ingredients and no fat. What with the appeal of this cake, I created a new rendition you can bake with the mixes today and even a better frosting—my chocolate pan frosting, worthy of a prize itself!

1. Place a rack in the center of the oven and preheat the oven to 350°F. Mist a 13 × 9-inch metal baking pan with oil and set the pan aside.

2. In a large mixing bowl, combine the cake mix, pie filling, eggs, and almond extract. Beat with an electric mixer on low speed until blended, about 30 seconds. Stop the machine and scrape down the sides of the bowl with a rubber spatula. Increase the mixer speed to medium and beat until the batter is nearly smooth (there will still be pieces of cherries), about 1 minute. Pour the batter into the prepared pan, smoothing the top with a rubber spatula.

3. Place the pan in the oven and bake until the cake springs back when gently pressed in the middle, 28 to 32 minutes.

4. Let the cake cool in the pan on a wire rack for 20 minutes. Pour the warm frosting over the top of the cake, smoothing it out quickly with a long metal spatula. Let the cake rest for 20 minutes before slicing and serving. Store, lightly covered, at room temperature up to 4 days.

VEGAN CHOCOLATE-COVERED CHERRY CAKE: Use 1/2 cup unsweetened applesauce instead of the eggs. Use plant-based butter and either almond or coconut milk in the frosting.

Chocolate Buttermilk Slab Cake
with Caramel Frosting

SERVES 16 TO 24

PREP: 25 TO 30 MINUTES

BAKE: 16 TO 21 MINUTES

CAKE

Vegetable oil spray, for misting the pan

1 cup (6 ounces) semisweet chocolate chips

1 (15.25-ounce) package chocolate cake mix

5 tablespoons (half a 3.9-ounce package) chocolate instant pudding mix

2 large eggs

1¼ cups buttermilk, preferably whole milk

½ cup vegetable oil

1 teaspoon vanilla extract

ASSEMBLY

Quick Caramel Frosting (page 364), warm

½ cup finely chopped lightly salted toasted pecans

COOK'S NOTE:
You can frost this cake in the pan or turn it out onto a long platter and then pour the warm caramel frosting over the top.

My friend Bette calls this her house cake. When people come over to her house for dinner, she wants to serve them a little something sweet to end the evening. But not too much. So she began baking chocolate cake in a half-sheet pan and smothering it in my caramel frosting for a sweet/salty combination. The salted nuts on top really bring out the sweetness in both the caramel and the chocolate.

1. Make the cake: Place a rack in the center of the oven and preheat the oven to 350°F. Mist an 18 × 13-inch half-sheet pan (rimmed baking sheet) with oil. Line the pan with parchment or wax paper. Set the pan aside.

2. Place the chocolate chips in a microwave-safe bowl and microwave on high power until nearly melted, 30 to 40 seconds. Stir until the chocolate is completely melted. Set aside for 10 minutes to cool.

3. In a large mixing bowl, stir together the cake mix and pudding mix. Add the melted chocolate, eggs, buttermilk, oil, and vanilla. Beat with an electric mixer on low speed until blended, about 30 seconds. Stop the machine and scrape down the sides of the bowl with a rubber spatula. Increase the mixer speed to medium and beat until the batter is smooth, about 1 minute. Pour the batter into the prepared pan, smoothing the top with a rubber spatula.

4. Place the pan in the oven and bake until the cake springs back when gently pressed in the middle, 16 to 21 minutes.

5. Transfer the pan to a wire rack. Pour the warm frosting over the top of the cake, smoothing it out quickly with a long metal spatula and spreading it nearly to the edges. Sprinkle with the chopped pecans. Let the cake rest at least 30 minutes longer before slicing and serving. Store, lightly covered, at room temperature for up to 4 days.

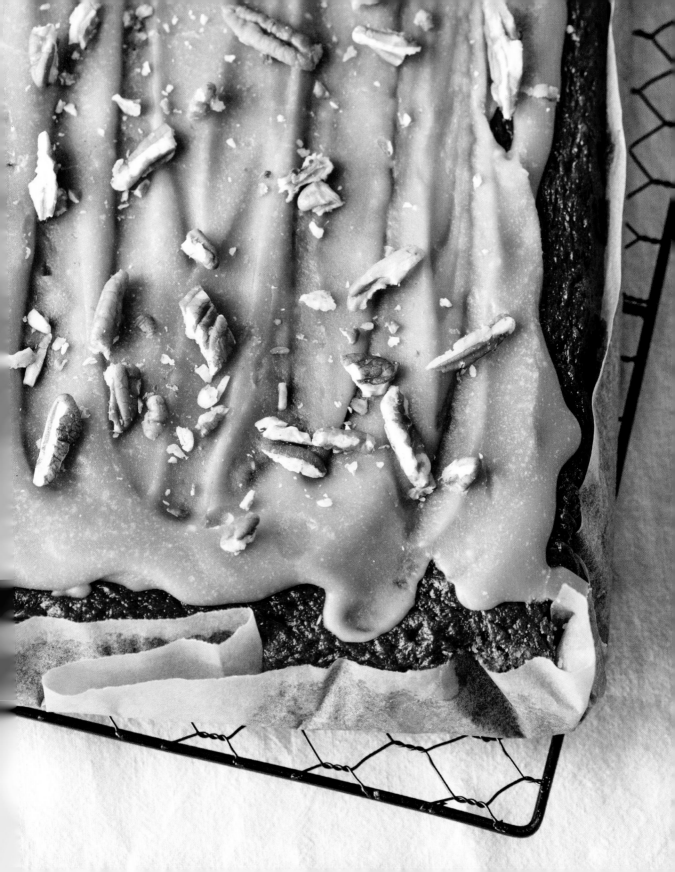

Basic Vanilla Cupcake
(page 268)

Cupcakes, Muffins, and More

Good things do come in small packages. This chapter shares the simple joy of baking cupcakes for a party (or for no reason at all), muffins to stash in the freezer for busy mornings, as well as little cakes baked in ice cream cones, cake pops, and other meringue-topped or sprinkle-dusted surprises sure to satisfy the child in all of us.

Basic Vanilla Cupcakes

MAKES SIXTEEN TO EIGHTEEN
2½-INCH CUPCAKES

PREP: 20 TO 25 MINUTES

BAKE: 18 TO 22 MINUTES

CUPCAKES

1 cup whole milk or full-fat canned coconut milk

8 tablespoons (1 stick) unsalted butter

1 (15.25- or 16.25-ounce) package butter or white cake mix

4 tablespoons (half a 3.4-ounce package) vanilla or white chocolate instant pudding mix

3 large eggs

2 teaspoons vanilla extract or ½ teaspoon almond extract

FROSTING CHOICES

Vanilla Buttercream Frosting (page 351), Leeann's Blackberry Frosting (page 360), Strawberry Cream Cheese Frosting (page 360), Chocolate Buttercream Frosting (page 355), or Quick Caramel Frosting (page 364)

This recipe is deliciously basic—like that white shirt—and goes with every frosting, whether it's chocolate, caramel, or a lemony buttercream.

1. Make the cupcakes: Place a rack in the center of the oven and preheat the oven to 350°F. Line 16 to 18 cups of two muffin tins with paper liners. Set the pans aside.

2. In a small saucepan, warm the milk and butter over medium-low heat until the butter melts, about 2 minutes. Remove the pan from the heat and set aside to cool slightly.

3. In a large mixing bowl, stir together the cake mix and pudding mix. Add the eggs, vanilla, and milk/butter mixture. Beat with an electric mixer on low speed until blended, about 30 seconds. Stop the machine and scrape down the sides of the bowl with a rubber spatula. Increase the mixer speed to medium and beat until the batter is smooth, about 1 minute. Spoon or scoop ⅓ cup (about 2 ounces) batter into each lined muffin cup, filling it three-quarters of the way full.

4. Place the pans in the oven and bake until the cupcakes are lightly golden and spring back when gently pressed in the middle, 18 to 22 minutes.

5. Let the cupcakes cool in the pans on wire racks for 3 minutes. Run a dinner knife around the edges of the cupcake liners, lever the bottom of the cupcakes up with the tip of the knife and carefully pick them out of the pan with your fingertips. Set the cupcakes on the wire racks to cool for 15 minutes before frosting.

6. Place a heaping tablespoon of frosting on each cupcake and spread it out with a short metal spatula or spoon. Store, lightly covered, at room temperature for up to 3 days.

3 large eggs, separated

½ teaspoon cream of tartar

1 (15.25-ounce) package yellow or butter cake mix

4 tablespoons (half a 3.4-ounce package) vanilla instant pudding mix

¾ cup orange juice

½ cup vegetable oil

1 teaspoon vanilla extract

Raspberry Buttercream (page 352)

16 to 18 raspberries, for garnish (optional)

Orange Vanilla Chiffon Cupcakes
with Raspberry Buttercream

You don't need a fresh orange in the house to bake chiffon cupcakes—a carton of OJ in the fridge is just fine. Thanks to the beaten egg whites, these cupcakes rise taller in the pan.

1. Place a rack in the center of the oven and preheat the oven to 350°F. Line 16 to 18 cups of two muffin tins with paper liners. Set the pans aside.

2. In a medium mixing bowl, combine the egg whites and cream of tartar. Beat with an electric mixer on high speed until stiff peaks form, about 3 minutes. Set aside.

3. In a large mixing bowl, combine the cake mix, pudding mix, egg yolks, orange juice, oil, and vanilla. Beat with an electric mixer on low speed until blended, about 30 seconds. Stop the machine and scrape down the sides of the bowl with a rubber spatula. Increase the mixer speed to medium and beat until the batter is smooth, about 1 minute. With a rubber spatula, fold the whipped egg whites into the batter until well combined but light. Spoon or scoop ⅓ cup (about 2 ounces) batter into each lined muffin cup, filling it three-quarters of the way full.

4. Place the pans in the oven and bake until the cupcakes are golden brown and spring back when gently pressed in the middle, 18 to 22 minutes.

5. Let the cupcakes cool in the pans on wire racks for 3 minutes. Run a dinner knife around the edges of the cupcake liners, lever the bottoms of the cupcakes up with the tip of the knife, then carefully pick them out of the cups with your fingertips. Cool on the wire racks for 15 minutes before frosting.

6. Place a heaping tablespoon of frosting on each cupcake and spread it out with a short metal spatula or spoon. Garnish each cupcake with a raspberry, if desired.

Vegan Dark Chocolate Cupcakes

MAKES SIXTEEN TO EIGHTEEN
2½-INCH CUPCAKES

PREP: 15 TO 20 MINUTES

BAKE: 19 TO 24 MINUTES

1 (15.25-ounce) package chocolate cake mix

5 tablespoons (half a 3.9-ounce package) chocolate instant pudding mix

1 cup (8 ounces) sparkling water or sparkling apple cider (see Cook's Note)

½ cup full-fat or light canned coconut milk or plain almond milk, preferably unsweetened

¼ cup applesauce

¼ cup vegetable oil

1 teaspoon vanilla extract

Vegan Vanilla Buttercream Frosting (page 353)

Vegan sprinkles (optional)

COOK'S NOTE:
Any sparkling water works in this recipe, even the flavored waters.

Begin this fast and fun vegan cupcake by opening the refrigerator and looking for something fizzy inside. Sparkling water, sparkling apple cider, even beer. While leavening in the cake mix does most of the work getting the cupcakes to rise, sparkling liquids seem to give it an extra boost in lieu of eggs.

1. Place a rack in the center of the oven and preheat the oven to 375°F. Line 16 to 18 cups of two muffin tins with paper liners. Set the pans aside.

2. In a large mixing bowl, stir together the cake mix and pudding mix. Add the sparkling water, coconut milk, applesauce, oil, and vanilla. Beat with an electric mixer on low speed until blended, about 30 seconds. Stop the machine and scrape down the sides of the bowl with a rubber spatula. Increase the mixer speed to medium and beat until the batter is smooth, about 1 minute. Spoon or scoop ⅓ cup (about 2 ounces) batter into each lined muffin cup, filling it three-quarters of the way full.

3. Place the pans in the oven and bake until the cupcakes spring back when gently pressed in the middle, 19 to 24 minutes.

4. Let the cupcakes cool in the pans on wire racks for 3 minutes. The cupcakes will shrink some as they cool. Run a dinner knife around the edges of the cupcake liners, lever the bottoms of the cupcakes up with the tip of the knife, then carefully pick them out of the cups with your fingertips. Set the cupcakes on the wire racks to cool for 15 minutes before frosting.

5. Place a heaping tablespoon of frosting on each cupcake and spread it out with a short metal spatula or spoon. Decorate with sprinkles, if desired. Store, lightly covered, in the refrigerator for up to 5 days.

Matcha Mint Cupcakes

MAKES SIXTEEN TO EIGHTEEN
2½-INCH CUPCAKES

PREP: 20 TO 25 MINUTES

BAKE: 18 TO 22 MINUTES

1 (15.25- or 16.25-ounce) package butter or white cake mix

3 large eggs

1 cup full-fat or light canned coconut milk

½ cup light olive oil

4 single-serve packets (about ⅓ teaspoon each) matcha green tea powder, plus more (optional) for sprinkling

½ teaspoon mint extract

Matcha Buttercream (page 352)

Before matcha green tea powder, if you wanted a cake to be green for St. Patrick's Day or another festive occasion, you used a package of pistachio pudding mix or food coloring. Emerald green matcha is so much nicer to tint a cake naturally green, and it is known for its antioxidant and health benefits, too.

1. Place a rack in the center of the oven and preheat the oven to 350°F. Line 16 to 18 cups of two muffin tins with paper liners. Set the pans aside.

2. In a large mixing bowl, combine the cake mix, eggs, coconut milk, olive oil, matcha, and mint extract. Beat with an electric mixer on low speed until blended, about 30 seconds. Stop the machine and scrape down the sides of the bowl with a rubber spatula. Increase the mixer speed to medium and beat until the batter is smooth, about 1 minute. Spoon or scoop ⅓ cup (about 2 ounces) batter into each lined muffin cup, filling it three-quarters of the way full.

3. Place the pans in the oven and bake until the cupcakes spring back when gently pressed in the middle, 18 to 22 minutes.

4. Let the cupcakes cool in the pans on wire racks for 3 minutes. Run a dinner knife around the edges of the cupcake liners, lever the bottoms of the cupcakes up with the tip of the knife, then carefully pick them out of the cups with your fingertips. Cool on the wire racks for 15 minutes before frosting.

5. Place a heaping tablespoon of frosting on each cupcake and spread it out with a short metal spatula or spoon. If desired, sprinkle the tops of the cupcakes with a little matcha powder. Store, lightly covered, at room temperature for up to 3 days.

    MINI MINT MATCHAS: Scoop 1 to 2 tablespoons batter into about 36 lined cups of two mini muffin tins and bake for 10 to 16 minutes, depending on the size.

FILLING

1 large egg

⅔ cup unsweetened shredded coconut

⅓ cup sugar

1 tablespoon cornstarch

¼ teaspoon coconut extract

CUPCAKES

1 (15-ounce) package gluten-free chocolate cake mix

5 tablespoons (half a 3.9-ounce package) chocolate instant pudding mix

3 large eggs

¾ cup canned coconut milk

½ cup vegetable oil

1 teaspoon vanilla extract

½ teaspoon coconut extract

½ cup (3 ounces) mini semisweet chocolate chips

TOPPING

⅓ cup slivered almonds

¼ cup unsweetened shredded coconut

2 to 3 tablespoons sugar

Gluten-Free Chocolate Macaroon Cupcakes

These little chocolate coconut cakes are sweet enough to pass as a cupcake and sturdy enough to resemble a muffin. So call them what you like! They're a perfect end to a festive meal and a gluten-free dessert tempting to everyone.

1. Place a rack in the center of the oven and preheat the oven to 350°F. Line 14 to 16 cups of two muffin tins with paper liners. Set the pans aside.

2. Make the filling: Crack the egg into a small bowl. Beat it gently with a fork, then stir in the coconut, granulated sugar, cornstarch, and coconut extract. Set the filling aside.

3. Make the cupcakes: In a large mixing bowl, stir together the cake mix and pudding mix. Add the eggs, coconut milk, oil, vanilla, and coconut extract. Beat with an electric mixer on low speed until blended, about 30 seconds. Stop the machine and scrape down the sides of the bowl with a rubber spatula. Increase the mixer speed to medium and beat until the batter is smooth, about 1 minute. Fold in the chocolate chips.

4. Spoon or scoop ¼ cup (about 1.5 ounces) batter into each lined muffin cup, filling it two-thirds of the way full. Using the back of a teaspoon, make a ½-inch well in the batter. Dollop a teaspoon of filling into each well. Piling in the center, sprinkle the toppings in this order: almonds, coconut, and sugar.

5. Place the pans in the oven and bake until the cupcakes spring back when gently pressed in the middle, 16 to 20 minutes.

6. Let the cupcakes cool in the pans on wire racks for 3 minutes. Run a dinner knife around the edges of the cupcake liners and pick them out of the cups with your fingertips. Set the cupcakes on the wire racks to cool for 15 minutes before serving.

1 cup (6 ounces) semisweet chocolate chips

1 (15.25-ounce) package chocolate cake mix

5 tablespoons (half a 3.9-ounce package) chocolate instant pudding mix

3 large eggs

1 cup warm water

½ cup sour cream

½ cup vegetable oil

Chocolate Ganache (page 362) or Cream Cheese Frosting (page 356)

COOK'S NOTE:
For a deeper flavor, add 1 teaspoon espresso powder to the batter.

Chocolate Sour Cream Cupcakes

Absolutely nothing beats a chocolate cupcake spread with homemade frosting. And this is a goodie, whether slathered with chocolate ganache or cream cheese frosting.

1. Place a rack in the center of the oven and preheat the oven to 350°F. Line 20 to 22 cups of two muffin tins with paper liners. Set the pans aside.

2. Place the chocolate chips in a small microwave-safe bowl and microwave on high power until nearly melted, 40 to 45 seconds. Stir until the chocolate is completely melted. Set aside to cool slightly.

3. In a large mixing bowl, stir together the cake mix and pudding mix. Add the melted chocolate, eggs, water, sour cream, and oil. Beat with an electric mixer on low speed until blended, about 30 seconds. Stop the machine and scrape down the sides of the bowl with a rubber spatula. Increase the mixer speed to medium and beat until the batter is smooth, about 1 minute. Spoon or scoop ⅓ cup (about 2 ounces) batter into each lined muffin cup, filling it three-quarters of the way full.

4. Place the pans in the oven and bake until the cupcakes spring back when gently pressed in the middle, 17 to 21 minutes.

5. Let the cupcakes cool in the pans on wire racks for 3 minutes. Run a dinner knife around the edges of the cupcake liners, lever the bottoms of the cupcakes up with the tip of the knife, then carefully pick them out of the cups with your fingertips. Set the cupcakes on the wire racks to cool for 15 minutes before frosting.

6. Place a heaping tablespoon of frosting on each cupcake and spread it out with a short metal spatula or spoon. Store, lightly covered, at room temperature for up to 3 days.

How to Make More Cupcakes

Fill with less batter. Most of the cupcake recipes in this chapter will yield 24 cupcakes if you fill the pans two-thirds instead of three-quarters full. Bake for slightly less time than the recipe suggests.

How to Turn Any Layer, Snack, or Bundt Cake into Cupcakes

Make the batter, scoop 2 ounces (⅓ cup) into cupcake liners, and bake at 350°F for 15 to 20 minutes. The cakes in this book will yield 16 to 24 cupcakes, give or take a cupcake.

How to Make Dozens of Mini Cupcakes

Depending on the size of your mini muffin pans, use a 1¼-inch scoop to place about 1 tablespoon of batter in the liners or a 1¾-inch scoop to place 2 tablespoons batter into the liners. The smaller minis bake in 10 to 12 minutes; the larger ones in 14 to 16 minutes. You yield twice as many minis as regular-size cupcakes.

2 ounces unsweetened
chocolate, chopped

1 (15.25-ounce) package
yellow or butter cake mix

5 tablespoons (half a
3.9-ounce package)
chocolate instant
pudding mix

3 large eggs

1¼ cups whole milk or full-
fat canned coconut milk

½ cup creamy peanut butter

⅓ cup vegetable oil

Martha's Chocolate Fudge
Icing (page 373), or Peanut
Butter Frosting (page 354),
or both

Chocolate Peanut Butter Cupcakes

You have the best of both worlds in this cupcake—peanut butter and chocolate. The peanut butter batter is made first and then chocolate is stirred into part of it. Both rise up in delicious harmony.

1. Place a rack in the center of the oven and preheat the oven to 350°F. Line 18 to 20 cups of two muffin tins with paper liners. Set the pans aside.

2. Place the chocolate in a medium microwave-safe bowl and microwave on high power until nearly melted, 45 to 50 seconds. Stir until the chocolate is completely melted. Set aside to cool.

3. In a large mixing bowl, stir together the cake mix and pudding mix. Add the eggs, milk, peanut butter, and oil. Beat with an electric mixer on low speed until blended, about 30 seconds. Stop the machine and scrape down the sides of the bowl with a rubber spatula. Increase the mixer speed to medium and beat until the batter is smooth, about 1 minute. Measure out 1 cup of the batter and stir it into the melted chocolate until well combined.

4. Spoon or scoop a generous ¼ cup (about 1.5 ounces) peanut butter batter into each lined muffin cup, filling it a little more than two-thirds of the way full. With a small scoop or tablespoon, dollop a spoonful of chocolate batter on top of each cupcake.

5. Place the pans in the oven and bake until the cupcakes spring back when gently pressed in the middle, 18 to 22 minutes.

6. Let the cupcakes cool in the pans on wire racks for 3 minutes. Run a dinner knife around the edges of the cupcake liners, lever the bottoms of the cupcakes up with the tip of the knife, then carefully pick them out of the cups with your fingertips. Cool on the wire racks for 15 minutes before frosting.

7. Place a heaping tablespoon of icing on each cupcake and spread it out with a short metal spatula or spoon. If using both, begin with peanut butter and swirl in the chocolate.

Sweet Tea Cupcakes
with Lemon Buttercream

MAKES EIGHTEEN TO TWENTY
2½-INCH CUPCAKES

PREP: 20 TO 25 MINUTES

BAKE: 17 TO 21 MINUTES

⅓ cup whole milk

12 tablespoons (1½ sticks)
unsalted butter

1 (15.25-ounce) package
yellow or butter cake mix

4 tablespoons (half a
3.4-ounce package) vanilla
instant pudding mix

½ teaspoon ground
cinnamon

¼ teaspoon ground allspice

¼ teaspoon ground cloves

3 large eggs

1 cup sweet tea
(see Cook's Note)

Lemon Buttercream
(page 352)

Curls of lemon zest,
for garnish

COOK'S NOTE:

Use tea punch or sweetened
tea in this recipe. If you
brew your own tea, let it
steep for several hours
to create a stronger,
more flavorful liquid.

*In the South, tea sweetened with sugar and served over ice
is the beverage of choice. I prefer my tea unsweetened, but I
love a good tea punch made with fruit juices, mint, and often
spices like cinnamon. These cupcakes mimic tea punch with a
hint of spice. The lemon buttercream adds that perfect note of
citrus, just like a lemon slice does to a glass of sweet tea.*

1. Place a rack in the center of the oven and preheat the oven to
   350°F. Line 18 to 20 cups of two muffin tins with paper liners.
   Set the pans aside.

2. In a small saucepan, warm the milk and butter over medium-
   low heat until the butter melts, 1 to 1½ minutes. Remove from
   the heat and set the pan aside.

3. In a large mixing bowl, stir together the cake mix, pudding
   mix, cinnamon, allspice, and cloves. Add the eggs, tea, and the
   slightly cooled milk/butter mixture. Beat with an electric
   mixer on low speed until blended, about 30 seconds. Stop the
   machine and scrape down the sides of the bowl with a rubber
   spatula. Increase the mixer speed to medium and beat until
   the batter is smooth, about 1 minute. Spoon or scoop ⅓ cup
   (about 2 ounces) batter into each lined muffin cup, filling it
   three-quarters of the way full.

4. Place the pans in the oven and bake until the cupcakes are
   lightly golden and spring back when gently pressed in the
   middle, 17 to 21 minutes.

5. Let the cupcakes cool in the pans on wire racks for 3 minutes.
   Run a dinner knife around the edges of the cupcake liners,
   lever the bottoms of the cupcakes up with the tip of the knife,
   then carefully pick them out of the cups with your fingertips.
   Cool on the wire racks for 15 minutes before frosting.

6. Place a big tablespoon of frosting on each cupcake and spread
   with a short metal spatula or spoon. Garnish with lemon zest.
   Store, covered, at room temperature for up to 3 days.

Wedding Cake Cupcakes

MAKES EIGHTEEN TO TWENTY 2½-INCH CUPCAKES

PREP: 35 TO 40 MINUTES

BAKE: 18 TO 22 MINUTES

1 (15.25- or 16.25-ounce) package white cake mix

⅓ cup all-purpose flour

¼ cup sugar

5 large egg whites

12 tablespoons (1½ sticks) unsalted butter, melted and cooled

1 cup sparkling wine, such as Prosecco or Champagne (see Cook's Note)

⅓ cup whole milk

2 teaspoons vanilla extract

Small-Batch Wedding Cake Frosting (page 356)

Small edible flowers and white sprinkles, for garnish

COOK'S NOTE:
You can use sparkling apple cider instead of sparkling wine, but reduce the sugar to 2 tablespoons.

If a wedding cake seems just too daunting to pull off, consider baking wedding-style cupcakes instead. Decorated with edible flowers or sprinkles, they not only look beautiful but taste good, too! They contain sparkling wine, the festive beverage of choice. Bake and serve these at showers, tea parties, and, of course, weddings!

1. Place a rack in the center of the oven and preheat the oven to 350°F. Line 18 to 20 cups of two muffin tins with paper liners. Set the pans aside.

2. In a large mixing bowl, stir together the cake mix, flour, and sugar. Add the egg whites, melted butter, sparkling wine, milk, and vanilla. Beat with an electric mixer on low speed until blended, about 30 seconds. Stop the machine and scrape down the sides of the bowl with a rubber spatula. Increase the mixer speed to medium and beat until the batter is smooth, about 1 minute. Spoon or scoop ⅓ cup (about 2 ounces) batter into each lined muffin cup, filling it three-quarters of the way full.

3. Place the pans in the oven and bake until the cupcakes are lightly golden and spring back when gently pressed in the middle, 18 to 22 minutes.

4. Let the cupcakes cool in the pans on wire racks for 3 minutes. Run a dinner knife around the edges of the cupcake liners, lever the bottoms of the cupcakes up with the tip of the knife, then carefully pick them out of the cups with your fingertips. Cool on the wire racks for 15 minutes before frosting.

5. Place a heaping tablespoon of frosting on each cupcake and spread it out with a short metal spatula or spoon. Decorate the tops with edible flowers and sprinkles. Store, lightly covered, at room temperature for up to 3 days.

Key Lime Pie Cupcakes

These cupcakes, filled with their own Key lime pie filling, blur the line between pie and cake. Because they are so light and citrusy, they make just the right end to a summer meal; and because they are topped with a fancy-looking soft meringue, they are appropriate for even a New Year's dinner party.

CUPCAKES

1 (15.25-ounce) package yellow or butter cake mix

4 tablespoons (half a 3.4-ounce package) vanilla instant pudding mix

3 large eggs

1 cup water or orange juice

8 tablespoons (1 stick) unsalted butter, melted and cooled

¼ cup vegetable oil

Grated zest and juice of 1 large lime

FILLING

1 cup sweetened condensed milk

⅓ cup Key lime juice (see Cook's Note)

COCONUT MERINGUE

3 large egg whites

¼ teaspoon cream of tartar

⅓ cup sugar

½ teaspoon coconut extract

1. Make the cupcakes: Place a rack in the center of the oven and preheat the oven to 350°F. Line 18 to 20 cups of two muffin tins with paper liners. Set the pans aside.

2. In a large mixing bowl, combine the cake mix, pudding mix, eggs, water, melted butter, oil, lime zest, and lime juice. Beat with an electric mixer on low speed until blended, about 30 seconds. Stop the machine and scrape down the sides of the bowl with a rubber spatula. Increase the mixer speed to medium and beat until the batter is smooth, about 1 minute. Spoon or scoop ¼ cup (about 1.5 ounces) batter into each lined muffin cup, filling it two-thirds of the way full.

3. Place the pans in the oven and bake until the cupcakes are lightly golden and spring back when gently pressed in the middle, 18 to 22 minutes.

4. Let the cupcakes cool in the pans on wire racks for 3 minutes. Run a dinner knife around the edges of the cupcake liners, lever the bottoms of the cupcakes up with the tip of the knife, then carefully pick them out of the cups with your fingertips. Cool on the wire racks for 15 minutes before filling. Leave the oven on.

5. Make the filling: In a small bowl, stir together the sweetened condensed milk and Key lime juice. Spoon the filling into a pastry bag or large plastic resealable bag with the corner cut, fitted with a medium tip. Press the tip ¼ inch into the top center of each cooled cupcake and squeeze in about 1 tablespoon filling. Scrape off any excess filling with a rubber spatula. Place the cooled cupcakes nearly side by side on one baking sheet or use two.

6. Make the coconut meringue: In a large mixing bowl, combine the egg whites and cream of tartar. Beat with an electric mixer on high speed until frothy, about 45 seconds. Add 1 tablespoon of the sugar and the coconut extract. Beat on high speed, adding the rest of the sugar 1 tablespoon at a time, until stiff peaks form, 1 to 2 minutes.

7. Spoon 2 tablespoons of the meringue on top of each cupcake and spread it just to the edges with a short metal spatula or spoon. Place the pan in the oven and bake until the meringue is lightly browned, 5 to 6 minutes. Serve at once or allow to cool for 10 minutes. They are best enjoyed freshly baked. Store, lightly covered, in the refrigerator for up to 3 days, but the meringue will soften.

COOK'S NOTE:
Key lime juice makes this recipe. It is tarter and fresher than the juice of Persian limes, the type found in supermarkets. Buy Key lime juice from the fruit juice aisle.

1 (15.25- or 16.25-ounce)
package white cake mix

4 tablespoons (half a
3.4-ounce package) vanilla
instant pudding mix

3 large eggs

1 cup buttermilk,
preferably whole milk

1 teaspoon grated
lemon zest

2 tablespoons fresh
lemon juice

⅓ cup lemon curd,
homemade (see page 365)
or store-bought

8 tablespoons (1 stick)
unsalted butter, at room
temperature

Leeann's Blackberry Frosting
(page 360)

22 small blackberries,
for garnish (optional)

Lemon Curd Cupcakes

with Leeann's Blackberry Frosting

*Each summer, Leeann Hewlett of Nashville goes blackberry
picking with her daughter and mother-in-law in Blairsville,
Georgia. They make sure to save enough berries to make
frosting for her daughter's August birthday cupcakes. It's
no surprise that her daughter's favorite color is purple!*

1. Place a rack in the center of the oven and preheat the oven to
350°F. Line 20 to 22 cups of two muffin tins with paper liners.
Set the pans aside.

2. In a large mixing bowl, combine the cake mix, pudding mix,
eggs, buttermilk, lemon zest, lemon juice, lemon curd, and
butter. Beat with an electric mixer on low speed until blended,
about 30 seconds. Stop the machine and scrape down the sides
of the bowl with a rubber spatula. Increase the mixer speed to
medium and beat until the batter is smooth, about 1 minute. The
batter will be thick. Spoon or scoop ⅓ cup (2 ounces) batter into
each lined muffin cup, filling it three-quarters of the way full.

3. Place the pans in the oven and bake until the cupcakes are
golden brown and spring back when gently pressed in the
middle, 18 to 22 minutes.

4. Let the cupcakes cool in the pans on wire racks for 5 minutes.
Run a dinner knife around the edges of the cupcake liners, lever
the bottoms of the cupcakes up with the tip of the knife, then
carefully pick them out of the cups with your fingertips. Cool
on the wire racks for 15 minutes before frosting.

5. Place a heaping tablespoon of frosting on each cupcake and
spread it out with a short metal spatula or spoon. If desired,
place a small blackberry on top of each cupcake. Store, lightly
covered, in the refrigerator for up to 3 days.

Chocolate Nutella Marbled Cupcakes

⅓ cup (2 ounces)
semisweet chocolate chips

¼ cup Nutella
(chocolate-hazelnut spread;
see Cook's Note)

1 (15.25- or 16.25-ounce)
package white cake mix

4 tablespoons (half a
3.4-ounce package) vanilla
instant pudding mix

3 large eggs

1 cup full-fat or light canned
coconut milk

10 tablespoons (1¼ sticks)
unsalted butter, at room
temperature

1 teaspoon vanilla extract

Chocolate Buttercream
Frosting (optional;
page 355)

COOK'S NOTE:

If you don't have Nutella,
omit it. You won't have the
chocolate-hazelnut flavor,
but you will still have a
chocolate marbled cupcake!

*The chocolate and hazelnut spread Nutella makes the most
interesting and yummy cupcakes. When you fold it into the batter,
it suspends and holds its shape, creating a marbled pattern.*

1. Place a rack in the center of the oven and preheat the oven to
    350°F. Line 18 to 20 cups of two muffin tins with paper liners.
    Set the pans aside.

2. Place the chocolate chips in a medium microwave-safe bowl
    and microwave on high power until nearly melted, 20 to
    25 seconds. Stir until the chocolate is completely melted. Stir in
    the Nutella and set aside to cool.

3. In a large mixing bowl, stir together the cake mix and pudding
    mix. Add the eggs, coconut milk, butter, and vanilla. Beat with
    an electric mixer on low speed until blended, about 30 seconds.
    Stop the machine and scrape down the sides of the bowl with
    a rubber spatula. Increase the mixer speed to medium and beat
    until the batter is smooth, about 1 minute. Spoon 1 cup of the
    batter into the bowl with the chocolate and Nutella and stir
    until well blended.

4. Spoon or scoop ¼ cup (about 1.5 ounces) of the plain batter
    into each lined muffin cup, filling it two-thirds of the way full.
    Dollop about 2 teaspoons of the chocolate batter on top of each
    and lightly swirl into the plain batter with a small metal spatula.

5. Place the pans in the oven and bake until the cupcakes spring
    back when gently pressed in the middle, 20 to 24 minutes.

6. Let the cupcakes cool in the pans on wire racks for 3 minutes.
    Run a dinner knife around the edges of the cupcake liners, lever
    the bottoms of the cupcakes up with the tip of the knife, then
    carefully pick them out of the cups with your fingertips. Set the
    cupcakes on the wire racks to cool for 15 minutes before frosting.

7. If using the chocolate buttercream, place a heaping tablespoon
    on each cupcake and spread it out with a spatula or spoon.

Butternut Cupcakes
with Cinnamon Buttercream

MAKES SIXTEEN TO EIGHTEEN
2½-INCH CUPCAKES

PREP: 40 TO 45 MINUTES

BAKE: 18 TO 22 MINUTES

1 medium butternut squash (1½ pounds) or 8 to 10 ounces butternut squash cubes

1 (15.25-ounce) package yellow or butter cake mix

4 tablespoons (half a 3.4-ounce package) vanilla instant pudding mix

2 teaspoons ground cinnamon

½ teaspoon ground allspice

½ teaspoon ground ginger

3 large eggs

½ cup vegetable oil

Cinnamon Buttercream (page 351)

Brown sugar, for garnish (optional)

The sight of pumpkin gets us in the mood for fall, but those other winter squash that arrive in the market—butternut and acorn—also have a place in baking. And when cooked (steamed in the microwave or roasted in the oven when you're cooking dinner) and pureed, they lend a lovely golden-orange hue to cupcakes. Slather on buttercream and pour the cider!

1. For the whole squash, halve lengthwise and remove the seeds. Place the halves, cut-side down, in a shallow glass dish and fill with about 1 inch of water. Microwave uncovered on high power until tender, 8 to 10 minutes. Let the squash rest for 15 minutes. For the squash cubes, toss them with ¼ cup water in a microwave-safe dish with fitting glass lid. Microwave covered on high power until tender, 4 to 5 minutes. Let rest 5 minutes.

2. When the squash halves are cool enough to handle, scoop the pulp into a large mixing bowl; for the cubes, just transfer to the bowl. Mash with a potato masher until smooth. You need 1¼ cups, so reserve leftovers for another use. Set the bowl aside.

3. Place a rack in the center of the oven and preheat the oven to 350°F. Line 16 to 18 cups of two muffin tins with paper liners. Set the pans aside.

4. Add the cake mix, pudding mix, cinnamon, allspice, ginger, eggs, and oil to the bowl with the squash. Beat with an electric mixer on low speed until blended, about 30 seconds. Stop the machine and scrape down the sides of the bowl with a rubber spatula. Increase the mixer speed to medium and beat until the batter is smooth, about 1 minute. Spoon or scoop ⅓ cup (about 2 ounces) batter into each lined muffin cup, filling it three-quarters of the way full.

5. Place the pans in the oven and bake until the cupcakes spring back when gently pressed in the middle, 18 to 22 minutes.

CONTINUED

6. Let the cupcakes cool in the pans on wire racks for 3 minutes. Run a dinner knife around the edges of the cupcake liners, lever the cupcakes up with the tip of the knife, then carefully pick them out of the cups with your fingertips. Cool on the wire racks for 15 minutes before frosting.

7. Place frosting on each cupcake and spread with a short metal spatula or spoon. Sprinkle with brown sugar, if desired. Store, lightly covered, at room temperature for up to 3 days.

Microwave Mug Sprinkle Cake

MAKES ENOUGH MIX
FOR 10 MUG CAKES

PREP: 5 MINUTES

COOK: 1 MINUTE 45 TO
50 SECONDS

MUG CAKE MIX

1 (15.25-ounce) package yellow cake mix

4 tablespoons (half a 3.4-ounce package) vanilla or lemon instant pudding mix

½ cup sprinkles

FOR ONE MUG CAKE

½ cup Mug Cake Mix (above)

3 tablespoons milk (whole milk, unsweetened plain almond milk, or full-fat or light canned coconut milk)

2 tablespoons vegetable oil or melted butter

Vegetable oil spray, for misting the coffee mug

Ice cream, for serving (optional)

Your favorite frosting and sprinkles (optional)

No need to purchase mug cake mixes when you can make your own at home. Just pour cake mix and pudding mix—plus sprinkles—into a plastic resealable bag and zap your own mug cake when the mood for cake strikes!

1. Make the mug cake mix: In a large bowl, whisk together the cake mix, pudding mix, and sprinkles until combined. Pour into a large glass jar or a plastic resealable bag and seal.

2. Make a mug cake: In a small bowl, stir together the mix, milk, and oil. Mist an 8- to 12-ounce microwave-safe coffee mug with oil. Pour in the batter. Microwave on high for 1 minute 45 to 50 seconds (for a 700-watt oven), until the cake springs back.

3. Remove the mug from the microwave and let it rest for 4 to 5 minutes. Run a knife around the cake and turn it out to cool. Or, leave the cake in the mug and add a scoop of ice cream. Frost if desired, add more sprinkles, and serve immediately. (To make more than one mug cake, repeat steps 2 and 3, but only 1 mug cake can be microwaved at a time.)

Ice Cream Cone Cakes

MAKES 20 TO 24 CONE CAKES

PREP: 40 TO 45 MINUTES

BAKE: 20 TO 25 MINUTES

20 to 24 flat-bottomed wafer ice cream cones

CUPCAKE BATTER (CHOOSE ONE)

Basic Vanilla Cupcakes (page 268)

Matcha Mint Cupcakes (page 272)

Chocolate Sour Cream Cupcakes (page 275)

ASSEMBLY

1 recipe Vanilla Buttercream Frosting (page 351) and 1 recipe Chocolate Buttercream Frosting (page 355), chilled

Sugar sprinkles or miniature candies, for garnish

This is a favorite way to fool the eye, baking a bit of cake inside an ice cream cone and then frosting it to look like ice cream. To get that ruffled look of freshly scooped ice cream using frosting, chill the frosting first. Vary the shades of frosting from chocolate to vanilla to pink. What a conversation piece!

1. Place a rack in the center of the oven and preheat the oven to 350°F. Wrap a small square of aluminum foil around the base of each ice cream cone and stand the cones in the ungreased cups of two muffin tins.

2. Prepare your cupcake batter of choice and spoon or scoop about ¼ cup (about 1.5 ounces) batter into each cone, filling it no more than halfway.

3. Place the pans in the oven and bake until the cupcakes spring back when gently pressed in the middle, 20 to 25 minutes.

4. Let the cupcakes cool in the pans on wire racks for 30 minutes before frosting.

5. Remove the foil from the base of each cone. Using a 2-ounce ice cream scoop, pile frosting onto the top of each cupcake to resemble a generous scoop of ice cream. Press some sprinkles onto the frosting while it is soft. Place the frosted cones back in the pan and refrigerate to set—about 30 minutes—or until time to serve. Place the cones on a platter or serve right from the cupcake pan. Store, lightly covered, at room temperature for up to 2 days.

Cake Pops

CAKE

Vegetable oil spray or shortening, for greasing the pans

All-purpose flour, for dusting the pans

½ cup (3 ounces) semisweet chocolate chips

1 (15.25- or 16.25-ounce) package white cake mix

2 large eggs

1 cup water

½ cup sour cream

½ cup vegetable oil

¼ teaspoon almond extract

2 tablespoons sprinkles

BUTTERCREAM FROSTING FOR CAKE POPS

¼ cup (1½ ounces) semisweet chocolate chips

8 tablespoons (1 stick) unsalted butter, at room temperature

2 cups confectioners' sugar

1 to 2 tablespoons whole milk or half-and-half

1 teaspoon vanilla extract

Cake bites, cake pops, cake lollipops—all names for these little bites of crumbled cake and frosting dipped in melted confectionary coating and decorated with sprinkles. And while they might look complicated to make at home, rest assured, they are not. Plus, they're economical—you can make close to 50 pops from one box of mix and one recipe of frosting.

1. Make the cake: Place a rack in the center of the oven and preheat the oven to 350°F. Grease and flour two 9-inch round cake pans. Set the pans aside.

2. Place the chocolate chips in a microwave-safe medium bowl and microwave on high power until nearly melted, 40 to 45 seconds. Stir until the chocolate is completely melted. Set aside to cool slightly.

3. In a large mixing bowl, combine the cake mix, eggs, water, sour cream, oil, and almond extract. Beat with an electric mixer on low speed until blended, 30 seconds. Stop the machine and scrape down the bowl with a rubber spatula. Increase the mixer to medium and beat until smooth, about 1 minute.

4. Pour half of the batter into the bowl of melted chocolate and stir until combined. Pour the chocolate batter into one of the prepared cake pans, smoothing it out with a rubber spatula. Stir the sprinkles into the remaining plain cake batter until combined, and pour the batter into the other cake pan.

5. Place the pans in the oven and bake until the cakes spring back when gently pressed in the middle, 23 to 27 minutes.

6. Let the cakes cool in the pans on wire racks for 10 to 15 minutes. Run a dinner knife around the edge of each pan, then invert each layer onto a rack. Invert the layers again so they are right-side up and allow the cakes to cool completely, about 20 minutes longer.

7. Meanwhile, make the buttercream frosting: Place the chocolate chips in a small microwave-safe bowl and microwave on high power until nearly melted, 35 to 40 seconds. Stir until chocolate is completely melted. Set aside to cool slightly.

1 bag (8 ounces) white confectionery coating (candy wafers)

1 bag (8 ounces) chocolate-flavored confectionery coating (candy wafers)

4 teaspoons vegetable oil

50 lollipop sticks

½ cup sprinkles, for garnish

COOK'S NOTES:

Feel free to experiment with different shades of candy coatings. You can find the coatings at bakery supply stores and online, where you will also find the lollipop sticks and sprinkles.

Stand the cake pops upright in a piece of Styrofoam or a shoebox punched with holes.

8. In a medium mixing bowl, combine the butter, confectioners' sugar, 1 tablespoon of the milk, and vanilla and beat with an electric mixer on low speed until fluffy, about 30 seconds. Stop the machine and add a little more milk if needed to make the frosting spreadable. Increase the mixer speed to medium and beat until the frosting is light and fluffy, about 1 minute. Place half of the frosting in a clean medium bowl and stir in the melted chocolate until combined. Set both bowls of frosting aside.

9. With your hands, crumble the white cake into the bowl with the vanilla frosting. Stir and set aside. Crumble the chocolate cake into the bowl with chocolate frosting and stir to combine.

10. Roll both mixtures into rounds 1¼ to 1½ inches in diameter and arrange them on a sheet pan. Refrigerate for 1 hour to chill.

11. Remove the rounds from the refrigerator and roll them between your hands or on the counter to form smoother, more perfect balls. Return them to the refrigerator to chill for at least 3 hours more, until they are well chilled.

12. Assemble the cake pops: Pour the white candy wafers and the chocolate candy wafers into two separate microwave-safe medium bowls or 2-cup glass measuring cups. One at a time, microwave for 5 to 6 minutes on the defrost setting, stopping to stir a few times. Add 2 teaspoons vegetable oil to each bowl of melted candy and stir to combine well. Keep the melted candy warm while dipping. If the kitchen is warm, this is not a problem, but if it begins to harden, place the bowl in a small saucepan filled with 1 inch of simmering water, and stir until melted again.

13. Remove 6 or 7 cake balls from the fridge at a time and drop them, one by one, into the melted candy coating, using a small spatula or spoon to help coat the surface. Stab the coated balls with lollipop sticks, pushing them about halfway through. Lift the coated balls out of the melted candy and stand them upright. Immediately scatter sprinkles over each cake pop and let set. Store, uncovered and upright, in the fridge for up to 1 week.

Chocolate Chunk Muffins

MAKES EIGHTEEN TO TWENTY
2½-INCH MUFFINS

PREP: 10 TO 15 MINUTES

BAKE: 16 TO 20 MINUTES

Vegetable oil spray,
for misting the pans

1 (15.25-ounce) package
chocolate cake mix

5 tablespoons (half a
3.9-ounce package)
chocolate instant
pudding mix

¾ teaspoon
ground cinnamon

¼ teaspoon cayenne pepper
(optional)

3 large eggs

1 cup sour cream or
full-fat Greek yogurt

½ cup vegetable oil

10 ounces coarsely chopped
semisweet chocolate
or chocolate chunks
(about 2 cups)

2 teaspoons confectioners'
sugar, for dusting (optional)

*These chocolate muffins are big and sturdy, seriously packed with
chunks of chocolate, and with a surprise hint of cayenne and
cinnamon. They pair well with coffee or cold milk, and use whatever
bittersweet or semisweet chocolate you've got in the pantry.*

1. Place a rack in the center of the oven and preheat the oven
    to 375°F. Mist 18 to 20 cups of two muffin tins with oil or line
    the cups with paper liners. Set the pans aside.

2. In a large mixing bowl, stir together the cake mix, pudding mix,
    cinnamon, and cayenne (if using). Make a well in the center
    and add the eggs, sour cream, and oil. Stir with a fork to break
    up the eggs and blend the wet ingredients. Stir the wet and dry
    ingredients together using a wooden spoon just to combine,
    about 30 strokes. Fold in 1½ cups of the chocolate and stir
    another 10 strokes until just combined. Spoon or scoop ⅓ cup
    (2 ounces) batter into each prepared muffin cup, filling it three-
    quarters of the way full. Sprinkle the top of each muffin with
    3 or 4 chocolate chunks.

3. Place the pans in the oven and bake the muffins until
    they spring back when gently pressed in the middle,
    16 to 20 minutes.

4. Let the muffins cool in the pans on a wire rack for 5 minutes.
    Run a dinner knife around the edges of the muffins (or paper
    liners), lever the bottoms of the muffins up with the tip of
    the knife, then carefully pick them out of the cups with your
    fingertips. Cool on the wire rack for 15 minutes. Dust with the
    confectioners' sugar, if desired, and serve. Store, lightly covered,
    at room temperature for up to 5 days.

Coffee Cake Muffins

MAKES SIXTEEN TO EIGHTEEN
2½-INCH MUFFINS

PREP: 20 TO 25 MINUTES

BAKE: 20 TO 25 MINUTES

TOPPING

½ cup all-purpose flour

⅓ cup granulated sugar

⅓ cup (packed) light
brown sugar

1 tablespoon ground
cinnamon

½ teaspoon ground
cardamom (optional; see
Cook's Note)

4 tablespoons (½ stick)
unsalted butter, cut into
½-inch pieces

½ cup finely chopped pecans

MUFFINS

1 (15.25-ounce) package
yellow or butter cake mix

4 tablespoons (half a
3.4-ounce package) vanilla
instant pudding mix

3 large eggs

1 cup sour cream

½ cup vegetable oil

½ cup water

*When there is just one of you—or two—and you crave the rich
flavor of coffee cake, make these coffee cake muffins. Freeze
whatever you don't eat, then anytime you crave a coffee cake treat,
reheat in a 300°F oven just until warm, about 20 minutes.*

1. Place a rack in the center of the oven and preheat the oven to
    375°F. Line 16 to 18 cups of two muffin tins with paper liners.
    Set the pans aside.

2. Make the topping: In a medium mixing bowl, stir together the
    flour, granulated sugar, brown sugar, cinnamon, and cardamom
    (if using). Cut the butter into the mixture with two dinner
    knives or a pastry cutter until it resembles small peas.
    Stir in the pecans and set aside.

3. Make the muffins: In a large mixing bowl, stir together the
    cake mix and pudding mix. Make a well in the center and add
    the eggs, sour cream, oil, and water. Stir with a fork to break
    up the eggs and blend the wet ingredients. Stir the wet and dry
    ingredients together using a wooden spoon just to combine
    the batter, 30 to 40 strokes. The batter will be smooth. Spoon
    2 tablespoons batter into each lined muffin cup, filling it one-
    third of the way full. Using half of the topping, sprinkle over the
    batter. Spoon 2 to 3 more tablespoons batter into each cup so
    the pans are now more than two-thirds full. Sprinkle the tops
    with the remaining topping.

4. Place the pans in the oven and bake the muffins until they
    spring back when gently pressed in the middle and are golden
    brown, 20 to 25 minutes.

5. Let the muffins cool in the pans on wire racks for 5 minutes.
    Run a dinner knife around the edges of the paper liners, lever
    the bottoms of the muffins up with the tip of the knife, then
    carefully pick them out of the cups with your fingertips. Cool
    on the wire racks for 15 minutes before serving. Store, lightly
    covered, at room temperature for up to 5 days.

MAKES SIXTEEN TO EIGHTEEN
2½-INCH MUFFINS

PREP: 15 TO 20 MINUTES

BAKE: 18 TO 22 MINUTES

1 (15.25-ounce) package
yellow or butter cake mix

4 tablespoons (half a
3.4-ounce package) lemon
instant pudding mix

1 teaspoon grated
lemon zest

2 tablespoons fresh
lemon juice

3 large eggs

1 cup buttermilk, preferably
full-fat

⅔ cup vegetable oil

1½ tablespoons poppy seeds

Lemon Buttermilk Poppy Seed Muffins

*Put lemon and poppy seeds in a bread, muffin, or cake,
and I'm in. It's a classic combination, and there is
absolutely nothing new about the matchup, but it works.
And it's simple. So it feels right. Tastes even better!*

1. Place a rack in the center of the oven and preheat the oven to
    375°F. Line 16 to 18 cups of two muffin tins with paper liners.
    Set the pans aside.

2. In a large mixing bowl, stir together the cake mix, pudding mix,
    and lemon zest. Make a well in the center and add the lemon
    juice, eggs, buttermilk, oil, and poppy seeds. Stir with a fork
    to break up the eggs and blend the wet ingredients. Stir the
    wet and dry ingredients together using a wooden spoon just
    to combine the batter, about 30 strokes. Spoon or scoop ⅓ cup
    (2 ounces) batter into each lined muffin cup, filling it three-
    quarters of the way full.

3. Place the pans in the oven and bake the muffins until they are
    golden brown and spring back when gently pressed in the
    middle, 18 to 22 minutes.

4. Let the muffins cool in the pans on wire racks for 5 minutes.
    Run a dinner knife around the edges of the muffin liners, lever
    the bottoms of the muffins up with the tip of the knife, then
    carefully pick them out of the cups with your fingertips. Cool
    on the wire racks for 15 minutes before serving. Store, lightly
    covered, at room temperature for up to 5 days.

Apple Butter Muffins

MAKES EIGHTEEN TO TWENTY
2½-INCH MUFFINS

PREP: 10 TO 15 MINUTES

BAKE: 16 TO 20 MINUTES

Vegetable oil spray, for
misting the pans

OAT TOPPING

⅓ cup quick-cooking oats

¼ cup (packed) light
brown sugar

¼ cup finely chopped pecans

½ teaspoon ground
cinnamon

3 tablespoons cold unsalted
butter, cut into ½-inch
pieces

MUFFINS

1 (15.25-ounce) package
yellow or butter cake mix

4 tablespoons (half a
3.4-ounce package) vanilla
instant pudding mix

3 large eggs

1¼ cups apple butter,
homemade (see page 369)
or store-bought

½ cup buttermilk, preferably
whole milk

8 tablespoons (1 stick)
unsalted butter, melted and
cooled

*There is nothing quite like the flavor of apple butter to say fall!
If you have a jar of apple butter—or pumpkin butter—this is
a perfect way to use it. And if you don't, I share how to make
spiced apple butter from applesauce on page 369. Apple butter
isn't really butter—it just has the rich, spreadable consistency
of butter since it's been cooked down until creamy.*

1. Place a rack in the center of the oven and preheat the oven to
   375°F. Mist 18 to 20 cups of two muffin tins with oil. Set the
   pans aside.

2. Make the oat topping: In a small bowl, stir together the oats,
   brown sugar, pecans, and cinnamon. Cut the butter into the
   sugar mixture using two dinner knives or a pastry cutter until
   the mixture is crumbly.

3. Make the muffins: In a large mixing bowl, stir together the
   cake mix and pudding mix. Make a well in the center and add
   the eggs, apple butter, buttermilk, and melted butter. Stir with
   a fork to break up the eggs and blend the wet ingredients.
   Stir the wet and dry ingredients together with a wooden spoon
   until just combined, about 30 strokes. Spoon or scoop ⅓ cup
   (2 ounces) batter into each prepared muffin cup, filling it three-
   quarters of the way full. Sprinkle 2 teaspoons of the topping
   over each muffin.

4. Place the pans in the oven and bake the muffins until
   they spring back when gently pressed in the middle, 16 to
   20 minutes.

5. Let the muffins cool in the pans on a wire rack for 5 minutes.
   Run a dinner knife around the edges of the muffins, lever
   the bottoms of the muffins up with the tip of the knife, then
   carefully pick them out of the cups with your fingertips.
   Cool on the wire racks for 15 minutes before serving. Store,
   lightly covered, at room temperature for up to 5 days.

Pear and Cardamom Muffins

MAKES SIXTEEN TO EIGHTEEN
2½-INCH MUFFINS

PREP: 20 TO 25 MINUTES

BAKE AND BROIL: 22 TO
24 MINUTES

Vegetable oil spray,
for misting the pans

COCONUT TOPPING

½ cup (packed)
light brown sugar

½ cup finely chopped
pecans or almonds

½ teaspoon ground
cinnamon

3 tablespoons half-and-half

1 cup unsweetened shredded
coconut

4 tablespoons (½ stick)
unsalted butter,
melted and cooled

MUFFINS

2 large pears,
such as Bartlett

1 (15.25-ounce) package
yellow or butter cake mix

4 tablespoons (half a
3.4-ounce package) vanilla
instant pudding mix

1½ teaspoons ground
cinnamon

I'm always looking for more ways to use pears in cooking and baking, especially in the fall when so many varieties of pears come into season. I appreciate their gentle, sweet flavor, which marries well with the cinnamon and cardamom and as well as the coconut in this recipe. Bartlett pears are a nice pear for baking because they have good flavor and retain their shape. Other pears like Comice will work, as long as they are firm and not overripe.

1. Place a rack in the center of the oven and preheat the oven to 375°F. Mist 16 to 18 cups of two muffin tins with oil or line the cups with paper liners. Set the pans aside.

2. Make the coconut topping: In a small bowl, combine the brown sugar, nuts, cinnamon, half-and-half, and coconut. Stir in the melted butter to combine. Set aside.

3. Make the muffins: Peel and core the pears, then cut them into ½-inch pieces to yield about 3 cups. Set aside.

4. In a large mixing bowl, stir together the cake mix, pudding mix, cinnamon, and cardamom. Make a well in the center and add the eggs, coconut milk, and oil. Stir with a fork to break up the eggs and blend the wet ingredients. Stir the wet and dry ingredients together using a wooden spoon just to combine the batter, about 30 strokes. Fold in 2 cups of the pears. Spoon or scoop ⅓ cup (2 ounces) batter into each prepared muffin cup, filling it three-quarters of the way full. Divide the remaining 1 cup pears on top of the batter, pushing the pieces into the batter.

5. Place the pans in the oven and bake the muffins until they spring back when gently pressed in the middle, 20 to 21 minutes.

6. Transfer the pans to wire racks while you preheat the broiler to high. Set a rack at least 10 inches away from the broiler element.

RECIPE AND INGREDIENTS CONTINUED

½ teaspoon ground cardamom or ginger

3 large eggs

1 cup full-fat or light canned coconut milk

⅔ cup vegetable oil

7. Spoon the topping onto the baked muffins, almost to the edges. The topping is loose, but you can push it together with your fingers to help it to stay on the muffins. Place the pans in the oven and broil the topping until it turns a deep golden brown, 2 to 3 minutes. Don't let it get too brown.

8. Let the muffins cool in the pans on the wire racks for 5 minutes. Run a dinner knife around the edges of the muffins (or the paper liners), lever the bottoms of the muffins up with the tip of the knife, then carefully pick them out of the cups with your fingertips. Cool on the wire rack for 15 minutes before serving. Store, lightly covered, at room temperature for up to 5 days.

Stash Some Muffins in the Freezer

Place cooled muffins in a plastic resealable freezer bag in the freezer for up to 3 months. You can pull frozen muffins from the bag and reheat in a low oven until warmed through or wrap individually in paper towels and microwave on high power for 10 seconds, or until warm.

Vegetable oil spray,
for misting the pans

1 (15.25-ounce) package
yellow or butter cake mix

4 tablespoons (half a
3.4-ounce package) vanilla
instant pudding mix

3 large eggs

10 tablespoons (1¼ sticks)
unsalted butter, melted
and cooled

1 cup full-fat or light canned
coconut milk or whole milk

2 teaspoons vanilla extract

1 cup fresh blueberries

1 cup frozen wild
blueberries
(see Cook's Note)

COOK'S NOTE:
Look for bags of frozen
wild blueberries (which
are smaller than regular
blueberries). You can
measure what you need and
return the bag to the freezer.

The Best Blueberry Muffins

We tested and retested this recipe, searching for big blueberry flavor, which in the beginning we didn't get from just fresh berries. But when we added those small frozen wild blueberries? Bingo. I fold them into the batter while they're still a little frozen—call me impatient for not waiting on them to thaw, perhaps—but doing this keeps the batter from turning purple.

1. Place a rack in the center of the oven and preheat the oven to 375°F. Mist 18 to 20 cups of two muffin tins with oil. Set the pans aside.

2. In a large mixing bowl, stir together the cake mix and pudding mix. Make a well in the center and add the eggs, melted butter, coconut milk, and vanilla. Stir with a fork to break up the eggs and blend the wet ingredients. Stir the wet and dry ingredients together with a wooden spoon just combined, about 30 strokes. Fold in the fresh and frozen blueberries until just combined. Spoon or scoop ⅓ cup (2 ounces) batter into each prepared muffin cup, filling it three-quarters of the way full.

3. Place the pans in the oven and bake the muffins until they spring back when gently pressed in the middle, 20 to 24 minutes.

4. Let the muffins cool in the pans on a wire rack for 5 minutes. Run a dinner knife around the edges of the muffins, lever the bottoms of the muffins up with the tip of the knife, then carefully pick them out of the cups with your fingertips. Serve warm or place on the wire rack to cool for 15 minutes longer. Store, lightly covered, at room temperature for up to 5 days.

Cookie Pops
(page 309)

Cookies, Bars, and Bites

Everybody is crazy about cookies. And using a cake mix makes the process easier because there's no measuring of flour or sugar, which means you have more time to get creative. So bake these peanut butter or chocolate chip drop cookies, cut-out sugar or gingerbread cookies, fruit bars, and possibly even petit fours when you feel like having fun and making someone happy.

Basic Sugar Cookies

MAKES SIXTEEN TO EIGHTEEN
2- TO 3-INCH COOKIES

PREP: 20 TO 25 MINUTES

BAKE: 8 TO 12 MINUTES
PER BATCH

1 (15.25-ounce) package
yellow or butter cake mix

6 tablespoons unsalted
butter, melted and cooled

1 large egg

1 teaspoon vanilla extract,
½ teaspoon almond extract,
or 2 teaspoons grated
lemon zest

1 to 2 tablespoons
all-purpose flour, if needed
for rolling

1 large egg white

Sugar sprinkles,
for decorating

COOK'S NOTE:

If you like to bake cookies
in a convection oven,
reduce the temp to 350°F
and reduce the baking
time by a few minutes.

*A quick sugar cookie recipe is a lifesaver during the holidays . . .
or on any day. And this method is so simple I'm a little embarrassed
to call it a "recipe." It's what you do with it that counts—roll
and cut into your favorite shapes. Or roll balls in coarse sugar
before baking. Form the dough into a log, then slice and bake.
Or turn them into snickerdoodles by adding cinnamon to the sugar
(see below). Or give these cookies a completely new look by folding
in ⅓ cup of sprinkles before baking. The possibilities are limitless!*

1. Place a rack in the center of the oven and preheat the oven
   to 375°F. Have ready two ungreased cookie sheets.

2. In a large mixing bowl, combine the cake mix, butter, egg,
   and vanilla. Beat with an electric mixer on low speed for
   30 seconds. Stop the machine and scrape down the sides of
   the bowl with a rubber spatula. Increase the mixer speed to
   medium and beat until the mixture comes together into a sticky
   ball, 30 to 45 seconds.

3. With a lightly floured rolling pin, roll the dough to ¼- to
   ⅜-inch thickness on a lightly floured board. Use cookie cutters
   to stamp out the shapes and place them spaced 2 inches apart
   on one cookie sheet. (You can reroll the dough scraps once and
   cut out more cookies.) Brush the cookies with egg white, and
   decorate with the sprinkles.

4. Place one pan in the oven at a time. Bake until the edges of the
   cookies are golden brown, 8 to 10 minutes for smaller cookies
   and 10 to 12 minutes for larger.

5. Let the cookies rest on the cookie sheet for 1 minute, then
   remove to wire racks with a metal spatula to cool completely,
   about 20 minutes. Store, lightly covered, at room temperature
   for 1 week.

   SNICKERDOODLES: Make the dough for Basic Sugar Cookies
   as directed. In a small bowl, stir together 1 tablespoon ground
   cinnamon (or to taste) and ¼ cup granulated sugar. Roll the
   dough balls into this mixture before baking as directed.

For nearly 4 dozen cookies, form ¾-inch (½-ounce) balls and bake 6 to 7 minutes.

For 2 dozen cookies, form 1½-inch (1-ounce) balls and bake 8 to 9 minutes.

For about a dozen cookies, form 2½-inch (2-ounce) balls and bake 10 to 12 minutes.

For 8 large 4-inch cookies, form 3-inch (3-ounce) balls and bake 12 to 14 minutes.

A FEW TIPS FOR BAKING CAKE MIX COOKIES

No need to grease the baking sheet unless the recipe calls for it.

•

Use a scoop and a scale to portion dough if you want cookies the same size.

•

Store chewy cookies in a tightly covered container and crisp ones lightly covered.

•

Freeze baked cookies in plastic resealable bags for up to 6 months. Or freeze the dough up to 1 month, thaw, and bake.

Old-Fashioned Drop Sugar Cookies

Make the dough for Basic Sugar Cookies, but increase the amount of butter to 12 tablespoons, which should be melted and cooled. Add 1 tablespoon flour to the dough if it seems sticky. Drop about twelve 2-inch (1½ ounce) balls of the dough spaced 2 inches apart on two cookie sheets. Place one pan in the oven at a time. Bake until the edges are golden brown, 9 to 11 minutes.

GLUTEN-FREE SLICE-AND-BAKE SUGAR COOKIES: Make the dough for Basic Sugar Cookies but use a 15-ounce package gluten-free yellow cake mix, increase the butter to 8 tablespoons (1 stick) butter and increase the vanilla to 1 tablespoon. Form the dough into a log about 10 inches long and 2 inches in diameter, wrap in parchment, and chill. Cut into slices ½ inch thick, sprinkle with sugar, and bake at 350°F for 9 to 13 minutes.

GLUTEN-FREE CHOCOLATE SLICE-AND-BAKE SUGAR COOKIES: Make the dough as directed in Gluten-Free Slice-and-Bake Sugar Cookies but add ⅓ cup chopped semisweet chocolate, melted, and fold in ½ cup mini semisweet chocolate chips. Bake as directed.

Decorating Icing

In a bowl, stir together 1 cup confectioners' sugar and 2 tablespoons water. Add food coloring, if desired, taking care only to add a drop at a time, because it goes a long way. The icing needs to be thick enough to set up but thin enough to spread on a cookie with a small knife. Or, you can place it in a clean squeeze bottle and pipe it onto cookies. You can outline cookies in icing, create patterns, or add dots. And for an added touch, sprinkle the wet icing with colored sugar sprinkles. Let iced cookies rest for 1 hour before you pack and store them.

Cookie Pops

MAKES ABOUT FORTY 2-INCH
COOKIES

PREP: 40 TO 45 MINUTES

BAKE: 8 TO 10 MINUTES
PER BATCH

1 (15.25-ounce) package
yellow or butter cake mix

12 tablespoons (1½ sticks)
unsalted butter,
at room temperature

1 large egg

1 teaspoon vanilla extract

1 tablespoon all-purpose
flour, if needed

¾ cup sprinkles

40 wooden craft sticks

*If you are the kind of person who likes to roam the aisles at a craft
store searching for rainy day projects, you probably already have
wooden "craft" sticks—aka Popsicle sticks—for this recipe. And
you probably already have a good stash of sprinkles, too. Meaning
cookie pops are ready to be made, decorated, and shared!*

1. Place a rack in the center of the oven and preheat the oven to
   375°F. Have ready two ungreased cookie sheets.

2. In a large mixing bowl, combine the cake mix, butter, egg,
   and vanilla. Blend with an electric mixer on low speed for
   30 seconds. Stop the machine and scrape down the sides of
   the bowl with a rubber spatula. Increase the mixer speed to
   medium and beat until the mixture comes together into a sticky
   ball, 30 to 45 seconds. If the mixture doesn't pull together,
   add the tablespoon of flour and beat until combined.

3. Divide the dough into forty 1-tablespoon (½-ounce) balls.
   Pour the sprinkles into a shallow bowl and roll the balls in the
   sprinkles, covering them. Place 12 balls about 2 inches apart on
   each of the cookie sheets.

4. Place one pan in the oven at a time. Bake until the edges of the
   cookies are golden brown, 8 to 10 minutes.

5. Let the cookies cool on the sheet on a wire rack for 5 minutes,
   then push a craft stick into the center of each cookie. Let the
   cookie pops rest on the pan a couple of minutes more, then
   carefully transfer them to wire racks to cool completely, 25 to
   30 minutes.

6. Repeat with the remaining dough, letting the pans cool to the
   touch before adding more balls of dough. Store, lightly covered,
   at room temperature for up to 5 days.

Slice-and-Bake Toffee Maple Cookies

MAKES THIRTY TO THIRTY-TWO 2¾-INCH COOKIES

PREP: 10 TO 15 MINUTES

BAKE: 10 TO 13 MINUTES PER BATCH

1 (15.25-ounce) package yellow or butter cake mix

12 tablespoons (1½ sticks) unsalted butter, at room temperature

1 large egg

1 teaspoon vanilla extract

½ teaspoon maple extract

¼ cup finely chopped pecans

¼ cup toffee bits

Jazz Up a Slice-and-Bake Cookie

Instead of the maple flavoring, pecan, and toffee bits, you could add grated lemon zest and chopped almonds and/or pistachios. Or, a little coconut extract along with toasted shredded coconut and mini chocolate chips.

Chewy, full of crispy pecans and crunchy toffee bits, these maple cookies are a perfect medley of textures. I love how the dough can be made ahead, rolled in wax paper, and chilled until time to slice and bake—meaning that as long as you have a log frozen and waiting, these cookies are ready to please anytime!

1. In a large mixing bowl, combine the cake mix, butter, egg, vanilla, and maple extract. Beat with an electric mixer on low speed for 30 seconds. Stop the machine and scrape down the sides of the bowl with a rubber spatula. Increase the mixer speed to medium and beat until the mixture comes together into a sticky ball, 30 to 45 seconds. Add the pecans and toffee bits and beat for 15 seconds longer.

2. Turn the dough out onto an 18-inch sheet of parchment or wax paper. Form the dough into a 14-inch log, about 2 inches in diameter. Roll the log up in the paper and twist the ends to seal. Roll the log of dough back and forth on the counter to smooth it. Chill the log in the refrigerator for 1 hour.

3. Place a rack in the center of the oven and preheat the oven to 375°F. Have ready two ungreased cookie sheets.

4. Slice the chilled dough into rounds ¼ to ½ inch thick. Place 10 to 12 rounds 2 inches apart on each cookie sheet.

5. Place one pan in the oven at a time. Bake until the cookies are lightly browned around the edges but a little soft in the center, 10 to 13 minutes.

6. Let the cookies rest on the cookie sheet for 1 minute, then remove them with a metal spatula to wire racks to cool completely, about 20 minutes.

7. Repeat with the remaining dough, letting the pan cool to the touch before adding the last slices of dough. Store, lightly covered, at room temperature for up to 5 days.

Cashew Thumbprints

MAKES ABOUT FORTY 2-INCH COOKIES

PREP: 25 TO 30 MINUTES

BAKE: 10 TO 12 MINUTES PER BATCH

1 (15.25-ounce) package yellow or butter cake mix

3 tablespoons all-purpose flour

12 tablespoons (1½ sticks) unsalted butter, at room temperature

1 large egg

2 teaspoons vanilla extract

1 cup finely chopped lightly salted cashews, pecans, or almonds

1 cup of your favorite jam, such as apricot, fig, strawberry, or marmalade

COOK'S NOTE:

If you use preserves (which is chunkier than jam), pulse briefly in the food processor to finely chop the fruit.

To experience the simple joy of baking, press your thumb into a soft ball of dough. It is no surprise that thumbprints are so many bakers' favorite, comfy, and homespun cookie, and just right for cleaning out all the half-empty jars of jam in your fridge!

1. Place a rack in the center of the oven and preheat the oven to 375°F. Have ready two ungreased cookie sheets.

2. In a large mixing bowl, combine the cake mix, flour, butter, egg, and vanilla. Beat with an electric mixer on low for 30 seconds. Stop the machine and scrape down the sides of the bowl with a rubber spatula. Increase the mixer speed to medium and beat until the mixture comes together into a sticky ball, 30 to 45 seconds.

3. Drop sixteen to twenty 1-inch (about ½-ounce) balls of the dough spaced 2 inches apart on each of the cookie sheets. Place the cashews in a small bowl. Pick up each ball of dough and roll it on all sides in the nuts to cover. Return it to the pan and press down gently with your thumb to form a thumbprint. Spoon a teaspoon of jam into the thumbprint.

4. Place one pan in the oven at a time. Bake until the cookies are golden brown, 10 to 12 minutes.

5. Let the cookies rest on the cookie sheet for 1 minute, then remove with a metal spatula to wire racks to cool completely, about 20 minutes.

6. Repeat with the remaining dough, letting the pans cool to the touch before adding more cookies. Store, lightly covered, at room temperature for up to 5 days.

Mix-and-Match Thumbprint Cookie Magic

Pecans + peach jam or fig preserves

Almonds + raspberry preserves or lemon curd

Walnuts + strawberry jam or blueberry jelly

Cashews + Banana Jam (see page 120) or apricot preserves

Pistachios + plum jam or orange marmalade

Peanut Butter Cookies

MAKES EIGHTEEN TO TWENTY
3-INCH COOKIES

PREP: 10 TO 15 MINUTES

BAKE: 12 TO 14 MINUTES

1 (15.25-ounce) package
yellow or butter cake mix

2 large eggs

1 cup peanut butter
(creamy or crunchy)

8 tablespoons (1 stick)
unsalted butter, melted
and cooled

1 teaspoon vanilla extract

¼ cup sugar, for rolling
(see Cook's Note)

COOK'S NOTE:
Instead of the usual
granulated sugar, upgrade to
a vanilla-scented sugar such
as one made by Beautiful
Briny Sea or make one
yourself by covering a vanilla
bean in granulated sugar and
storing in a sealed container
in a dark spot in your pantry
for a couple of weeks.

Whether you bit into your first peanut butter cookie in a school lunchroom or in your grandmother's kitchen, this cookie forms deep memories. Here's how to make it from a cake mix for those busy times, even with the distinctive crosshatch marks in the center!

1. Place a rack in the center of the oven and preheat the oven to 375°F. Have ready two ungreased cookie sheets.

2. In a large mixing bowl, combine the cake mix, eggs, peanut butter, melted butter, and vanilla. Beat with an electric mixer on low speed for 30 seconds. Stop the machine and scrape down the sides of the bowl with a rubber spatula. Increase the mixer speed to medium and beat until the mixture comes together into a ball, 30 to 45 seconds.

3. Divide the dough into eighteen to twenty 2-inch (1½-ounce) balls. Place the sugar in a small bowl and roll the balls of the dough in the sugar. Arrange the balls, spaced 2 inches apart, on the cookie sheets. Lightly press down on the center of each ball with a fork. Turn the fork 90 degrees and press down again to form a crosshatch pattern.

4. Place one pan in the oven at a time. Bake until the cookies are golden brown, 12 to 14 minutes.

5. Let the cookies rest on the cookie sheet for 1 minute, then remove with a metal spatula to wire racks to cool completely, about 20 minutes. Store, lightly covered, at room temperature for up to 1 week.

Almond Sandwich Cookies

MAKES ABOUT FIFTY-FOUR
2-INCH SANDWICH COOKIES

PREP: 40 TO 45 MINUTES

BAKE: 8 TO 10 MINUTES
PER BATCH

COOKIES

**1 cup sliced almonds
(3 ounces)**

**1 (16-ounce) package
angel food cake mix**

½ cup water

**1½ teaspoons
almond extract**

**2 cups sweetened
shredded coconut**

FILLING CHOICES

**Half recipe of Chocolate
Buttercream Frosting
(page 355), Small-Batch
Chocolate Ganache Topping
(page 362), or half recipe of
Vanilla Buttercream Frosting
(page 351)**

*You would never guess that these delightfully sophisticated
cookies start with an angel food cake mix! What began
as a simple retest of an old macaroon recipe ended up
being a completely new recipe filled with chocolate.*

1. Make the cookies: Place a rack in the center of the oven and preheat the oven to 350°F. Line two cookie sheets with parchment paper and set aside.

2. Grind half of the almonds by pulsing in a food processor for 15 to 20 seconds and set aside. Coarsely chop the other half and set aside with the ground almonds.

3. In a large mixing bowl, combine the cake mix, water, and almond extract. Beat with an electric mixer on low speed for 15 seconds. Stop and scrape down the sides of the bowl. Increase the mixer speed to medium and beat, about 1 minute. Fold in the ground and chopped almonds and the coconut.

4. Drop about twenty ½-tablespoon (¼-ounce) balls of dough spaced 2 inches apart on each of the cookie sheets.

5. Place one pan in the oven at a time. Bake until the edges of the cookies are lightly golden brown, 8 to 10 minutes.

6. Remove the pan from the oven and slide the parchment with cookies onto a cooling rack. Let the cookies cool on the parchment for 5 minutes, then remove with a metal spatula to wire racks to cool completely, about 20 minutes.

7. Repeat with the remaining dough, baking about 5 batches and letting the pans cool before adding more cookies. To reuse parchment, scrape off cookie bits before adding more dough.

8. Fill the sandwich cookies: Place a teaspoon of frosting on the flat side of one cookie and sandwich it with the flat side of a second cookie. Store, tightly covered, at room temperature for up to 5 days.

Brown Butter Chocolate Chip Cookies

MAKES EIGHTEEN TO TWENTY
3-INCH COOKIES

PREP: 10 TO 15 MINUTES

BAKE: 11 TO 13 MINUTES
PER BATCH

10 tablespoons (1¼ sticks)
unsalted butter

1 (15.25-ounce) package
yellow or butter cake mix

⅓ cup quick-cooking or
instant unflavored oats

½ teaspoon ground
cinnamon

2 large eggs

1 teaspoon vanilla extract

½ cup chopped walnuts or
pecans (optional)

½ cup (3 ounces)
bittersweet chocolate chips
or chunks

Now, this is a fabulous cookie because everything you need is likely already in your pantry. Aside from opening a box of mix, all you need to do is melt butter and let it brown. It's amazing how such a simple technique yields such deep and delicious results.

1. In a small heavy saucepan, heat the butter over low heat until melted, 1 to 2 minutes. Increase the heat just a bit and cook until the butter begins to brown, 7 to 8 minutes. Remove from the heat and strain the browned butter into a small bowl to cool.

2. Place a rack in the center of the oven and preheat the oven to 375°F. Have ready two ungreased cookie sheets.

3. In a large mixing bowl, combine the cake mix, oats, cinnamon, eggs, vanilla, and the cooled browned butter. Beat with an electric mixer on low speed for 30 seconds. Stop the machine and scrape down the sides of the bowl with a rubber spatula. Increase the mixer speed to medium and beat until the mixture comes together into a sticky ball, 30 to 45 seconds. Fold in the nuts (if using) and chocolate.

4. Drop 2-inch (1½-ounce) balls of the dough spaced 2 inches apart on the cookie sheets.

5. Place one pan in the oven at a time. Bake until the edges of the cookies are golden brown but the cookies are still soft to the touch, 10 to 13 minutes.

6. Let the cookies rest on the cookie sheet for 1 minute, then remove with a metal spatula to wire racks to cool completely, about 20 minutes. Store, lightly covered, at room temperature for up to 5 days.

CHOCOLATE CHIP ICE CREAM COOKIE SANDWICHES: Bake and cool the cookies as directed. Remove 1 pint of chocolate or caramel ice cream from the freezer to soften. Place 2 generous tablespoons of ice cream on the flat side of one cookie and sandwich it with a second cookie. Wrap each cookie sandwich in plastic wrap and freeze until firm, about 30 minutes. Makes 9 or 10 cookie sandwiches.

Double Chocolate Drop Cookies

MAKES ABOUT TWENTY 3-INCH
COOKIES

PREP: 10 TO 15 MINUTES

BAKE: 11 TO 14 MINUTES
PER BATCH

1 (15.25-ounce) package
chocolate cake mix

2 large egg yolks

6 tablespoons (¾ stick)
unsalted butter, melted
and cooled

½ cup Nutella
(chocolate-hazelnut spread)

3 tablespoons water or
brewed strong coffee

Pinch of salt

1 cup (5 ounces) chopped
bittersweet chocolate or
semisweet chocolate chunks

These easy cookies are fabulous either on their own or turned into
ice cream cookie sandwiches covered in sprinkles (see opposite).
I love their chewiness, which is likely due to the addition of Nutella, a
powerful and yummy flavor add-in that offers quick flavor and texture.

1.   Place a rack in the center of the oven and preheat the oven to
     375°F. Have ready two ungreased cookie sheets.

2.   In a large mixing bowl, combine the cake mix, egg yolks, melted
     butter, Nutella, water, and salt. Beat with an electric mixer on
     low speed for 30 seconds. Stop the machine and scrape down
     the sides of the bowl with a rubber spatula. Increase the mixer
     speed to medium and beat until the mixture comes together
     into a sticky ball, 30 to 45 seconds. Fold in the chocolate.

3.   Drop 2-inch (1½-ounce) balls of the dough spaced 2 inches
     apart on the cookie sheets.

4.   Place one pan in the oven at a time. Bake until the edges of the
     cookies are crispy but the cookies are still soft to the touch,
     11 to 14 minutes.

5.   Let the cookies rest on the cookie sheet for 1 minute, then
     remove with a metal spatula to wire racks to cool completely,
     about 20 minutes. Store, lightly covered, at room temperature
     for up to 5 days.

Ice Cream Sprinkle Cookie Sandwiches

Bake and cool the cookies as directed. Remove 1 pint of vanilla ice cream from the freezer to soften. Place 2 generous tablespoons of ice cream on the flat side of one cookie and sandwich it with a second cookie. Scatter sprinkles around the sides to stick to the ice cream. Wrap each cookie sandwich in plastic wrap and freeze until firm, about 30 minutes. Makes about 10 cookie sandwiches.

Easy Chocolate Walnut Cookies

MAKES ABOUT TWENTY 3-INCH
COOKIES

PREP: 10 TO 15 MINUTES

BAKE: 11 TO 14 MINUTES
PER BATCH

1 (15.25-ounce) package
chocolate cake mix

1 tablespoon unsweetened
cocoa powder

2 large eggs

½ cup vegetable oil

1 teaspoon vanilla
extract (optional)

1 cup semisweet
chocolate chips

½ cup coarsely chopped
walnuts

*This super-simple recipe was inspired by some cookies made by
Mart Stovall of Nashville. Mart adds ½ cup vegetable oil, 2 eggs,
and 1 cup chocolate chips to a cake mix to make his easy cookies,
and I added the cocoa and walnuts. It's such a nice blueprint way
of making chocolate cookies from a mix, which you could vary
by using a light olive oil and possibly pecans if you have them.*

1. Place a rack in the center of the oven and preheat the oven to
    375°F. Have ready two ungreased cookie sheets.

2. In a large mixing bowl, combine the cake mix, cocoa, eggs, oil,
    and vanilla (if using). Beat with an electric mixer on low speed
    for 30 seconds. Stop the machine and scrape down the sides
    of the bowl with a rubber spatula. Increase the mixer speed to
    medium and beat until the mixture comes together into a ball,
    30 to 45 seconds. Fold in the chocolate chips and walnuts.

3. Drop 2-inch (1½-ounce) balls of the dough spaced 2 inches
    apart on the cookie sheets.

4. Place one pan in the oven at a time. Bake until the edges of the
    cookies are crispy but the centers are still soft, 11 to 14 minutes.

5. Let the cookies rest on the cookie sheet for 1 minute, then
    remove with a metal spatula to wire racks to cool completely,
    about 20 minutes. Store, lightly covered, at room temperature
    for up to 5 days.

Gingerbread People

MAKES ABOUT TWENTY-FOUR
4-INCH COOKIES

PREP: 15 TO 20 MINUTES

CHILL: 2 HOURS

BAKE: 6 TO 8 MINUTES
PER BATCH

COOKIES

1 (15.25-ounce) package
butter cake mix

1 teaspoon ground ginger

½ teaspoon ground
cinnamon

½ teaspoon ground cloves

1 large egg

4 tablespoons (½ stick)
unsalted butter, at room
temperature

¼ cup molasses

1 tablespoon grated orange
zest (from 1 medium orange)

All-purpose flour, for rolling

GLAZE AND DECORATION

4 to 5 teaspoons water

1 cup confectioners' sugar

3 tablespoons sprinkles,
currants, or mini semisweet
chocolate chips, for eyes or
buttons (optional)

No cookie says the winter holidays better than gingerbread, or possibly, gingerbread people! The cutter I used for stamping these cookies is about 4 inches tall. So if your cutter is larger, that's fine, but count on fewer cookies. You can also cut the dough into rounds, stars, diamonds, or whatever shape you like.

1. Make the cookies: In a large mixing bowl, stir together the cake mix, ginger, cinnamon, and cloves. Add the egg, butter, molasses, and orange zest. Beat with an electric mixer on low speed for 30 seconds. Stop the machine and scrape down the sides of the bowl with a rubber spatula. Increase the mixer speed to medium and beat until the mixture begins to come together into a ball, 45 seconds to 1 minute. It will be crumbly.

2. Turn the dough out onto a piece of plastic wrap. With your hands, work the dough into a disk. Wrap the dough and refrigerate it for 2 hours to chill.

3. Place a rack in the center of the oven and preheat the oven to 400°F. Line two cookie sheets with parchment paper.

4. Divide the dough into two pieces. Wrap one half back in the plastic wrap and return it to the refrigerator. Place the other half on a counter dusted with 1 tablespoon flour. Press down on the dough with your hands to flatten it as much as possible. Lightly flour a rolling pin and gently roll out the dough from the center to the edges until it is ⅛ to ¼ inch thick. Dip a cookie cutter in flour and cut out shapes. Slide a long metal spatula underneath the shapes and place them on the cookie sheets about 2 inches apart. Collect the dough scraps, form them into a ball, wrap in plastic, and place in the fridge.

5. Place one pan in the oven at a time. Bake until the edges of the cookies are crispy but the centers are still a little soft, 6 to 8 minutes. If you want a crispier cookie, one that is more reminiscent of a gingersnap, bake until the edges have browned, 9 to 10 minutes.

CONTINUED

GLUTEN-FREE GINGERBREAD PEOPLE: Make the dough for Gingerbread People, but use a 15-ounce package gluten-free yellow cake mix, increase the ginger to 1¼ teaspoons, decrease the butter to 2 tablespoons, add 2 tablespoons vegetable shortening (this will make the cookies softer), and replace the orange zest with 1 to 2 teaspoons vanilla extract. Use rice flour for rolling out the dough. Bake at 350°F for 9 to 11 minutes. Makes 18 cookies.

COOK'S NOTES: For crispy but still chewy cookies, use as little flour as possible when cutting and rolling out the cookies—just enough to keep the dough from sticking to the counter.

Work quickly to keep the dough cold. If the dough is soft and your kitchen is hot, chill the cookie sheet of cut cookies before baking.

6. Let the cookies rest on the cookie sheet for 1 minute, then remove with a metal spatula to wire racks to cool completely, about 20 minutes.

7. Repeat with the remaining dough. (It will take rerolling the dough about 3 times to stamp out all these cookies. Discard any remaining scraps after you have cut out the cookies you need.) Be sure to let the pans cool to the touch before adding more cookies. You can reuse the parchment paper from earlier batches.

8. Meanwhile, make the glaze: In a small glass bowl, stir the water into the confectioners' sugar until the glaze is smooth and spreadable.

9. Spread the icing over the top of the cooled cookies or pour the icing into a squeeze bottle and use the icing like glue to decorate the cookies with sprinkles, currants, or mini chocolate chips. Let the glazed cookies set for 20 minutes before serving. Store, lightly covered, at room temperature for up to 5 days.

Brown Butter Blondies

MAKES SIXTEEN 2-INCH
SQUARES

PREP: 20 TO 25 MINUTES

BAKE: 19 TO 23 MINUTES

12 tablespoons (1½ sticks)
unsalted butter

1 (15.25-ounce) package
butter cake mix

¼ cup (packed)
dark brown sugar

Pinch of salt

2 large eggs

1½ teaspoons vanilla extract

¼ cup chopped pecans

COOK'S NOTE:
If you miss chocolate,
scatter ¼ cup mini
semisweet chocolate
chips on top when you
add the pecans.

Martha's husband, Rusty, generously toted many of this book's recipes to work with him, but he would not take these blondies. He said they were too good to share. And I agree. They remind me of my mother's chess cake with pecans. Rich, buttery, and once they cool, chewy like a blondie should be.

1. In a heavy medium saucepan, melt the butter over medium heat. Continue to cook until the butter turns amber-golden brown, 8 to 12 minutes. Watch closely and do not let the butter burn. Remove from the heat and immediately pour the butter through a fine-mesh sieve into a small bowl. Let cool.

2. Place a rack in the center of the oven and preheat the oven to 350°F.

3. In a large mixing bowl, combine the cake mix, brown sugar, salt, eggs, vanilla, and cooled brown butter. With a wooden spoon, stir for about 30 strokes, until well combined. The batter will be thick. Turn the batter out into an ungreased 9-inch square metal baking pan and spread to the edges with a small metal spatula. Sprinkle the pecans over the top.

4. Place the pan in the oven and bake until the blondies are lightly golden brown, 19 to 23 minutes. The center will still be soft; be careful to not overbake.

5. Transfer the pan to a wire rack to cool for 20 minutes before cutting into squares. Store, lightly covered, at room temperature for up to 5 days.

Spiced Tea Cakes
with Chai Glaze

MAKES TWENTY-EIGHT TO
THIRTY 2½-INCH COOKIES

PREP: 25 TO 30 MINUTES

BAKE: 10 TO 12 MINUTES
PER BATCH

STEEP: 3 HOURS

1 chai tea bag

⅓ cup boiling water

TEA CAKES

1 (15.25-ounce) package
yellow or butter cake mix

1 teaspoon ground
cinnamon

½ teaspoon ground allspice

¼ teaspoon ground ginger

¼ teaspoon ground nutmeg

1 large egg

8 tablespoons (1 stick)
unsalted butter, melted
and cooled

½ cup apple butter,
homemade (see page 369)
or store-bought

⅓ cup golden raisins
(optional)

CHAI GLAZE

1 cup confectioners' sugar

Baked in a hot oven, these soft tea cakes really do melt in your mouth. The hotter oven temperature crisps the edges but keeps the interior soft and cakey. Use either homemade or store-bought apple butter. You can leave these unglazed but you will miss out on the wonderfully spiced topping flavored with chai masala, an Indian style of black tea infused with warm spices.

1. Place the tea bag in a small glass bowl and pour the boiling water over. Set aside to steep for at least 3 hours.

2. Make the tea cakes: Place a rack in the center of the oven and preheat the oven to 400°F. Line two cookie sheets with parchment paper and set aside.

3. In a large mixing bowl, stir together the cake mix, cinnamon, allspice, ginger, and nutmeg. Add the egg, butter, and apple butter. Beat with an electric mixer on low speed until smooth, about 30 seconds. Stop the machine and scrape down the sides of the bowl with a rubber spatula. Increase the mixer speed to medium and beat for 1 minute. Fold in the raisins, if desired.

4. Drop about fifteen 1-tablespoon balls of dough spaced 2 inches apart onto each prepared cookie sheet.

5. Place one pan in the oven at a time. Bake until the cookies are lightly browned around the edges but still soft in the center, 10 to 12 minutes.

6. Let the cookies rest on the cookie sheet for 1 minute, then remove to wire racks to cool completely, 20 minutes.

7. Meanwhile, make the chai glaze: Remove the tea bag from the tea. Place the confectioners' sugar in a small glass bowl and stir in 4 to 5 teaspoons of the tea, until the glaze is smooth and spreadable. You will not use all the tea.

8. Spoon the glaze over each cookie. Let the cookies set for 20 minutes before serving. Store, covered, for up to 5 days.

Easy and Good Lemon Squares

MAKES 24 SQUARES OR BARS, ABOUT 2 INCHES EACH

PREP: 20 TO 25 MINUTES

BAKE: 48 TO 54 MINUTES

1 (15.25-ounce) package yellow or butter cake mix

10 tablespoons (1¼ sticks) unsalted butter, melted and cooled

7 large eggs

2½ cups granulated sugar

4 teaspoons grated lemon zest

½ cup fresh lemon juice (about 2 large lemons)

1 to 2 teaspoons confectioners' sugar, for dusting (optional)

A good—make that great—lemon square is loaded with lemon topping, and this recipe delivers, plus is quick to make using a mix. They taste wonderful made with regular lemons or Meyer lemons and if you slip in a ½ cup or more of fresh blueberries, all the better. The squares bake and freeze well, too. And they can be sliced any way you like: in diamonds, squares, or in longer, more rectangular bars.

1. Place a rack in the center of the oven and preheat the oven to 350°F.

2. Set aside 2 tablespoons of the cake mix for the filling.

3. In a large mixing bowl, combine the remaining cake mix and the melted butter. Separate one of the eggs and add the egg white to the mixing bowl (save the yolk for the filling). Beat on low speed with an electric mixer until well combined, 45 to 60 seconds. The dough will be thick. Press the dough evenly over the bottom and 1¼ inches up the sides of an ungreased 13 × 9-inch metal baking pan.

4. Place the pan in the oven and bake until the crust is golden brown, 18 to 22 minutes.

5. While the crust bakes, in a medium bowl, combine the reserved 2 tablespoons cake mix, granulated sugar, lemon zest, lemon juice, reserved egg yolk, and remaining 6 whole eggs. Beat with an electric mixer on low speed until just combined but not frothy, about 1 minute.

6. Remove the pan from the oven. Pour the lemon mixture over the warm crust. Return the pan to the oven and bake until the lemon squares are lightly golden and the center is set, 30 to 32 minutes.

7. Transfer the pan to a wire rack to cool to room temperature, about 1 hour. Cut into squares or triangles. Dust with confectioners' sugar, if desired. Store, tightly covered, at room temperature for up to 4 days or in the refrigerator for up to 1 week.

Whoopie Pies

MAKES FIVE 4-INCH "PIES"

PREP: 40 TO 45 MINUTES

BAKE: 14 TO 17 MINUTES
PER BATCH

WHOOPIE PIES

1 (15.25-ounce) package
chocolate cake mix

1 large egg

8 tablespoons (1 stick)
unsalted butter, melted
and cooled

FILLING

½ cup vegetable shortening

8 tablespoons (1 stick)
unsalted butter, at room
temperature

2 cups confectioners' sugar

2 cups marshmallow creme

2 teaspoons vanilla extract

Whoopie pies, made from two pillowy chocolate cakes and sandwiched with a marshmallow creme filling, are delightful. Thanks to Joan Linthicum of North Carolina for sending me her recipe years back. I've baked them larger for this book and piled them with more filling because they are meant to be shared. In lieu of the cream filling, you can always fill them with ice cream instead, and stash them in the freezer!

1. Make the whoopie pies: Place a rack in the center of the oven and preheat the oven to 350°F. Have ready two ungreased cookie sheets.

2. In a large mixing bowl, combine the cake mix, egg, and melted butter. Beat with an electric mixer on low speed until the ingredients come together in a stiff mass, about 1 minute.

3. Form the dough into 10 balls about ¼ cup (2 ounces) each. Place 6 balls on one pan and 4 on the other, spaced about 2½ inches apart. Press down on the balls with your hands until they form 2½-inch rounds.

4. Place one pan in the oven at a time. Bake until the tops of the cakes are puffy and a toothpick comes out clean, 14 to 17 minutes.

5. Let the cakes cool on the pan for 2 to 3 minutes. Then remove with a metal spatula to a wire rack to cool completely, about 30 minutes.

6. Make the filling: In a large mixing bowl, combine the shortening, butter, confectioners' sugar, marshmallow creme, and vanilla. Beat with an electric mixer on medium-high speed until the mixture is smooth and well blended, 1½ to 2 minutes.

7. Spread the flat side of half of the cooled cakes with ½ cup filling. Sandwich with the flat side of the remaining cakes. Wrap each whoopie pie in plastic wrap until ready to serve. Store, lightly covered, at room temperature for up to 5 days.

WHOOPIE PIE FILLING VARIATIONS: Try peanut butter, almond butter, ice cream, frosting, mascarpone cheese, or whipped cream.

SMALL WHOOPIE PIES: Make the dough for Whoopie Pies and form it into 1-inch (½-ounce) balls. Arrange on the cookie sheets and press down on them until they are 1¾ inches in diameter. Bake at 350°F for 10 to 12 minutes. Let cool. Spread about 2 tablespoons of filling on half of the cakes, then place the flat side of the remaining cakes on top. Makes 18 to 20 small whoopie pies.

Petit Fours

MAKES FORTY 1½-INCH
PETIT FOURS

PREP: 3 HOURS

BAKE: 28 TO 32 MINUTES

CAKE

Vegetable oil spray,
for misting the pan

1 (15.25-ounce) package
butter cake mix

1 (8-ounce) package cream
cheese, at room temperature

3 large eggs

½ cup warm water

½ cup vegetable oil

1 teaspoon vanilla extract

1 teaspoon almond extract

ICING

1 cup granulated sugar

Pinch of cream of tartar

½ cup hot tap water

2 cups confectioners' sugar,
sifted if needed

¼ teaspoon vanilla or
almond extract (optional)

DECORATIONS

Small edible flowers,
white chocolate curls,
sprinkles, lemon curd, small
blueberries, or sliced almonds

It was always a dream to be able to make petit fours using a cake mix. I wondered as I was decorating a recent batch if anyone still cares about these precious bite-size French tea cakes drenched in icing and decorated with something delicate and wonderful like edible flowers from your herb garden or tiny curls of white chocolate. So I posted a photo on Instagram and found out immediately that there is still strong love for petit fours. They're so easy to love!

1. Make the cake: Place a rack in the center of the oven and preheat the oven to 350°F. Mist the bottom and sides of a 13 × 9-inch pan. Line the bottom with parchment paper. Set the pan aside.

2. In a large mixing bowl, combine the cake mix, cream cheese, eggs, water, oil, vanilla, and almond extract. Beat with an electric mixer on low speed until blended, about 30 seconds. Stop the machine and scrape down the sides of the bowl with a rubber spatula. Increase the mixer speed to medium and beat until the batter is smooth and fluffy, about 1 minute. Pour the batter into the prepared pan, smoothing the top with a rubber spatula.

3. Place the pan in the oven and bake until the cake is golden brown and the top springs back when gently pressed in the middle, 28 to 32 minutes.

4. Let the cake cool in the pan on a wire rack for 15 minutes. Run a long sharp knife around the edges of the cake, shake the pan gently, and invert the cake onto a wire rack and remove the parchment paper. Invert it again so it is right-side up. Let the cake cool at least 20 minutes longer.

5. With a long serrated or slicing knife, trim the cake to a 12 × 7½-inch rectangle (discard the scraps). Cut the rectangle into forty 1½-inch squares. Trim the top off each square so they are level and about the same height. Arrange the cubes on a sheet pan and transfer to the freezer until they are firm, at least 30 minutes.

6. Meanwhile, make the icing: In a heavy medium saucepan, combine the granulated sugar, cream of tartar, and hot water. Whisk over medium heat to combine. Increase the heat to

medium-high and let the mixture boil until it reaches 225°F on a candy thermometer, 6 to 8 minutes. Remove from the heat and let cool for about 15 minutes, then whisk in the confectioners' sugar, ½ cup at a time, until the icing is pourable. Whisk in the vanilla, if using.

7. Remove only 6 to 8 frozen cake cubes from the freezer at a time; keep the others frozen (when the cake is frozen, crumbs don't fall out into the icing). Then, working with one cube at a time, dip each one, top-side down, into the icing to cover the top and sides.

Pull the cube out of the icing and carefully transfer it to a wire rack to set. Repeat until all the frozen cubes are iced. If the icing gets too cool, gently warm the bowl set over a pan filled with an inch of simmering water.

8. Decorate the tops of the petit fours with any of the suggested decorations. They adhere best when the icing is still a little sticky. Store, tightly covered, at room temperature for up to 2 days. They keep longer if garnished with nuts and sprinkles than with fresh fruit or flowers.

Cranberry-Orange Biscotti

MAKES 14 TO 16 BISCOTTI

PREP: 55 MINUTES TO 1 HOUR

BAKE: 43 TO 47 MINUTES

BISCOTTI

1 cup (4 ounces) sweetened dried cranberries

6 tablespoons fresh orange juice

1 (15.25-ounce) package butter cake mix

8 tablespoons (1 stick) unsalted butter, melted and cooled

2 large eggs

1 cup all-purpose flour

1 tablespoon grated orange zest

DRIZZLE (OPTIONAL)

1 cup confectioners' sugar

1 teaspoon grated orange zest

The idea that you can create the Italian twice-baked cookies with a cake mix appeals to all of us who love biscotti and want to bake them easily at home. I am sharing a new cranberry-orange version of my tried-and-true biscotti method as well as an option for making chocolate biscotti, too (see the Variation, opposite).

1. Make the biscotti: Place a rack in the center of the oven and preheat the oven to 350°F. Line a cookie sheet with parchment paper and set aside.

2. Cut the cranberries in half and place in a small bowl. Add the orange juice and stir to coat. Set aside for 10 minutes for the cranberries to soak up the juice

3. Reserving the orange juice, drain the cranberries. (Set the juice aside for the drizzle if you're making it.) In a large mixing bowl, combine the cake mix, butter, eggs, flour, orange zest, and the cranberries. Beat with an electric mixer on low speed until well combined, about 1 minute. The dough will be thick. Turn the dough onto the prepared cookie sheet and shape it into a rectangle about 15½ by 4 inches and ½ inch thick. Mound the dough so it is slightly higher than ½ inch in the center.

4. Place the pan in the oven and bake until the dough rectangle feels firm when gently pressed in the middle and a toothpick inserted in the center comes out clean, 33 to 37 minutes.

5. Let cool on the pan on a wire rack for 10 minutes. Leave the oven on.

6. Leaving it on the cookie sheet, use a sharp serrated bread knife to slice the rectangle on the diagonal into 1-inch-thick slices. You should get 14 to 16. Carefully turn the slices onto their sides.

7. Return the pan to the oven and bake the sliced biscotti for 10 minutes. Turn off the oven and leave the biscotti in the oven until they are crisp, about 30 minutes longer.

8. Transfer to wire racks to cool completely, about 1 hour.

9. If desired, make the drizzle: In a small bowl, whisk 2 to 3 tablespoons of the reserved orange juice into the confectioners' sugar until you have a smooth but pourable glaze. Fold in the orange zest.

10. With a spoon, drizzle the mixture over the biscotti. Let the glaze set for 20 minutes before serving. Store, lightly covered, at room temperature for up to 1 week. You can freeze them unglazed for up to 2 months.

How to Make Chocolate-Almond Biscotti

Replace the butter cake mix with a (15.25-ounce) package of chocolate cake mix. And replace the cranberries and orange zest with ½ cup chopped slivered almonds and ½ teaspoon almond extract. The rectangle of dough bakes a little more quickly—in 25 to 30 minutes. The slices bake in 10 minutes. You can dip these biscotti into melted white or dark chocolate once they are cool.

Plum Linzer Bars

MAKES TWENTY-FOUR
2¼ × 2-INCH BARS

PREP: 20 TO 25 MINUTES

BAKE: 38 TO 45 MINUTES

1⅓ cups (6 ounces)
slivered almonds

1 (15.25-ounce) package
yellow or butter cake mix

10 tablespoons (1¼ sticks)
unsalted butter, melted
and cooled

¼ cup whole milk

½ teaspoon ground
cinnamon

¼ teaspoon ground nutmeg

1⅔ cups (18 ounces)
plum jam (or raspberry,
strawberry, peach, or
apricot)

1 teaspoon grated lemon
zest

1¼ cups (7½ ounces) white
chocolate chips

At first I didn't feel comfortable adapting such a classic recipe like the Linzer torte to be cake mix friendly. But doing some research I found that the addition of raspberry jam to the torte—and later the bars—was an American touch; the original jam used was black currant. So I felt a bit better about including plum jam in this recipe once shared with me by Laura Cunningham of New Jersey.

1. Place a rack in the center of the oven and preheat the oven to 350°F.

2. Measure ¾ cup of the almonds and finely chop them to make 1 cup. Set aside. Set aside the unchopped almonds for the topping.

3. In a large mixing bowl, combine the cake mix, melted butter, milk, cinnamon, nutmeg, and chopped almonds. Beat on low speed with an electric mixer until well combined, 45 seconds to 1 minute. The dough will be thick. Set aside one-third (about 1 cup) of the dough for the topping.

4. Place the remaining dough in an ungreased 13 × 9-inch metal baking pan and press it evenly over the bottom of the pan but not up the sides. Place the pan in the oven and bake until the crust is lightly browned around the edges, 10 to 13 minutes.

5. While the crust bakes, in a small saucepan, combine the jam and lemon zest and warm over low heat for a couple of minutes. (Alternatively, heat them in a microwave-safe glass bowl in the microwave for 30 to 45 seconds, until the jam is spreadable.)

6. Remove the pan from the oven and immediately sprinkle the white chocolate chips evenly over the crust. Spoon the warm jam on top. Crumble the reserved dough into ½-inch pieces on top of the jam, leaving spaces in between for the jam to show. Sprinkle the reserved unchopped almonds on top.

7. Return the pan to the oven and bake until golden brown and bubbling, 28 to 32 minutes.

8. Let cool in the pan on a rack for 30 minutes. Cut into 24 bars. Store, tightly covered, at room temperature for up to 5 days.

Orange Ricotta Cheesecake Bars

MAKES TWENTY-FOUR
3 X 1½-INCH BARS

PREP: 30 TO 35 MINUTES

BAKE: 55 MINUTES TO 1 HOUR

Vegetable oil spray or
1 teaspoon melted butter,
for greasing the pan

1 (15.25-ounce) package
butter cake mix

1 cup graham cracker
crumbs

12 tablespoons (1½ sticks)
unsalted butter, melted
and cooled

4 large eggs

2 cups (16 ounces) full-fat
ricotta cheese

1 (14-ounce) can sweetened
condensed milk

1 tablespoon grated
orange zest

3 tablespoons fresh
orange juice

1 teaspoon vanilla extract

¼ teaspoon almond extract
(optional)

Don't want to commit to baking a whole cheesecake? Make cheesecake bars. This is a lovely recipe for any occasion, which you can bake ahead and freeze. The addition of ricotta instead of the usual cream cheese makes a lighter bar; orange zest and juice add a wonderfully fresh flavor, and the graham crackers in the crust add that old-fashioned icebox pie touch everyone will love.

1. Place a rack in the center of the oven and preheat the oven to 350°F. Lightly grease the bottom and sides of a 13 × 9-inch metal baking pan. Set the pan aside.

2. Measure out ⅓ cup of the cake mix and set it aside for the filling.

3. In a large mixing bowl, combine the remaining cake mix, graham cracker crumbs, and melted butter. Separate one of the eggs and add the egg white to the mixing bowl. (Reserve the yolk for the filling.) Beat with an electric mixer on low speed until just combined, about 1 minute. Turn the dough into the prepared baking pan and press it evenly over the bottom and 1 inch up the sides.

4. Place the pan in the oven and bake until the crust is lightly browned, about 15 minutes.

5. Meanwhile, in a large mixing bowl, combine the ricotta, condensed milk, orange zest, and orange juice and beat with the electric mixer (no need to clean the beaters) on low speed until well blended and smooth, about 1 minute. Stop the machine and scrape down the sides of the bowl with a rubber spatula. Add the reserved ⅓ cup cake mix, the reserved egg yolk, the remaining 3 whole eggs, vanilla, and almond extract (if using). Beat on medium speed until blended, about 1 minute.

6. Remove the crust from the oven and reduce the oven temperature to 325°F. With a metal spatula or a smaller pan, press down on the baked crust to flatten it as soon as it is out of the oven. Pour the filling into the crust, smoothing the top with the rubber spatula.

7. Return the pan to the oven and bake until the filling is mostly set when you jiggle the pan, 40 to 45 minutes.

8. Transfer the pan to a wire rack to cool to room temperature, about 1 hour. Slice into bars and serve. Store, tightly covered, in the refrigerator for up to 1 week.

Classic Gooey Butter Cake

MAKES TWENTY-FOUR 2-INCH
SQUARES

PREP: 20 TO 25 MINUTES

BAKE: 42 TO 47 MINUTES

Vegetable oil spray or
1 teaspoon melted butter,
for greasing the pan

1 (15.25-ounce) package
butter cake mix

8 tablespoons (1 stick)
unsalted butter, melted
and cooled

4 large eggs

2½ teaspoons vanilla
extract

12 ounces cream cheese,
at room temperature

4 cups confectioners' sugar,
sifted

*Legend has it that the first recipe for gooey butter cake was an
accident—the baker was in a hurry and left out a key ingredient—
yeast—so the results were, well, gooey. It has since become a beloved,
signature cake of St. Louis. I've always loved the scratch version
of this cake but found the cake mix variations just too sweet.
So I revisited the classic gooey butter cake for this book, increasing
the filling and decreasing the sugar. You will love this recipe.*

1. Place a rack in the center of the oven and preheat the oven
   to 350°F. Lightly grease the bottom and sides of a 13 × 9-inch
   metal baking pan. Set the pan aside.

2. In a large mixing bowl, combine the cake mix, melted butter,
   1 of the eggs, and 1 teaspoon of the vanilla. Beat with an electric
   mixer on low speed until blended and the mixture comes
   together in a ball, about 1 minute. Press the dough into the
   bottom of the prepared pan and set the pan aside.

3. In the same bowl, combine the cream cheese, remaining 3 eggs,
   and 1½ teaspoons vanilla. With the same beaters (no need to
   clean), beat the mixture on medium speed until smooth and
   fluffy, about 1 minute. Stop the machine and scrape down the
   sides of the bowl with a rubber spatula. Reduce the mixer speed
   to low and beat in the confectioners' sugar, 1 cup at a time, and
   continue to beat until smooth, about 1 minute. Pour the filling
   over the crust, spreading it to the edges with the spatula.

4. Bake until the cake is very lightly browned and the center
   still jiggles a little if you shake the pan, 42 to 47 minutes.

5. Transfer the pan to a wire rack to cool for 30 minutes. Slice into
   triangles or squares and serve. Store, tightly covered, at room
   temperature for up to 3 days or in the refrigerator for 1 week.

Chocolate Brownie Gooey Butter Cake

Make the Classic Gooey Butter Cake crust as directed, but use a (15- to 18.3-ounce) package brownie mix instead of the butter cake mix and fold in ½ cup chopped walnuts. Press the crust into a greased 9-inch square pan and bake at 350°F for 10 to 12 minutes or until nearly firm. For the topping, reduce the cream cheese to 8 ounces, reduce the eggs to just 1, the vanilla to ¾ teaspoon, and the confectioners' sugar to 2 cups. Pour over the crust and top with ¼ cup mini semisweet chocolate chips. Bake until firm, 30 to 35 minutes. Let cool in the pan before cutting into 16 squares.

Chocolate Pecan Pie Squares

MAKES TWENTY-FOUR 2-INCH
SQUARES

PREP: 20 TO 25 MINUTES

BAKE: 43 TO 47 MINUTES

CRUST

1 (15.25-ounce) package
yellow or butter cake mix

1 large egg white

12 tablespoons (1½ sticks)
unsalted butter, melted
and cooled

TOPPING

1 large egg yolk

3 large eggs

¾ cup sugar

1 cup light corn syrup

12 tablespoons (1½ sticks)
unsalted butter, melted
and cooled

Pinch of salt

1½ teaspoons vanilla
extract or 2 tablespoons
bourbon

2 cups (6½ ounces) chopped
pecans

1½ cups (9 ounces)
semisweet chocolate chips

*A yellow cake mix makes an easy crust for bar cookies.
You blend the mix with some butter and an egg or egg white
and you've got the simple cookie crust ready to be topped with
all types of wonderful fillings, like this one for pecan pie.*

1. Place a rack in the center of the oven and preheat the oven
    to 375°F.

2. Make the crust: Set aside 1½ tablespoons of the cake mix for
    the topping. In a large mixing bowl, combine the remaining
    cake mix, egg white, and melted butter. Beat with an electric
    mixer on low speed until well combined, about 1 minute. The
    dough will be thick. Press the dough evenly into the bottom
    and 1¼ inches up the sides of an ungreased 13 × 9-inch metal
    baking pan.

3. Place the pan in the oven and bake until lightly golden brown,
    15 to 17 minutes.

4. Meanwhile, make the topping: In a medium bowl, combine the
    reserved 1½ tablespoons cake mix, the egg yolk, whole eggs,
    sugar, corn syrup, melted butter, salt, and vanilla. Beat with an
    electric mixer on low speed until just combined but not frothy,
    about 1 minute. Fold in the pecans and chocolate chips.

5. Remove the crust from the oven and press down on the crust
    with a metal spatula or small metal baking pan to flatten it.
    Pour the topping over the warm crust.

6. Return the pan to the oven and bake until the center is set and
    the top is dark golden brown, 28 to 30 minutes.

7. Transfer the pan to a wire rack to cool to room temperature,
    about 1 hour. Cut into squares and serve. Store, tightly covered,
    at room temperature for up to 3 days or in the refrigerator for
    up to 1 week.

Chocolate Fudge Peppermint Sticks

MAKES EIGHTEEN 3 × 1½-INCH
STICKS OR TWENTY-SEVEN
3 × 1-INCH STICKS

PREP: 40 TO 45 MINUTES

BAKE: 20 TO 25 MINUTES

Vegetable oil spray,
for misting the pan

1 (15- to 18.3-ounce)
package brownie mix

2 large eggs

10 tablespoons (1¼ sticks)
unsalted butter, at room
temperature

2 cups confectioners' sugar

2 tablespoons half-and-half
or evaporated milk

½ teaspoon peppermint
extract

Small-Batch Chocolate Pan
Frosting (page 361), warm

Recipes get passed along in unusual ways—I have more than my share of cocktail napkins and sticky notes with great recipes scribbled on them by friends. This one came from a Texas cake decorator I met at a trade show in Detroit many years ago. I have since adapted these to a brownie mix and love their flavor, especially during the holidays. Note to self: You never know who you will meet and what recipe they will have to share. Bring cocktail napkins and sticky notes just in case!

1. Place a rack in the center of the oven and preheat the oven to 350°F. Lightly mist a 9-inch square metal baking pan with oil and set the pan aside.

2. In a large mixing bowl, combine the brownie mix and eggs and set aside.

3. In a small saucepan, melt 8 tablespoons of the butter over low heat, 1 to 2 minutes. Pour the melted butter into the large bowl and stir with a wooden spoon until blended, 35 to 40 strokes. Pour the batter in the prepared pan and spread it to the edges.

4. Place the pan in the oven and bake the brownies until they are set but still a little soft, 20 to 25 minutes.

5. Meanwhile, in a medium mixing bowl, combine the confectioners' sugar, remaining 2 tablespoons butter, the half-and-half, and peppermint extract. Beat with an electric mixer on low speed to combine, about 30 seconds. Increase the mixer speed to medium and beat until fluffy, about 1 minute.

6. Remove the brownie layer from the oven. Dollop the peppermint topping over the warm brownies when they come out of the oven, spreading it to the edges and taking care to not disturb the top crust of the brownies. Set aside so the topping can set.

7. Use a spoon to drizzle the pan frosting over the filling so you leave the filling showing. Let the brownies rest for 30 minutes, then slice and serve. Store, tightly covered, at room temperature, for up to 3 days or in the refrigerator for up to 1 week.

Kahlúa Marbled Cheesecake Brownies

MAKES SIXTEEN 2-INCH
BROWNIES

PREP: 20 TO 25 MINUTES

BAKE: 28 TO 33 MINUTES

Vegetable oil spray,
for misting the pan

1 (8-ounce) package cream
cheese, at room temperature

13 tablespoons unsalted
butter, at room temperature

¼ cup sugar

3 large eggs

¼ cup plus 1 tablespoon
Kahlúa

1 (15- to 18.3-ounce)
package brownie mix

¼ cup (1½ ounces) mini
semisweet chocolate chips

*One of my favorite ways to doctor up a brownie mix, this recipe
has been with me for a while. Sometimes I use ricotta instead
of cream cheese. Sometimes I sprinkle mini chocolate chips on
top before baking, and sometimes not. But I always add the
coffee liqueur Kahlúa—it just makes the brownies so special.
These are great to bake ahead and freeze, and in fact, slicing is
neater when they are semifrozen. They're party-perfect cut into
small squares when you just want to offer a bite of chocolate.*

1. Place a rack in the center of the oven and preheat the oven to
   350°F. Lightly mist a 9-inch square metal baking pan with oil
   and set the pan aside.

2. In a large mixing bowl, combine the cream cheese, 5 tablespoons
   of the butter, the sugar, 1 of the eggs, and 1 tablespoon of the
   Kahlúa. Beat with an electric mixer on low speed until smooth
   and combined, about 1 minute. Transfer the cream cheese
   mixture to a small bowl and set aside.

3. In a small saucepan, melt the remaining 8 tablespoons butter
   over low heat, 1 to 2 minutes. When the butter has melted,
   pour it into the same mixing bowl—no need it clean it. Add the
   brownie mix and the remaining 2 eggs and ¼ cup Kahlúa. Stir
   with a wooden spoon until the ingredients are combined and
   the batter lightens, about 50 strokes. Pour the batter into the
   prepared pan and spread it out with a rubber spatula. Dollop
   the cream cheese mixture on top of the brownie batter. As you
   spread it to the edges of the pan with a small metal spatula,
   swirl it into the batter to create a marbled effect. Scatter the
   chocolate chips over the top.

4. Place the pan in the oven and bake until the brownies are
   very lightly browned and the center is still a little soft,
   28 to 33 minutes.

5. Transfer the pan to a wire rack to cool for 30 minutes, then slice and serve. Store, tightly covered, at room temperature for up to 3 days or in the refrigerator for up to 1 week.

Peanut Butter Chocolate Bars

MAKES TWENTY-FOUR
3- × 1½-INCH BARS

PREP: 15 TO 20 MINUTES

BAKE: 30 TO 35 MINUTES

1 (15.25-ounce) package yellow or butter cake mix

1 cup creamy peanut butter

8 tablespoons (1 stick) unsalted butter, melted and cooled

2 large eggs

2 cups (12 ounces) semisweet chocolate chips

1 (14-ounce) can sweetened condensed milk

2 teaspoons vanilla extract

Our go-to dessert to bake for last-minute parties and our surefire contribution to a bake sale, these bars have been a part of our family for two decades. We have varied them in all sorts of ways, but this modern, streamlined version is better without the coconut and pecans in the original recipe. These are the best yet.

1. Place a rack in the center of the oven and preheat the oven to 350°F.

2. In a large mixing bowl, combine the cake mix, peanut butter, melted butter, and eggs. Beat with an electric mixer on low speed until combined, about 1 minute. Stop the machine and scrape down the sides of the bowl with a rubber spatula. The mixture will be thick. Measure out and set aside 1 cup for the topping. Using your fingers, press the rest of the mixture into the bottom and 1 inch up the sides of an ungreased 13 × 9-inch metal baking pan. Set the pan aside.

3. In a large microwave-safe bowl, combine the chocolate chips and condensed milk and microwave on high power for 1 minute. Remove the bowl and stir until the chocolate melts. Stir in the vanilla. Pour the filling over the crust, spreading it to reach the sides. Crumble the reserved topping into ½-inch pieces and scatter on top. It will not completely cover the filling; you want the filling to peek through.

4. Place the pan in the oven and bake until the bars are golden brown, 30 to 35 minutes.

5. Transfer the pan to a wire rack to cool for 30 minutes, then slice and serve. Store, tightly covered, at room temperature for up to 3 days or in the refrigerator for up to 1 week.

Little Brownie Pizza

SERVES 8

PREP: 15 TO 20 MINUTES

BAKE: 17 TO 21 MINUTES

Who knew you could make a pizza from a brownie mix? If you have pizza decorators at your house who will search the kitchen for fruit, nuts, chocolate, sprinkles, and anything edible that goes with chocolate, then you, too, can have an absolutely adorable brownie pizza. And the leftovers are great for breakfast!

CRUST

8 tablespoons (1 stick) unsalted butter, melted and cooled

1 (15- to 18.3-ounce) package brownie mix

1 large egg

TOPPING

1 (8-ounce) container whipped cream cheese spread, at room temperature

2 cups frozen whipped topping (Cool Whip), thawed

2 tablespoons confectioners' sugar

DECORATIONS

Sliced kiwi, sliced strawberries, blackberries, sliced bananas, blueberries, raspberries, M&M's candies, Reese's Pieces, sweetened shredded coconut, chopped nuts, toffee bits, chopped candy bars

1. Place a rack in the center of the oven and preheat the oven to 350°F. Cut an 11-inch round from a sheet of parchment paper and place it on a cookie sheet or baking sheet. Set the pan aside.

2. Make the crust: In a large mixing bowl, combine the melted butter, brownie mix, and egg. Beat with a wooden spoon until smooth, 25 to 30 strokes. The batter will be thick. Turn the batter out onto the parchment round and, with clean hands, spread the batter out to within 1 inch of the edge. (The brownie will expand as it bakes.)

3. Place the pan in the oven and bake the brownie crust until it is firm around the edges but still slightly soft in the center, 17 to 21 minutes.

4. Remove the pan from the oven and slide the parchment sheet with the brownie on it onto a wire rack to cool completely, about 40 minutes.

5. Meanwhile, make the topping: In a large bowl, whisk together the cream cheese spread, whipped topping, and confectioners' sugar. Store in the fridge while the crust cools.

6. When the brownie crust has cooled, spread the topping over the crust. To decorate, score the pizza with a pizza cutter into 8 wedges by drawing a line through the topping but not through the crust. This will be the guide. Add different toppings to each slice, or let the decorators at your house create their own pizza masterpiece. (Or you can slice the wedges all the way through the crust and let everyone have their own slice to decorate. For presentation, after the slices are decorated, slide them back into place to make a complete pizza round.)

7. Serve at once! Then store leftover pizza, lightly covered, in the refrigerator for up to 2 days. Fruit shortens the shelf life, so omit the fruit if you want to make the pizza ahead and store it in the fridge.

Buttermilk Spice Doughnuts

MAKES 28 DOUGHNUTS AND
28 HOLES

PREP: 2 HOURS

COOK: 1 TO 1½ MINUTES
PER BATCH

DOUGHNUTS

2 (7g) packages active dry
yeast (4½ teaspoons total)

½ cup hot tap water

1½ cups buttermilk,
preferably whole milk,
at room temperature

3⅓ cups all-purpose flour,
plus more for dusting

1 (15.25-ounce) package
butter cake mix

1 tablespoon ground
cinnamon

½ teaspoon ground allspice

½ teaspoon ground ginger

½ teaspoon ground nutmeg

½ teaspoon salt

Vegetable oil, for greasing
the baking sheets and
for frying

CINNAMON SUGAR

½ cup sugar

2 tablespoons ground
cinnamon

*Nothing beats the aroma of freshly fried doughnuts, especially
ones infused with spices and dredged in cinnamon and sugar.
This recipe was once shared with me by reader Christine
Urban of California. It belonged to her grandmother who used
to make doughnuts with a cake mix. I've updated it a little
to include buttermilk, and I've added more spices. Just make
sure you've got warm cocoa ready to wash them down.*

1. Make the doughnuts: In a large glass bowl, stir together the yeast
    and hot water until dissolved. Stir in the buttermilk. Set aside.

2. In a separate large bowl, stir together the flour, cake mix,
    cinnamon, allspice, ginger, nutmeg, and salt. Turn the dry
    ingredients into the yeast mixture and stir with a wooden
    spoon until smooth, about 50 strokes. Cover the bowl with a
    kitchen towel and place in a warm spot in the kitchen to rise
    until doubled in volume, about 1 hour.

3. Meanwhile, lightly grease 3 or 4 baking sheets with vegetable
    oil or line with parchment paper. Set aside.

4. Lightly flour a clean work surface. Punch down the dough
    with your fist and turn half of the dough out onto the surface.
    Knead the dough, dusting with a little more flour if the
    dough is sticky, then roll it out to a ½-inch thickness. Cut out
    doughnuts using a 2½- to 3-inch cutter or the rim of a glass. Use
    a 1¼-inch cutter to cut out the center from each round. Place
    the doughnuts and holes on the prepared pans, cover with the
    kitchen towel, and place in a warm spot to rise for 30 minutes.
    Repeat the process with the remaining dough and scraps.

5. Pour 1½ inches vegetable oil into a Dutch oven or deep
    cast-iron skillet and heat over medium-high heat until the oil
    reaches 340° to 350°F, using a candy thermometer.

6. Working in batches (do not crowd the pan), gently ease the
    doughnuts and holes into the hot oil. They will cook quickly.

Let them brown for 30 to 45 seconds, then turn them over to fry on the other side for 30 seconds. Remove with a slotted spatula and drain on wire racks or sheets of brown paper.

7. Make the cinnamon sugar: In a shallow pan, stir together the sugar and cinnamon. While the doughnuts are still warm, dredge them in the cinnamon sugar.

8. Serve warm. Store, lightly covered, at room temperature for up to 3 days.

Frostings, Fillings, and Glazes

Frosting is the first and last thing you taste on cake, and that's why it's so important to make it homemade. I've assembled my favorites here—buttercreams, cream cheese frostings, ganache and pan frostings, fillings, and glazes.

Basic Vanilla Cupcakes
(page 268)

Vanilla Buttercream Frosting

MAKES 3½ CUPS, ENOUGH TO FROST A TWO- OR THREE-LAYER CAKE, A 13 × 9-INCH CAKE, OR 20 TO 24 CUPCAKES

PREP: 10 TO 15 MINUTES

8 tablespoons (1 stick) unsalted or salted butter, at room temperature

2½ to 3 cups confectioners' sugar, sifted

3 to 4 tablespoons whole milk, as needed

2 teaspoons vanilla extract

Pinch of salt (if using unsalted butter)

For the creamiest and most delicious frosting, add the confectioners' sugar and milk in increments to get the consistency right. If you use unsalted butter, add a pinch of salt to balance the sugar. But if you use salted butter, omit the salt. Sift the sugar after measuring for the best results, but if you are in a hurry, just check to see if your confectioners' sugar has any lumps in it before making the frosting, and if it does, press those through a sifter or mesh sieve.

1. In a medium mixing bowl, beat the butter with an electric mixer on low speed until smooth, about 30 seconds. Add 2 cups of the sugar, 2 tablespoons of the milk, the vanilla, and the salt (if using) and beat on low until the sugar is incorporated. Add ½ cup more sugar and another tablespoon of milk and beat until smooth. If the frosting is spreadable, do not add any more sugar. Increase the mixer speed to medium and beat until the frosting is light and fluffy, about 1 minute. If the frosting is too thick to spread, beat in another tablespoon of milk.

2. Frost your cake or cupcakes right away, or store the frosting, covered, in the refrigerator for up to 2 days. Let the frosting come to room temperature before using.

    CANDY CANE BUTTERCREAM: Fold in ½ cup crushed peppermint candy. If desired, add a dash of peppermint extract, too.

    CINNAMON BUTTERCREAM: Add 1 teaspoon good-quality ground cinnamon (like Ceylon or Saigon) to the recipe along with the sugar.

    CINNAMON FAUX BUTTERCREAM: Replace the butter with plant butter and replace the milk with coconut milk or almond milk. Add 1 teaspoon good-quality ground cinnamon to the frosting.

CONTINUED

CEREAL MILK FROSTING: Pour whole milk over a bowlful of sweetened cereal and place the bowl in the fridge for 2 hours. Strain and use the cereal milk to make the Vanilla Buttercream Frosting and omit the vanilla. To use cereal milk with a chocolate frosting, make it with Cocoa Puffs or Cocoa Krispies and use it in Milk Chocolate Buttercream (page 355). Good cereal milk matchups for the frostings on some of the cakes in the book are: Cinnamon Toast Crunch for the Snickerdoodle Cake (page 91), Fruit Loops for the Confetti Cake (page 71), and Reese's Puffs for the Reese's Peanut Butter Cake (page 68).

MATCHA BUTTERCREAM: Add 1 single-serve packet of matcha green tea powder for a pale green color. Add 2 packets for a vivid green.

COFFEE BUTTERCREAM: Heat ¼ cup milk or coconut milk and stir in 2 tablespoons espresso or instant coffee to dissolve. Let cool. Substitute for the milk in the recipe.

RASPBERRY BUTTERCREAM: Substitute ½ cup (3 ounces) fresh raspberries, pureed and strained (1½ to 2 tablespoons) for the milk.

LEMON BUTTERCREAM: Use the juice and grated zest of 1 small lemon, plus enough milk to make 3 tablespoons. Omit the vanilla, if desired.

LIME BUTTERCREAM: Use the juice and grated zest of 1 lime, plus enough milk to make 3 tablespoons. Use 2 to 2½ cups sugar. Add a pinch of salt, if desired.

PINK CHAMPAGNE FROSTING: Increase the butter to 12 tablespoons (1½ sticks). Substitute pink champagne for the milk. Reduce the vanilla to 1 teaspoon and add a dab of pink food coloring.

Vegan Vanilla Buttercream Frosting

MAKES 2½ CUPS, ENOUGH TO FROST A TWO-LAYER CAKE, A 13 × 9-INCH CAKE, OR 16 TO 18 CUPCAKES

PREP: 10 TO 15 MINUTES

8 tablespoons (1 stick) plant butter (made with avocado or olive oil)

2½ cups confectioners' sugar, sifted

2 to 3 tablespoons liquid of your choice (lemon juice, orange juice, almond milk, or pureed fruit like mango)

½ teaspoon vanilla extract

Grated citrus zest (optional)

Plant-based butter substitutes work well for the butter in a frosting. It is more watery than butter and makes a softer frosting, too, so store the frosted cake in a cool place in the kitchen or in the refrigerator until time to serve. Thanks to cookbook author and vegan cook Kristen Hartke for turning me on to plant butters!

1. In a medium mixing bowl, combine the plant butter, 2 cups of the sugar, 1 tablespoon of the liquid, the vanilla, and citrus zest (if using). Beat with an electric mixer on low speed until smooth, about 30 seconds. Add the remaining ½ cup sugar and 1 tablespoon of the liquid and beat again until smooth. Increase the mixer speed to medium and beat until the frosting is light and fluffy, about 1 minute. If the frosting is too thick to spread, beat in another 1 tablespoon liquid.

2. Frost your cake or cupcakes right away, or store the frosting, covered, in the refrigerator for up to 2 days. Let the frosting come to room temperature before using.

   VEGAN CHOCOLATE BUTTERCREAM: Add ⅔ cup unsweetened cocoa powder and use a total of 4 to 5 tablespoons almond, coconut, or oat milk. Increase the vanilla to 2 teaspoons and add a pinch of salt, if desired. Frost your cake or cupcakes right away, or store the frosting, covered, in the refrigerator for up to 2 days.

Peanut Butter Frosting

MAKES 3 CUPS, ENOUGH TO
FROST A TWO-LAYER CAKE,
A 13 × 9-INCH CAKE, OR
20 TO 24 CUPCAKES

PREP: 10 TO 15 MINUTES

1 cup creamy peanut butter

8 tablespoons (1 stick)
unsalted butter,
at room temperature

2½ cups confectioners'
sugar, sifted

2 to 3 tablespoons whole
milk or full-fat canned
coconut milk, plus more
as needed

2 teaspoons vanilla extract

*A family favorite, this frosting is fabulous slathered on
chocolate cake, peanut butter cake, or cupcakes.*

1. In a medium mixing bowl, combine the peanut butter and
   butter and beat with an electric mixer on low speed until
   fluffy, about 30 seconds. A bit at a time, add 2 cups of the
   sugar, 2 tablespoons of the milk, and the vanilla, beating with
   the mixer on low speed until the sugar is well incorporated,
   about 1 minute. Increase the mixer speed to medium and beat
   the frosting until it is light and fluffy, about 1 minute, adding
   up to ½ cup more sugar if the frosting is too thin or up to
   1 tablespoon more milk if it seems too stiff.

2. Frost your cake or cupcakes right away, or store the frosting,
   covered, in the refrigerator for up to 2 days. Let the frosting
   come to room temperature before using.

EASY TIPS FOR MAKING FROSTING

1. Have all of the ingredients at room temperature for
   buttercreams and cream cheese frostings.

2. If the frosting tastes too sweet, add a pinch of sea or kosher salt.

3. Frost the top of a layer cake before the sides if you are worried
   about running out of frosting. If you don't have enough for the
   sides, just call the cake "naked."

4. Spoon pan frostings onto cakes warm so you have a smooth
   finish—they will set as they cool.

Chocolate Buttercream Frosting

MAKES 2¾ CUPS, ENOUGH TO
FROST A TWO-LAYER CAKE, A
13 × 9-INCH CAKE, OR
20 CUPCAKES

PREP: 10 TO 15 MINUTES

8 tablespoons (1 stick)
unsalted butter,
at room temperature

Pinch of salt

⅔ cup unsweetened
cocoa powder

2¼ cups confectioners'
sugar, sifted

1 teaspoon vanilla extract

4 to 5 tablespoons milk,
half-and-half, or canned
coconut milk

*Every family needs a go-to chocolate buttercream, and this
one is my family's favorite. I've made it more chocolaty and
less sweet through the years. Add a little espresso powder
or pinch of cinnamon if you like. I like to use this as the
filling for the Almond Sandwich Cookies (page 315).*

1. In a medium mixing bowl, combine the butter and salt and
    beat with an electric mixer on low speed until fluffy, about
    30 seconds. Add the cocoa, 2 cups of the sugar, the vanilla, and
    4 tablespoons of the milk and beat on low until the sugar and
    cocoa are incorporated, about 1 minute. Add the remaining
    ¼ cup sugar, increase the mixer speed to medium, and beat
    until light and fluffy, adding another 1 tablespoon milk if the
    frosting seems too stiff.

2. Frost your cake or cupcakes right away, or store the frosting,
    covered, in the refrigerator for up to 2 days. Let the frosting
    come to room temperature before using.

    MILK CHOCOLATE BUTTERCREAM: Decrease the cocoa
    to ½ cup. Add ¼ teaspoon ground cinnamon and use 5 to
    6 tablespoons whole milk or full-fat canned coconut milk.

Cream Cheese Frosting

MAKES 3½ CUPS, ENOUGH
TO FROST A TWO- OR
THREE-LAYER CAKE, A
13 × 9-INCH CAKE, OR TO
THINLY FROST A SLAB CAKE
OR 20 TO 24 CUPCAKES

PREP: 10 TO 15 MINUTES

1 (8-ounce) package
cream cheese,
at room temperature

8 tablespoons (1 stick)
unsalted butter,
at room temperature

1 teaspoon vanilla extract

3 to 3½ cups
confectioners' sugar,
sifted

Make sure both the cream cheese and butter are soft and at room temperature before making. If you need to soften them quickly, do so in the microwave. Unwrap both and place them on a plate, microwaving at 10- to 15-second increments on high power.

1. In a medium mixing bowl, combine the cream cheese and butter and beat with an electric mixer on low speed until smooth, about 30 seconds. Add the vanilla and 3 cups of the sugar, beating on low until the sugar is blended, about 1 minute. Blend in the remaining ½ cup sugar, if desired. Increase the mixer speed to medium and beat until fluffy, about 1 minute.

2. Frost your cake or cupcakes right away, or store the frosting, covered, in the refrigerator for up to 2 days. Let the frosting come to room temperature before using.

VEGAN CREAM CHEESE FROSTING: Substitute 8 ounces vegan cream cheese and plant butter. Use 4 cups confectioners' sugar. Add 1 teaspoon grated lemon or orange zest, if desired. Refrigerate the cake or cupcakes after frosting.

WHITE CHOCOLATE CREAM CHEESE FROSTING: Place 6 ounces white chocolate, either chopped or white chocolate chips, in a small microwave-safe bowl and microwave on high power until melted, 50 to 55 seconds. Stir the chocolate until smooth, then set aside to slightly cool. Reduce the butter to 4 tablespoons. Add the melted white chocolate to the cream cheese and butter and proceed with the recipe as written.

SMALL-BATCH WEDDING CAKE FROSTING: Reduce the cream cheese to 6 ounces and the butter to 3 tablespoons. Use 3 cups confectioners' sugar. The vanilla stays the same, but add ½ teaspoon almond extract. Use whole milk as needed to thin the frosting and make it spreadable. Makes enough for a 9-inch two-layer cake or 18 to 20 cupcakes.

Buttermilk Devil's
Food Cake
(page 50)

MASCARPONE FROSTING: Reduce the cream cheese to 2 ounces and the unsalted butter to 4 tablespoons. Add 8 ounces room-temperature mascarpone. Reduce the confectioners' sugar to 2 cups and increase the vanilla to 1 tablespoon. Add a pinch of salt.

LIGHTER CREAM CHEESE FROSTING: Reduce the cream cheese to 4 ounces; the butter stays the same. Reduce the vanilla to ½ teaspoon and the confectioners' sugar to 2 to 2½ cups. Add 1 tablespoon whole milk (to make up for using less cream cheese). Makes enough for an 8- or 9-inch two-layer cake.

SMALL-BATCH CREAM CHEESE FROSTING: Reduce the cream cheese to 4 ounces, the butter to 2 tablespoons. Reduce the vanilla to ½ teaspoon and the confectioners' sugar to 1½ cups. Add 1 teaspoon whole milk. Makes enough for an 8- or 9-inch one-layer cake.

Creamy Nutella Frosting

MAKES ABOUT 1½ CUPS, ENOUGH TO FROST A TWO-LAYER 8-INCH CAKE, SNACK CAKE, OR 12 CUPCAKES

PREP: 5 MINUTES

1 cup Nutella (chocolate-hazelnut spread)

½ cup peanut butter or almond butter

1 teaspoon vanilla extract

4 to 6 tablespoons unsweetened plain almond milk

Nutella, the delightful chocolate and hazelnut spread, is already sweetened, so no need to add extra sugar to this frosting.

1. In a medium mixing bowl, combine the Nutella, peanut butter, vanilla, and 4 tablespoons of the milk and beat with an electric mixer on low speed until blended, about 30 seconds. Add another 2 tablespoons milk, or as needed to make it spreadable and beat on low speed until the mixture is creamy, about 1 minute.

2. Frost your cake or cupcakes right away, or store the frosting, covered, in the refrigerator for up to 2 days. Let the frosting come to room temperature before using.

Brown Sugar Cream Cheese Frosting

MAKES ABOUT 2 CUPS, ENOUGH TO FROST A BABY CAKE, OR TO THINLY FROST A TWO-LAYER LAYER CAKE, A 13 × 9-INCH CAKE, OR 12 CUPCAKES

PREP: 10 MINUTES

1 (8-ounce) package cream cheese, at room temperature

8 tablespoons (1 stick) unsalted butter, at room temperature

Pinch of salt

1 cup (packed) light brown sugar

1 teaspoon vanilla extract

This is one of my favorite frostings, given to me by reader Kathy Lambert. Spread it on the Little Brown Sugar–Grapefruit Cake (page 124).

1. In a medium mixing bowl, combine the cream cheese, butter, and salt and beat with an electric mixer on low speed until creamy, about 30 seconds. Add the brown sugar and vanilla, increase the mixer speed to medium, and beat until light and fluffy, 1 to 2 minutes.

2. Frost your cake or cupcakes right away, or store the frosting, covered, in the refrigerator for up to 2 days. Let the frosting come to room temperature before using.

Chocolate Cream Cheese Frosting

MAKES 3½ CUPS, ENOUGH
TO FROST A TWO- OR
THREE-LAYER CAKE, A SLAB
CAKE, OR 20 TO 24 CUPCAKES

PREP: 10 TO 15 MINUTES

1 (8-ounce) package cream cheese, at room temperature

8 tablespoons (1 stick) unsalted butter, at room temperature

Pinch of salt

½ cup unsweetened cocoa powder

1 teaspoon vanilla extract

3 to 3½ cups confectioners' sugar, sifted

I first tasted this frosting when judging a cake baking contest at the Tennessee State Fair. Since then it has become my go-to and often I'll add a little almond extract with the vanilla.

1. In a medium mixing bowl, combine the cream cheese, butter, and salt and beat with an electric mixer on low speed until creamy, about 30 seconds. Add the cocoa, vanilla, and 3 cups of the sugar, 1 cup at a time, beating on low until smooth. Add the remaining ½ cup sugar, if needed to make a spreadable frosting. Increase the speed to medium and beat until fluffy, about 1 minute.

2. Frost your cake or cupcakes right away, or store the frosting, covered, in the refrigerator for up to 2 days. Let the frosting come to room temperature before using.

VEGAN CHOCOLATE CREAM CHEESE FROSTING:
Substitute vegan cream cheese and plant butter and use 3½ cups confectioners' sugar. Frost your cake or cupcakes right away, or store the frosting, covered, in the refrigerator for up to 2 days.

Leeann's Blackberry Frosting

MAKES ABOUT 2¾ CUPS,
ENOUGH TO FROST A
TWO-LAYER CAKE, A
13 × 9-INCH CAKE, OR
20 CUPCAKES

PREP: 20 TO 25 MINUTES

½ cup blackberries
(3 ounces)

4 ounces cream cheese,
at room temperature

4 tablespoons (½ stick)
unsalted butter,
at room temperature

½ teaspoon vanilla extract

Pinch of salt

2½ cups confectioners'
sugar, sifted

We slather this frosting on Lemon Curd Cupcakes (page 285), and it goes well with all lemon and vanilla cakes.

1. In a food processor, process the blackberries to a puree, about 10 seconds. Strain the puree through a fine-mesh sieve to remove the seeds to yield 1½ to 2 tablespoons strained puree. Set aside.

2. In a medium mixing bowl, combine the cream cheese and butter and beat with an electric mixer on low speed until creamy, about 30 seconds. Add the blackberry puree, vanilla, salt, and 2 cups of the confectioners' sugar and beat with the mixer on low until smooth, about 1 minute. Add the remaining ½ cup sugar, increase the mixer to medium, and beat until fluffy, about 1 minute.

3. Frost your cake as desired, or store, covered, in the refrigerator for up to two days. Let the frosting come to room temperature before using.

STRAWBERRY CREAM CHEESE FROSTING: Make a strawberry puree from ½ cup of strawberries and use instead of the blackberry puree. Increase the confectioners' sugar to 3 cups. The rest of the recipe is the same.

ORANGE CREAM CHEESE FROSTING: Omit the blackberry puree and add 1 to 2 teaspoons grated orange zest. Use 1 teaspoon orange juice or as needed to make it spreadable.

Chocolate Pan Frosting

MAKES 3 CUPS, ENOUGH FOR A TWO-LAYER CAKE, A 13 × 9-INCH CAKE, OR 20 TO 24 CUPCAKES

PREP: 10 TO 15 MINUTES

8 tablespoons (1 stick) unsalted butter

¼ cup unsweetened cocoa powder

Pinch of salt

⅓ cup whole milk, half-and-half, or full-fat canned coconut milk, plus more as needed

2 to 2½ cups confectioners' sugar, sifted

This was the frosting of my childhood. I've made it slightly less sweet than the version that I have shared before. Spread it over chocolate cake, brownies, or pretty much anything.

1. In a medium saucepan, melt the butter over low heat, about 2 minutes. Stir in the cocoa, salt, and milk. Cook, stirring, until the mixture thickens and just begins to come to a boil, about 1 minute.

2. Remove the pan from the heat. Stir in 2 cups of the sugar, a bit at a time, and adding up to ½ cup more sugar or more milk if needed to make the frosting smooth and begin to thicken. It will set once it gets on the cake.

3. Spread the frosting over the cake while the frosting is still warm. It will set as you frost the cake.

BIG-BATCH CHOCOLATE PAN FROSTING: Use 12 tablespoons (1½ sticks) unsalted butter, 6 tablespoons unsweetened cocoa powder, pinch of salt, ½ cup whole milk (or half-and-half or coconut milk), plus more as needed, and 3¾ to 4 cups confectioners' sugar, sifted. Makes 4 cups, enough for a three-layer cake or a 18 × 13-inch slab cake.

SMALL-BATCH CHOCOLATE PAN FROSTING: Use 2 tablespoons unsalted butter, 1 tablespoon unsweetened cocoa powder, pinch of salt, 1½ tablespoons whole milk (or half-and-half or coconut milk), plus more as needed, and ¾ cup confectioners' sugar, sifted. Makes ¾ cup, enough to top an 8- to 9-inch snack cake or Bundt.

Chocolate Ganache

MAKES 1¾ CUPS, ENOUGH TO
THINLY FROST A TWO-LAYER
CAKE OR 20 TO 24 CUPCAKES

PREP: 5 MINUTES

COOK: 5 MINUTES

COOL: 45 MINUTES TO 1 HOUR

8 ounces semisweet
chocolate, chopped, or
semisweet chocolate chips
(1⅓ cups)

¾ cup heavy cream

1 tablespoon liqueur
of your choice or 1 teaspoon
vanilla extract (optional)

Chocolate ganache is truly the simplest frosting on earth. With just two ingredients—heavy cream and semisweet chocolate— you create a smooth and silky sauce to pour warm over ice cream and cake. And if you let the ganache firm up a bit you've got a spreadable frosting. Flavor it with vanilla or your favorite liqueur.

1. Place the chocolate in a stainless-steel medium bowl.

2. In a small heavy saucepan, heat the cream over medium heat, stirring, and bring just to a boil. Immediately remove from the heat and pour over the chocolate. Using a wooden spoon or silicone spatula, stir until the chocolate is melted, 3 to 4 minutes. Stir in the liqueur or vanilla, if desired.

3. Use at once for pouring like a sauce or let cool to room temperature for spreading.

SMALL-BATCH CHOCOLATE GANACHE TOPPING: Use 4 ounces chopped semisweet chocolate or chocolate chips (⅔ cup) and 6 tablespoons heavy cream. Use 1½ teaspoons liqueur or ½ teaspoon vanilla. Makes enough to frost the top of a Bundt cake or a one-layer cake.

MORE CHOCOLATY GANACHE: Use bittersweet chocolate or Ghirardelli 60% cacao chips.

Pour hot cream over chocolate.

Stir until the chocolate melts.

Stir in the liqueur or vanilla, if desired.

Chocolate-Mint Ganache

MAKES ABOUT 2 CUPS,
ENOUGH TO FROST A
TWO-LAYER CAKE OR
20 TO 24 CUPCAKES

PREP: 25 MINUTES

COOK: 5 MINUTES

COOL: 45 MINUTES TO 1 HOUR

1 cup (lightly packed)
fresh mint leaves

1 cup heavy cream

10 ounces semisweet
chocolate, chopped, or
chocolate chips (1⅔ cups)

*A wonderful way to infuse cream with herbal flavors,
which go perfectly with chocolate cake.*

1. Tear the mint leaves in half. In a small heavy saucepan, combine the mint and cream. Bring to a boil over medium heat, then remove the pan from the heat and let rest for 20 minutes to infuse the cream with the mint.

2. Place the chocolate in a large stainless-steel bowl and set a fine-mesh sieve over the bowl. Set the pan with the infused cream over medium heat and bring just to a boil. Immediately remove from the heat and pour through the sieve into the bowl of chocolate (discard the mint). Using a wooden spoon, stir the hot cream into the chocolate until the chocolate melts completely, 3 to 4 minutes.

3. Use at once for pouring like a sauce or let it cool to room temperature for spreading.

Whipped Chocolate Ganache

MAKES 3 CUPS, ENOUGH TO
FROST A TWO-LAYER CAKE,
A 13 × 9-INCH CAKE, OR
20 TO 24 CUPCAKES

PREP: 15 TO 20 MINUTES

COOK: 5 MINUTES

CHILL: 1 HOUR

Chocolate Ganache
(opposite)

*No secrets or surprises here, although the results are so fabulous
you'll think there must be something more to this recipe.*

1. Prepare the chocolate ganache as directed. Place the bowl, uncovered, in the refrigerator to chill for at least 30 minutes or preferably 1 hour. Place electric mixer beaters in the refrigerator to chill, too.

2. Remove the bowl and beaters from the refrigerator. Using the chilled beaters, whip the ganache on high speed until the frosting lightens in color and triples in volume, 2 to 3 minutes.

Quick Caramel Frosting

MAKES ENOUGH FOR A THREE-
OR TWO-LAYER CAKE,
18 TO 20 CUPCAKES, OR
A 13 × 9-INCH CAKE

PREP: 15 TO 20 MINUTES

This frosting takes a little practice to perfect. In the beginning you need to pay attention and spread frosting warm onto the cake, where it will set. As you make this frosting more often, you'll get better at it.

FOR A THREE-LAYER CAKE

12 tablespoons (1½ sticks) unsalted butter

¾ cup (packed) light brown sugar

¾ cup (packed) dark brown sugar

⅓ cup whole milk

2½ cups confectioners' sugar, sifted

1 teaspoon vanilla extract

½ teaspoon salt

FOR A TWO-LAYER CAKE

8 tablespoons (1 stick) unsalted butter

½ cup (packed) light brown sugar

½ cup (packed) dark brown sugar

¼ cup whole milk

1½ to 2 cups confectioners' sugar, sifted

½ teaspoon vanilla extract

¼ teaspoon salt

1. In a heavy medium saucepan, combine the butter and both brown sugars. Cook over medium heat, stirring, until the mixture simmers, about 2 minutes. Stir in the milk and let the mixture come to a boil, then remove the pan from the heat.

2. Add 2 cups of the confectioners' sugar (or 1½ cups for the two-layer recipe), the vanilla, and salt and whisk until the frosting is smooth. Whisk in up to ½ cup of the remaining sugar, but not so much that the frosting thickens and hardens.

3. Spread the frosting over cake layers, cupcakes, or sheet cake while the frosting is still warm. It will set as you frost the cake.

Triple-Layer Caramel Cake
(page 84)

1 tablespoon grated
citrus zest

¼ cup fresh citrus juice
(from 2 lemons, 3 to 4 limes
or clementines, or 1 medium
grapefruit)

¾ cup sugar

2 large eggs

6 tablespoons unsalted
butter, melted and cooled

Homemade Fruit Curd
(Lemon, Lime, Clementine, or Grapefruit)

Here is a blueprint method for making curd—a creamy custardy type of filling—from all kinds of citrus. Different fruit yields different amounts of juice, and limes are the least generous, so have a few extra on hand if you are making lime curd. You will find the curds in recipes throughout this book, but they are also wonderful just spread on a gingersnap cookie or piece of morning toast.

1. In a medium mixing bowl, combine the citrus zest and citrus juice. Whisk in the sugar and eggs and beat well until the mixture is well blended and lightens in color, 2 to 3 minutes. Whisk in the melted butter.

2. Transfer the mixture into a heavy 2-quart saucepan. Set over medium heat and cook, whisking constantly, until the mixture slowly thickens and comes to a simmer, 8 to 12 minutes. Remove the pan from the heat as soon as the mixture simmers. Continue to whisk for 2 to 3 minutes off the heat until it cools down.

3. Immediately pour the curd through a fine-mesh sieve set over a medium bowl to remove the zest. Press with a silicone spatula until all the curd is through the sieve. Scrape the curd off the underside of the sieve and into the bowl.

4. Allow the curd to cool at room temperature for about 5 minutes, then cover the bowl with plastic wrap and place in the refrigerator to chill for 3 hours. Remove when ready to assemble a cake. Curd keeps in the refrigerator for up to 1 week.

Sweetened Whipped Cream

MAKES 2 CUPS, ENOUGH TO
LIGHTLY FROST A TWO-LAYER
OR A 13 × 9-INCH CAKE

PREP: 5 MINUTES

1 cup heavy cream

2 to 4 tablespoons
confectioners' sugar

½ teaspoon vanilla extract

It takes minutes to whip a bowlful of cream to firm peaks, and it takes far longer than that to thaw a container of frozen whipped topping. So just from a time perspective, it pays to whip real cream. Two bits of advice—don't oversweeten and don't overbeat. I prefer 2 tablespoons sugar to 1 cup of cream, but sweeten to your taste.

1. Chill a large mixing bowl and electric mixer beaters in the freezer for a few minutes or in the refrigerator for 15 minutes while you measure the ingredients.

2. Pour the cream into the chilled bowl and beat with the electric mixer on high speed until it thickens, about 1½ minutes. Stop the machine and add the confectioners' sugar and vanilla. Beat on high speed until firm (but not stiff) peaks form, 1 to 2 minutes.

3. Use this right away to frost or fill a cake or store the whipped cream, covered, in the refrigerator for several hours.

    CHOCOLATE WHIPPED CREAM: Melt 1 cup (6 ounces) semisweet chocolate chips in a microwave-safe medium bowl in the microwave on high power for 50 seconds, or over low heat on the stove. Let the chocolate cool. Whip the cream until firm peaks form. Do not add sugar or vanilla. Fold the whipped cream into the cooled chocolate.

    KAHLÚA WHIPPED CREAM: Add 1 tablespoon Kahlúa and, if desired, a pinch of cinnamon.

    COOKIE WHIPPED CREAM: Fold 1 cup crushed chocolate sandwich cookies into the whipped cream.

    BOURBON WHIPPED CREAM: Add 1 tablespoon bourbon instead of the vanilla, and use 2 tablespoons sugar. Add a dash of nutmeg if you like.

SMALL-BATCH WHIPPED CREAM FILLING: Use ½ cup heavy cream, 1 heaping tablespoon confectioners' sugar, and a dash of vanilla. Makes enough to fill a two-layer cake.

BIG-BATCH WHIPPED CREAM FROSTING: Use 2 cups cream, a generous ¼ cup confectioners' sugar, and 1 teaspoon vanilla. Makes enough to frost a three-layer cake.

1½ tablespoons water

½ teaspoon
unflavored gelatin

1 cup heavy cream

¼ cup confectioners' sugar

½ teaspoon vanilla extract

Homemade Cool Whip
aka Stabilized Whipped Cream

There are so many reasons to use this whipped cream that's been stabilized with unflavored gelatin. You are making the cake ahead of time and chilling it. You are frosting a cake topped or layered with fruit. You are taking this dessert to a party. Or you are using this cream to pipe decorations on a cake.

1. Chill a medium mixing bowl and electric mixer beaters in the refrigerator for 15 minutes or freezer for several minutes.

2. In a small microwave-safe bowl, stir to combine the water and gelatin. Leave on the counter for the gelatin to partially dissolve, about 5 minutes. Place the bowl in the microwave for 5 to 10 seconds on high power to completely dissolve the gelatin. Set aside to cool.

3. Meanwhile, remove the bowl and beaters from the fridge or freezer. Pour the cream into the bowl and beat on high speed until the cream holds soft peaks, 2 to 3 minutes, adding the confectioners' sugar and vanilla halfway through. Scrape down the sides of the bowl. Add the gelatin mixture. Continue to beat on high until firm peaks form, about 45 seconds. Place the bowl in the fridge until ready to use.

Vegan Whipped Topping
(Whipped Aquafaba)

MAKES ABOUT 1¾ CUPS

PREP: 10 MINUTES

½ cup liquid drained from a 15-ounce can of chickpeas

⅛ teaspoon cream of tartar

½ cup confectioners' sugar, sifted

1 teaspoon vanilla extract

This faux meringue is like whipped topping in that you can dab it onto cakes, berries, anything where you might use whipped cream. The liquid in the can of chickpeas or white beans is called aquafaba, *which means "bean water," and this starchy liquid mimics egg whites in vegan cooking. The whipped aquafaba has the shiny consistency of marshmallow creme, but the texture is short-lived as it separates if you try to store it in the refrigerator, so this is a make and serve kind of recipe.*

1. In a large mixing bowl, combine the chickpea liquid and cream of tartar and beat with an electric mixer on medium speed until foamy, about 30 seconds. Increase the speed to high and beat until stiff peaks form, about 3 minutes. Add the sugar and vanilla. Beat on high until the mixture is fluffy and smooth, about 1 minute.

2. Use at once as you would whipped cream.

How to Make Apple Butter from Applesauce

Pour 2 cups sweetened applesauce into a medium saucepan and stir in 1 teaspoon ground cinnamon and ¼ teaspoon each ground nutmeg, allspice, and ginger. Bring the mixture to a boil, stirring over medium heat, then reduce the heat to medium-low and simmer, stirring occasionally, until reduced to 1¼ cups, 40 to 45 minutes. Transfer the apple butter to a heatproof glass bowl and let cool for 15 minutes. Cover and refrigerate for up to 2 weeks.

Dark Chocolate Glaze

MAKES ABOUT 1 HEAPING CUP,
ENOUGH FOR 12 CUPCAKES,
ONE LOAF, OR TO THINLY
FROST A 13 × 9-INCH CAKE

PREP: 10 TO 15 MINUTES

1 cup sweetened
condensed milk

2 ounces unsweetened
chocolate, coarsely chopped

Pinch of salt

½ teaspoon vanilla extract

2 to 3 tablespoons heavy
cream, or as needed

*More luxurious than Shiny Chocolate Glaze (opposite),
this glaze is spreadable like ganache but not quite so rich.
It's perfect for cupcakes, loaves, tortes, and sheet cakes.*

1. In a small saucepan, combine the condensed milk and chocolate. Stir constantly over low heat until the chocolate melts. Add the salt and vanilla. After several minutes, when the chocolate is nearly melted, remove from the heat. Continue stirring until completely melted. Whisk in the cream as needed to create a spreadable glaze.

2. Use immediately or reheat gently before spreading over the cake.

White Chocolate Glaze

MAKES ABOUT 1 CUP, ENOUGH
TO GLAZE THE WHITE
CHOCOLATE–PEPPERMINT
CHIFFON CAKE (PAGE 137)
OR 12 CUPCAKES

PREP: 15 MINUTES

½ cup sugar

¼ cup whole milk

4 tablespoons (½ stick)
unsalted butter

1 cup (6 ounces) white
chocolate chips

Pinch of salt (optional)

*This is a super-useful glaze as it can be poured over
the top of a cake or spread like a frosting.*

1. In a small saucepan, combine the sugar, milk, and butter and bring to a boil over medium heat, stirring constantly, about 2 minutes. Continue stirring at a low boil for 1 minute longer, until the butter fully melts. Remove the pan from the heat and stir in the white chocolate chips until they are melted. Taste the glaze; if it needs a little salt, add a pinch.

2. Let the glaze cool for 2 to 3 minutes before spooning it over a cake or cupcakes. If not using immediately, reheat gently before pouring over a cake.

DOUBLE WHITE CHOCOLATE GLAZE: Use the method above, but double all the ingredients: Use 1 cup sugar, ½ cup whole milk, 8 tablespoons (1 stick) unsalted butter, and 2 cups (12 ounces) white chocolate chips. Add a pinch of salt. Makes 2 cups, enough to pour over a slab cake or to generously frost a two-layer cake.

Shiny Chocolate Glaze

MAKES ABOUT 1 CUP, ENOUGH
TO GLAZE A BUNDT OR TUBE
CAKE, THE TOP OF A BOSTON
CREAM PIE, OR 12 CUPCAKES

PREP: 10 MINUTES

¾ cup (4½ ounces)
semisweet chocolate chips

3 to 4 tablespoons heavy
cream

1 tablespoon light corn
syrup

½ teaspoon vanilla extract

When you want just a thin coat of chocolate,
nothing to distract you from the cake, this is the recipe.

1. In a small saucepan, combine the chocolate chips, 3 tablespoons of the cream, and the corn syrup. Whisk over medium-low heat until smooth, 3 to 4 minutes. When the chocolate has melted, pull the pan off the heat and stir in the vanilla. Add another 1 tablespoon cream if needed to thin the glaze for pouring.

2. Use immediately or reheat gently before pouring over the cake.

Boston Cream Pie
(page 64)

Lemon Drizzle

MAKES ⅓ CUP, ENOUGH
TO TOP A BUNDT, LOAF, OR
POUND CAKE

PREP: 5 TO 7 MINUTES

2 to 3 tablespoons fresh
lemon juice

1 cup confectioners' sugar,
sifted

1 teaspoon grated
lemon zest

*Just what you need to dress up lemon,
orange, spice, or pumpkin cake.*

In a small bowl, whisk the lemon juice into the confectioners' sugar until smooth but pourable. Fold in the zest. With a spoon, drizzle the mixture over a cake and let the glaze set before slicing or serving.

Maple Caramel Drizzle

MAKES ¾ CUP, ENOUGH TO
GLAZE THE TOP OF A BUNDT,
POUND, OR ONE-LAYER CAKE

PREP: 15 TO 20 MINUTES

2 tablespoons unsalted butter

2 tablespoons
light brown sugar

2 tablespoons
dark brown sugar

1½ tablespoons whole milk

½ cup confectioners' sugar,
sifted

¼ teaspoon vanilla extract

2 drops maple extract

*A variation of my caramel frosting, this is just enough
for a topper, and it's scented with maple.*

1. In a small heavy saucepan, combine the butter and both brown sugars. Cook over medium heat, stirring, until the mixture comes to a boil, about 1 minute. Stir in the milk and let the mixture return to a boil, then remove the pan from the heat. Add the confectioners' sugar, vanilla, and maple extract and whisk until smooth.

2. Ladle warm over the top of a cake. It will set as it cools.

SALTED CARAMEL DRIZZLE: Omit the maple flavoring and add a large pinch of sea salt instead.

Vanilla Drizzle

MAKES ABOUT ¼ CUP,
ENOUGH TO TOP A BUNDT OR
LOAF CAKE

PREP: 5 TO 7 MINUTES

1 tablespoon whole milk
or fresh lemon juice

½ teaspoon vanilla extract
(if using milk)

½ cup confectioners' sugar,
sifted

When all else fails, there's vanilla drizzle! No, seriously, this glaze goes with everything and adds that little something extra.

In a small bowl, whisk the milk and vanilla (if using) into the confectioners' sugar until smooth. Use at once. If the drizzle sets, stir it vigorously to thin out; if needed, heat it briefly in the microwave.

Martha's Chocolate Fudge Icing

MAKES ABOUT 1½ CUPS,
ENOUGH TO FROST A BUNDT,
A 13 × 9-INCH CAKE,
OR 12 TO 16 CUPCAKES

PREP: 20 TO 25 MINUTES

½ cup (packed) dark
brown sugar

½ cup granulated sugar

6 tablespoons
unsalted butter

⅓ cup whole milk

1 cup (6 ounces) semisweet
chocolate chips

1 tablespoon unsweetened
cocoa powder

1 teaspoon vanilla extract

¼ teaspoon salt

My friend and recipe tester Martha shared this recipe with me years ago. It now has a stronger chocolate flavor, a little salt, and brown sugar for depth.

1.   In a medium saucepan, combine the brown sugar, granulated sugar, butter, and milk. Stir over medium heat until the mixture comes to a boil, 3 to 4 minutes. Let it boil for 1 minute, stirring to make sure all the sugar dissolves. Remove the pan from the heat and stir in the chocolate chips, cocoa, vanilla, and salt.

2.   Continue to stir until the chocolate has melted and the icing is smooth and satiny, 3 to 4 minutes. Use immediately because the icing sets up quickly.

The Cake Pantry

Old Favorites and Some New Flavors

Whether it's a last-minute batch of cupcakes or a special birthday cake, it's much easier to bake when you open the pantry and everything you need is there. Here are my must-haves in alphabetical order. Many of these have been a mainstay in my pantry, and some others are new favorites I especially enjoy baking with today.

BUTTER All my cakes, bars, and cookies call for unsalted butter because cake mixes have salt in them. If you have salted butter, go ahead and use it, but don't add salt to the frosting. If you like the rich European butters, save them for the frosting.

(PLANT) BUTTER Nondairy plant butters made from avocado and olive oil are white in color, softer in texture, and come to room temperature more quickly than dairy butter. Feel free to substitute them whenever I call for butter, but as they are more watery, you need a bit more confectioners' sugar to pull a frosting together.

BUTTERMILK Buttermilk adds flavor and moistness to a cake—use whole-milk buttermilk if you can find it. To make 1 cup of homemade buttermilk, pour 1 cup whole milk into a glass measuring cup and stir in 1 tablespoon lemon juice or white vinegar. Let the mixture rest about 10 minutes until it begins to curdle.

CAKE MIXES I always have a couple of packages of yellow, butter, chocolate, white cake, and brownie mix on hand. I prefer butter over yellow in most recipes because it has less food coloring. Chocolate comes in various forms—devil's food, chocolate fudge, etc.—but they're all chocolate to me!

CHOCOLATE Can't imagine a day without chocolate! Here is what I keep on hand:

- UNSWEETENED CHOCOLATE Also called "baking" or "bitter" chocolate, it contains no sugar and has big flavor. It's how I swirl marble cake with the deep, dark chocolate color and flavor.

- SEMISWEET AND BITTERSWEET CHOCOLATE They do it all in cakes and frostings and can be used interchangeably. Bittersweet is, as the name suggests, less sweet.

- SEMISWEET CHOCOLATE CHIPS When I don't want to chop semisweet chocolate, I use the chips. One cup weighs about 6 ounces, and the chips melt easily into glazes and sauces. The mini chips are invaluable for folding into batter—they don't sink!—or to scatter on top. There is a difference between brands, so do some taste-testing. I like Ghirardelli 60% cacao chips. No chocolate chips? Chop semisweet chocolate into small pieces.

- GERMAN'S SWEET CHOCOLATE A mild chocolate needed for Favorite German Chocolate Cake (page 57) and Stacy's Chocolate Chip Cake (page 134).

- MILK CHOCOLATE You need it for the Hershey's Bar Pound Cake (page 132).

- WHITE CHOCOLATE Make sure the label says "cocoa butter" or "milk solids," which indicate cocoa butter and flavor. If the bar is called "confectionery coating," it has no cocoa butter but works for Cake Pops (page 292). Buy real white chocolate for White Cake with White Frosting (page 102).

CITRUS I love all citrus fruit in baking—lemons, limes, Cara Cara oranges, blood oranges, clementines, and grapefruit. I use the zest and juice extensively throughout this book, from cakes to fillings to frostings and glazes. For citrus to last longer, store it in the refrigerator.

COCOA I like regular unsweetened cocoa because of the warm brown color and pleasant flavor it gives to cakes and frostings. The Dutch process cocoas make a darker frosting with a deeper flavor.

COCONUT MILK You can use full-fat or light canned coconut milk in baking my cakes. In testing these recipes I found both worked really well. When you want the recipe to be richer, use full-fat. But I am not talking about the coconut milk beverage, by the way. If you open a can of coconut milk and find fat collected at the top of the can, turn the contents into a small bowl and whisk until smooth.

CREAM CHEESE, MASCARPONE, AND RICOTTA All are wonderful ways to add density, structure, and moistness to cake. Because of the salt in cream cheese, frostings tend to taste less sweet. Mascarpone is loaded with fat, and that's why it is so delicious in a frosting. Whole-milk ricotta substitutes for sour cream if you need one and adds moistness and rich texture to cakes. And ricotta makes a wonderful frosting when added to an equal part of whipped cream.

EGGS Buy large eggs for baking these cakes. If you are in doubt about what size your eggs are—perhaps they are fresh eggs from a farmers' market or a neighbor's hen—put them on a scale. Large eggs weigh about 2 ounces in the shell.

EGG SUBSTITUTES My favorite substitute for an egg is unsweetened applesauce—about ¼ cup per large egg called for in the recipe. But you can also use whipped aquafaba—the liquid drained from a can of beans—or egg substitutes found on the baking aisle. Cake mixes have leavening built into them, so they will rise a bit on their own but not enough without some help!

EXTRACTS AND FLAVORINGS Choose pure extracts of vanilla, almond, and peppermint. While maple and coconut extracts are artificial flavorings, I use them often but am careful not to add too much.

FLOUR To ensure cakes release easily, I dust the pans with all-purpose flour after greasing. In some recipes, I call for a little flour to bulk up smaller mixes and make a more substantial cake.

GELATINS I keep lemon Jell-O on hand for lemon cake and strawberry Jell-O for strawberry cake. And I use unflavored, unsweetened gelatin in making a stabilized whipped cream that holds up like store-bought whipped topping.

HONEY As a shortcut, spread creamed or whipped honey over cupcakes instead of frosting.

INSTANT PUDDING MIX This is a key ingredient for improving the smaller cake mixes. It gives the Bundt cake a dense and moist texture, helps sheet cakes and layers slice without crumbling, and suspends raisins and chocolate chips in batters. I use half of a box of vanilla or chocolate—and sometimes lemon or white chocolate—pudding mix for one package of cake mix.

MILK AND CREAM I use whole milk, half-and-half, and cream for baking because you need the fat to make a richer cake and frosting. Fat-free milk works, but whole is better.

MILK SUBSTITUTES Unsweetened plain almond, coconut, and other nut milks, as well as soy, oat, and rice milk work instead of cow's milk. Canned coconut is the clear stand-out because of its higher fat content. These alternatives also work in buttercream frostings.

NUTS Pecans, almonds, walnuts, cashews, pistachios, and hazelnuts keep best in the freezer. (They will oxidize and turn rancid if left at room temp too long.) Buy nuts in as large pieces as possible because they freeze better and you can always chop them into smaller pieces.

OIL AND VEGETABLE SHORTENING Oil adds richness and plays nicely with chocolate, giving cake a dense and moist texture. I use canola and light olive oil. Vegetable shortening is my go-to for greasing layer and Bundt pans.

SALT It's not in my cake recipes because it's already in cake mixes. But I find it is essential in frostings where it balances sweetness (the exception being cream cheese frosting because cream cheese is salty). I love kosher and sea salt, especially with chocolate.

SOUR CREAM AND GREEK YOGURT Use both and use them interchangeably. They add acidity and richness to everything.

SUGAR Cake mixes have sugar in them, but for frostings and glazes I use granulated sugar, light brown, dark brown, and confectioners'—aka powdered—sugar.

With Gratitude/Acknowledgments

Writing a cookbook in 2020 gave me focus during one of our country's most unsettling times. Like many of you, I couldn't visit family and missed seeing my friends, but I could bake and write this book. Groceries for testing filled my dining room, and I am thankful to my husband, John, for buying eggs and butter whenever he was out. My friend Martha Bowden helped me test these recipes, and we would meet on my porch or hers to share cake and conversation about baking, the news, our children, and how many miles we had to walk to burn off the calories from this project! I am grateful for her enthusiasm and steadfastness. I am also grateful for my agent, David Black, who understood why I wanted to write this book. And thank you to Clarkson Potter and my editor, Raquel Pelzel, for welcoming me with open arms.

We all learned during the pandemic how important a pantry is and how nice it is to be able to bake a cake. Baking is a skill, something we get better at through life, and finally we had time to bake. And we realized, too, how important family is. I can tell you that in my years of being published, family members have been my best cheerleaders. I am grateful to John, Kathleen, Hugh, Litton, and John, as well as Susan and Mark, Ginger, Flowerree and Steve, Lawson, and cousins in Nashville and across the country. I am also grateful to Martha's husband, Rusty, who became like family during this project. He and my husband share the good trait of eating anything and offering critique afterward!

I don't know what I'd do without my friends who make life a lot more fun, and you know who you are. I encourage you to show up very soon on my porch for a glass of wine and a slice of cake. Thank you also to all the readers out there whom I have met, emailed with, and spoken to via social media. Or even if we haven't made contact, thank you for buying my books—and now this new book—for your kitchen shelf. I hope my recipes have brought you enjoyment and my words have made you a more confident cook.

Lastly, thanks to the team of people who, in spite of social distancing and working from home, got this book photographed, styled, designed, and edited in such a beautiful way—Marysarah Quinn, Catherine Casalino, Danielle Atkins, Teresa Blackburn, Patricia Shaw, Jessica Heim, Merri Ann Morrell, Kate Slate, Elizabeth T. Parson, Kristin Casemore, Samantha Simon, and Bianca Cruz. We'll never forget this year, and I won't forget the people who made this new book possible. Love to all, and happy baking!

Index